Samuel Carter Hall

A week at Killarney

With descriptions of the routes thither from Dublin, Cork

Samuel Carter Hall

A week at Killarney
With descriptions of the routes thither from Dublin, Cork

ISBN/EAN: 9783337147181

Printed in Europe, USA, Canada, Australia, Japan

Cover: Foto ©Andreas Hilbeck / pixelio.de

More available books at **www.hansebooks.com**

A
WEEK AT KILLARNEY,
WITH
Descriptions of the Routes thither,
FROM
DUBLIN, CORK, &c.

BY
MR. AND MRS. S. C. HALL.

LONDON:
VIRTUE BROTHERS AND CO.,
1, AMEN CORNER.
1865.

ADVERTISEMENT.

THE Authors of this Work have the satisfaction to issue A NEW EDITION, in which the reader will find notices of all recent changes and improvements in the district described; and, generally, in the South of Ireland.

In the autumn of 1864 they revisited "THE LAKES," in order to be enabled to communicate to the Tourist information concerning all matters with which it is important he should be made acquainted; studying to obtain such knowledge as might facilitate his progress while visiting districts assuredly more attractive—because more abundant in natural beauties—than any other portions of the British Islands.*

The leading purpose of the Authors is to induce VISITS TO IRELAND. Those who require relaxation from labour, or may be advised, to seek health under the influence of a mild climate, or search for sources of novel and rational amusement, or draw from change of scene a stimulus to wholesome excitement, or covet acquaintance with the charms of Nature, or wish to study a people full of original character—cannot project an excursion to any part of Europe that will afford a more ample recompense.

To the ENGLISH, therefore, a country in which they cannot fail to be deeply interested, holds out every temptation the traveller can need. A cordial and hearty welcome will be given, at all times and in all places, to the "STRANGER," who will

---

* A railroad to Dunmanway (fifty-three miles from Cork en route to Bantry and Glengariff will be immediately opened; and very soon a railway to Macroom (twenty-four miles from Cork) both towns being en route to Bantry and Glengariff. The reader will be pleased to bear these facts in mind for his guidance when arranging his Tour from Cork.

there journey in security such as he can meet in no other portion of the globe. Ireland will unquestionably supply every means of enjoyment that may be obtained in any Continental kingdom, and without calling for the sacrifices of money and comfort that will be exacted in Germany, Switzerland, France, or Italy.

The Authors are fully aware they have failed in giving to the reader more than a very limited idea of the grandeur and loveliness of THE KILLARNEY LAKES, and the wild magnificence of the sea-coasts so easily accessible from them. They trust, however, they have succeeded in presenting to the Tourist a COMPANION that—accompanying him during the several routes—may supply needful information during his progress, and be a pleasant reminiscence of his Tour, when it is over, and he is seated at home, reviewing his journeyings to the beautiful districts through which he has been travelling.

The Authors desire to lay continual stress on the advantages that must ensue from intercourse between the two countries—countries so naturally connected, and whose interests must be, while the world lasts, mutual and inseparable.

The Tourist will, of a surety, return from his Tour, brief or prolonged, with increased esteem for the Irish people of all grades, with enlarged ideas of their capabilities, and an augmented desire to draw closer and closer the bond of union between England and Ireland, by enabling the latter to participate more and more in the prosperity which the former enjoys.

Various unhappy circumstances have hitherto combined to postpone the on-progress of Ireland; but they are all rapidly departing—some of them are already matters of gone-by history. No one can visit that richly-endowed and most interesting country without conviction that its dark days are over; that it is, even now, giving promise to fulfil the poet's prophecy:—

"The Star of the West may yet rise in its glory,
And the land that was darkest be brightest in story!"

THE ILLUSTRATIONS.

ENGRAVINGS ON STEEL,

FROM DRAWINGS BY T. CRESWICK, R.A., AND W. H. BARTLETT.

		PAGE
1.	COOME DHUV: THE BLACK VALLEY . . . . *to face title.*	
2.	GOUGANE BARRA	38
3.	GLENGARIFF	43
4.	THE LOWER AND TORC LAKE	94
5.	MACGILLICUDDY'S REEKS	105
6.	THE GAP OF DUNLOE	121
7.	THE UPPER LAKE	121
8.	THE LOWER LAKE	127
9.	ROSS CASTLE	131
10.	INISFALLEN	142
11.	TORC MOUNTAIN	147
12.	TORC CASCADE	159
Map.	THE ROADS FROM CORK TO KILLARNEY	23
„	THE LAKES OF KILLARNEY	71

ENGRAVINGS ON WOOD.

	PAGE		PAGE
The Title-page.			
Dublin and its Harbour	4	The Cemetery, Cork	20
Testimonial to George the Fourth . . .	5	Blarney Castle	21
The Dublin University	6	Tail-piece	22
Bank of Ireland	7	Lough Hyne	25
The Birmingham Tower	8	Inisherken	26
Clondalkin Round Tower	9	Dunamore Castle	26
Kildare	10	Tail-piece	27
Dunamase	11	Bianconi's Car	29
Rock of Cashel	12	Covered Jaunting-Car	30
Iron Gate at Kilmallock	13	Inside Jaunting-Car	30
Ruins at Kilmallock	13	Outside Jaunting-Car	31
Ruins at Kilmallock	14	Old Car of the Peasant	31
Kilcoleman Castle	15	Old Irish Road	32
Tail-piece	15	Kilcrea Castle	34
Cork and its Harbour	16	Kilcrea Abbey	34
Haulbowlin Harbour	17	Macroom Bridge	35
Arms of the City of Cork	18	Gougane Barra	37
Doorway, St. Finn Bar	19	Keim-an-Eigh	39

LIST OF ENGRAVINGS ON WOOD.

	PAGE		PAGE
Tail-piece	40	Keeners	95
Bantry Bay	42	The Keener	96
The Legend-Stone	44	Tail-piece	97
View at Glengariff	46	Shores of the Lakes	98
Cromwell's Bridge	48	Vendor of Goat's Milk	102
Tail-piece	49	Devil's Punch-bowl	103
Castle at Limerick	50	Common Bagpipes	105
The Treaty Stone	51	Union Pipes	105
St. Mary's Church	52	Tail-piece	106
The Shannon Boat	53	The Islands	107
Dunmore Lighthouse	55	Aghadoe	108
The Saltees	56	The Gap of Dunloe	111
Dunbrody Abbey	57	The "Logan Stone"	112
Lough Coom-Shinawin	59	Garameen Bridge	113
Tubber Grieve	60	The Long Range	115
St. Mary's, Clonmel	61	The Eagle's Nest	116
Cahir Castle	62	Old Weir Bridge	118
Golden Bridge	63	The Devil's Island	119
Tail-piece	64	The Cottage at Glena	120
Killarney	67	In Glena Bay: Mrs. Hall's Point	121
The Railway Hotel	69	Tail-piece	122
View from Victoria Hotel	71	The Avenue to Mucross	123
The Arbutus	73	Ross Castle	125
The Flesk Bridge	77	Ross Island	127
The Old Guide	80	The Spirit of O'Donoghue	128
Tail-piece	82	O'Donoghue's Horse	129
View of the Upper Lake	83	Tail-piece	142
View from the Police Barracks	84	Druidic Remains	143
The Tunnel	86	Clough-na-Cuddy	147
Killarney Mountains	87	Tail-piece	153
Torc Waterfall	88	Blackwater Bridge	156
Killaghie church	89	The House in which O'Connell was Born	158
Brickeen Bridge	90	Valencia	160
Cottage in Dinis Island	90	In Dingle Bay	164
Mucross Abbey	92	Ferriter's Castle	166
Entrance to Mucross	93	Ardfert Abbey	167
The Fire-place at Mucross	93	Tail-piece	169
A Tomb at Mucross	94	Tail-piece	174

THE VOYAGE TO IRELAND.

STEAM-BOATS have done more than either Time or Legislation to unite England and Ireland: they facilitate intercourse almost as much as a bridge across St. George's Channel could do; and render the voyage, in summer time, a pleasure excursion. Little more than the third of a century ago, it was a serious business,—of so uncertain a duration that not unfrequently weeks were spent between the opposite ports. The "sailing packet" was a small schooner; the cabin, usually measuring 20 feet by 12, was lined with "berths," a few of which were "curtained off," and apportioned to ladies. A miserable paucity of accommodation, and utter indifference to the comforts of passengers, made the voyage an intolerable evil, to be endured only in cases of absolute necessity.* Ireland was, therefore, rarely visited. Under such circumstances, it is not surprising that little or no acquaintance existed between the two countries,—that England and Ireland were almost as much strangers to each other, as if the channel that divided them had been as broad as the Atlantic. The introduction of steam has made them, as it were, one island; and the Irish lakes are scarcely more distant from London than are those of Westmoreland.

The results of increased facilities for intercourse have been, that prejudices and popular errors are passing away from both countries; that a more just and rational estimate has been formed by the one of the other; that the vast natural resources of Ireland have been increased and developed; and that the moral and social condition of the people has been essentially improved. The upper orders of both countries have more thoroughly amalgamated, while the humbler classes have still more considerably benefited by the change.

Hitherto, however, although steam has so largely aided in inducing visits from Ireland to England, visitors to Ireland from England have not, in the same ratio, increased. Happily, many of the causes that produced this evil exist no more, others are rapidly disappearing, and ere long the current of travel must set more strongly in that direction. The English will be induced to see and judge for themselves, and no

---

* The voyage was not the only evil. Immediately on arrival—in Ireland—the luggage and the passenger were both taken to the Custom-house. No passport was required; but that was his only advantage on landing in Ireland over landing at a foreign port. All imported goods paid duty; and his portmanteau was rigidly searched for articles on which that duty was to be paid. He tendered his shillings and sixpences in payment; but they were no current coin in that part of the realm—they must be exchanged for "tenpennies" and "fivepennies" before he could obtain warrant to proceed to his hotel.

longer incur the reproach of being better acquainted with the Continent, than with a country in which they cannot fail to be deeply interested, and which holds out to them every temptation the traveller can need; a people, rich in original character, scenery, abundant in the wild and beautiful, a cordial and hearty welcome for the "stranger," and a degree of safety and security in his journeyings, such as he can meet in no other portion of the globe.* Ireland will, unquestionably, supply every means of enjoyment that may be obtained in any of the Continental kingdoms, and without calling for the sacrifices of money and comfort that will inevitably be exacted by the leeches of Germany, France, and Italy. Irish civility and hospitality to strangers have been proverbial for ages—existing even to a fault. Strangers will find, wherever they go, a ready zeal and anxiety, among all classes, to produce a favourable impression for the country; and in lieu of roguish couriers, insolent douaniers, dirty inns, and people courteous only that they may rob with greater certainty and impunity, they will encounter a people naturally kind and intelligent, in whom it is impossible not to feel interested. Even where discomfort is to be endured, it will be deprived of its character of annoyance by the certainty that every effort has been, or will be, exerted to remove it.

We shall rejoice if our statements be the means of inducing English travellers to direct their course westward, knowing well, that for every new *visitor*, Ireland will obtain a new Friend.

We have said that facilities for travelling to, and in, Ireland, have, of late years, largely increased; recently, however, they have been much more augmented: a railway conveys the tourist to Holyhead in seven hours, and a packet, across the Channel, in four hours. Another railway, traversing South Wales, takes him by large and admirably managed steam-boats across the sea into the beautiful bay of Waterford, a voyage from harbour to harbour of barely nine hours; railways also conduct him through several parts of the country, and all the way—either from Dublin, Cork, or Waterford—to Killarney.

There are many inducements to visit Ireland; one of them, assuredly, is the smallness of the cost at which the enjoyment may be purchased; the English and Irish railway companies have combined to bring the expenses of the journey within very narrow limits. Most happily, the agitation for "Repeal" is but a sad theme of history; poverty and misery are operating in Ireland with diminished power; a conviction of its approaching prosperity is daily becoming more and more strong;

---

* To the "safety" and "security" of travelling in Ireland it may seem superfluous to refer; but there are many who, in utter ignorance of the country and its people, have formed unaccountably erroneous opinions on the subject. It may, therefore, be well to lay peculiar stress upon the testimony supplied by every writer concerning the country, and the report of every Tourist by whom it has been visited. For ourselves, we have never hesitated to make journeys at all hours of the day or night, through any part of the island, upon ordinary jaunting-cars, under the full conviction that we were as safe as we should have been between Kensington and Hyde Park. It is not enough to say that we never encountered insult or injury; we never met with the smallest interruption, incivility, or even discourtesy, that could induce a suspicion that wrong or rudeness was intended. During our various wanderings, we have been located at all sorts of "Houses of Entertainment;" from the stately hotel of the city, to the poor "cabaret" of a mountain village; we never lost the value of a shilling by misconduct on the part of those to whom our property was entrusted. We should, indeed, ill discharge our duty, if we did not testify, as strongly as language enables us to do, to the generosity and honesty of the Irish character. To our own testimony we add that of a still better "authority." At a meeting of "the Social Science" at Leeds, Mr. Bianconi, one of the best benefactors of Ireland, whose public cars travel night and day through every high road of the island, made this statement:—

"I repeat with pleasure the testimony I gave in 1857, namely, that my conveyances have been in existence now forty-six years, many of them carrying very important mails, having been travelling during all hours of the day and night, often in lonely and unfrequented places, yet the slightest injury has never been done by the people to my property or that entrusted to my care!"

There is no other country in the world of which so much could, with truth, be said.

there is greater trust in its natural advantages, and less apprehension of its forlorn destiny than there used to be. The tourist is more often cheered than depressed as he travels either its highways or its byways. Seldom now does he encounter that terrible sight which formerly lowered his spirits at every step he took—of unemployed labour and unproductive soil; of misery that neither benevolence nor legislation could lessen or relieve; of lands wanting hands, and hands wanting lands: in short, to the mere passer-by, but infinitely more so to the observer and inquirer, there is much to excite hope, and much to induce conviction, that Ireland has seen its "worst days," and that the time is not distant when Ireland will be the right arm of England!

Let, therefore, those who are pondering how a week or a month may be most pleasantly and most profitably spent during the summer or autumn, consider the claims of Ireland, and believe that nowhere can there be found so large a recompence at so little cost.

Although the main purpose of this book is to show the Tourist how best he may enjoy the Lakes of Killarney,—and, with that view, full details are given concerning roads, inns, guides, cars, boats, &c., and all the minor matters upon which so much of his comfort and consequent pleasure will depend,—that is not the only object of the writers. They desire to lay before him the several facilities for "progressing" through the southern districts of the country, and to explain that many sources of enjoyment may be opened up to him on his way to or from the Lakes other than those he will more immediately derive from the beautiful and magnificent scenery at Killarney, and the parts adjacent to it.

They therefore conduct the Tourist to Dublin by the Dublin and Holyhead railway; to Cork, either by steam-boat from Bristol, or by railroad from Dublin; to Dublin from Liverpool; and to Waterford, by railway to Milford Haven, and steam-boat across; making Cork, generally, the starting-point; although in voyaging either from Dublin or Waterford, there is no necessity for taking Cork *en route*—the railway to Killarney now proceeding from Mallow, to which there are lines both from Waterford, Cork, and Dublin.

The voyage from Holyhead to Kingstown is nearly always made within four hours; Kingstown is seven miles, by railway, from Dublin. The steam-boats are of huge size, and fitted up with all possible care to comfort. Passengers embark both at Kingstown and Holyhead at the pier: there is no state of the tide that renders intermediate boats necessary.

It is obvious that by either of these routes to the Lakes much of the most interesting districts of "the South" will be passed through, and a fair general idea of the country and its peculiarities be thus obtained.

We shall, therefore, proceed with him, first to Dublin, then to Cork, and then to Waterford, conveying him by the routes thence to

The Killarney Lakes.

UBLIN AND ITS HARBOUR.

DUBLIN is the capital city of Ireland. There are few cities in the world, and perhaps none in Great Britain, so auspiciously situated. The ocean rolls its waves within ten miles of the quays; the Bay is at once safe, commodious, and magnificent, with every variety of coast, from the soft beach of sand to the rough sea promontory,—from the undulating slope to the terrific rock; and several lighthouses guide the vessels into harbour. On one side is the rich pasture-land of Meath; on the other are the mountains and valleys of Wicklow. A noble river flows through it. Breezes from the ocean and the hills both contribute to keep it healthy. Scenery of surpassing beauty is within an hour's walk of its crowded streets. But no description of Dublin can so aptly and pithily characterise it as the few quaint lines of old Stanihurst, who says, in tracing its origin to the sea-king Avellanus, and giving him credit for wisdom in selecting so advantageous a site,—" The seat of this city is of all sides pleasant, comfortable, and wholesome: if you would traverse hills, they are not far off; if champaign ground, it lieth of all parts; if you be delighted with fresh water, the famous river called the Liffey runneth fast by ; if you will take a view of the sea, it is at hand."

What a glorious impression of Ireland is conveyed to the eye and mind upon approaching the noble and beautiful bay of Dublin! It is, indeed, inexpressibly lovely; and on entering it after the voyage, the heart bounds with enthusiasm at the sight of its capacious bosom, enclosed by huge rocks, encompassed in turn by high and picturesque mountains. To the south, varied into innumerable forms, are "the Wicklow Hills;" but nearer, rising, as it were, out of the surface of old ocean, is the ever-green island of Dalkey. To the north, a bolder coast is commenced by "the Hill of Howth," on a leading pinnacle of which stands the most picturesque of the Irish beacons; at the other side of the promontory, are seen a village, with another lighthouse, a martello tower, an ancient abbey, and a calm, though now deserted, harbour—for a long period the first landing-place upon Irish ground.

Leaving to the left the pretty island of DALKEY, we enter the channel, between two huge sand-banks called, from the perpetual roaring of the sea that rolls over them, "the Bulls," north and south. But the place of ordinary debarkation is KINGSTOWN, formerly Dunleary, which received its modern name in honour of His Majesty George the Fourth, who took ship-board here on leaving Ireland in 1821. To commemorate the event of the king's visit, an obelisk was erected on the spot where he last stood; with an inscription setting forth the fact. The harbour of Kingstown is safe, commodious, and exceedingly picturesque. From the quay at which the passengers land, the railway carriages start, and convey passengers a distance of seven miles, in about twenty minutes, to the terminus, within a few hundred yards of the centre of the city; leaving to the right a long and narrow range of stone-work, known as the South Wall, which runs for above three miles into the sea, and nearly midway in which is an apology for a battery, called "the Pigeon-house,"—but keeping in sight all the way the opposite coast, speckled with villages, and beautifully varied by alternate hill and dale.

TESTIMONIAL TO GEORGE THE FOURTH.

The stranger cannot fail to receive a most agreeable impression of Dublin, no matter in what part of it, out of the mere suburbs, he chances to be set down; for its principal streets and leading attractions lie within a comparatively narrow compass; and his attention is sure to be fixed upon some object worthy of observation—to be succeeded, almost immediately, by some other of equal note. If he arrive sea-ward he will have fully estimated the magnificence of the approach, which nature has formed, and which art has improved; and there is scarcely one of the roads that conduct to it, on which he will not have journeyed through beautiful scenery, and obtained a fine view of the city as he nears it. But we must place him, at once, nearly in its centre—upon Carlisle Bridge; perhaps from no single spot of the kingdom can the eye command so great a number of interesting points. He turns to the north and looks along a noble street, Sackville Street; midway, is Nelson's Pillar, a fine Ionic column, surmounted by a statue of the hero; directly opposite to this is the Post-office, a modern structure built in pure taste; beyond, are the Lying-in Hospital, and the Rotunda; and, ascending a steep hill, one of the many fine squares. He has within ken the far-famed Bank of Ireland, and the University; "the Four Courts"—the courts of law—and the several bridges; to the east, the Custom-house, a superb though a lonesome building, and the quays. Towering above all are numerous steeples, of which no city, except the metropolis of England, can boast so many.

THE DUBLIN UNIVERSITY.

We must limit ourselves to a very brief notice of the principal public buildings. The front of "the College" faces Dame Street, and by its architectural beauty harmonises with the magnificent structure formerly occupied by the Irish Parliament. The Bank of Ireland—the "Parliament House" before "the Union"—is universally classed among the most perfect examples of British architecture in the kingdom; and indeed is, perhaps, unsurpassed in Europe. Yet, strange to say, little or nothing is known of the architect—the history of the graceful and beautiful structure being wrapt in obscurity almost approaching to mystery. It is built entirely of Portland stone, and is remarkable for an absence of all meretricious ornament, attracting entirely by its pure and classic, and rigidly simple, architecture.

The Exchange may, perhaps, rank in beauty next to the Bank; it was commenced in 1769 and finished in 1779, under the immediate direction of Mr. Thomas Cooley, an architect to whom Dublin is indebted for other fine structures. The Custom-house was designed and erected by Mr. James Gandon; the foundation-stone having been laid in 1781. "The Four Courts"—the building which contains the several Irish courts of law—was commenced by the architect, Mr. Thomas Cooley, in 1786; and in consequence of his death, continued by Mr. James Gandon. It is situated on the north side of the Liffey: and is an exceedingly beautiful and attractive object, seen either from an adjacent point, or from a distance. Of the other buildings the most important is "the Post-office," the first stone of which was laid in 1815. It was built after a design by Mr. Francis Johnson, and is one of the finest and most convenient public structures in the kingdom; the College of Surgeons may be ranked next; and next, the Lying-in Hospital. The National Gallery, prominent on one side of Merrion Square, is a structure of much architectural grace and beauty; it

BANK OF IRELAND.

contains a choice collection of paintings and works in sculpture, and it is free to the public. To these must be added the latest structure, the work of an eminent architect, Mr. Alfred Jones, where has been held the International Exhibition in 1865; it is "a winter garden," as well as a Hall for concerts, lectures, and so forth. The want of such an edifice had long been felt in Dublin; there is nothing in Great Britain at once so convenient, commodious, complete, and really elegant, as an example of modern architecture.

There are many public buildings of great merit, besides those we have mentioned, but we must be content with reference—and that a slight one only—to the more remarkable. It will be observed that of all these edifices there are none, except the College, much above a century old. But "The Castle" is of great antiquity. Its history is, in fact, the history of Dublin. To trace the progress of the city from the period when a band of invaders destroyed it by fastening matches to the tails of swallows, and so communicating fire to the thatched roofs of the houses, to its present extensive size and fine architectural character, would be a task—however interesting —that would far exceed our limits.

The Castle has undergone so many and such various changes from time to time, as circumstances justified the withdrawal of its defences, that the only portion of it which now bears a character of antiquity is the Birmingham Tower; and even that has been almost entirely rebuilt, although it retains its ancient form.

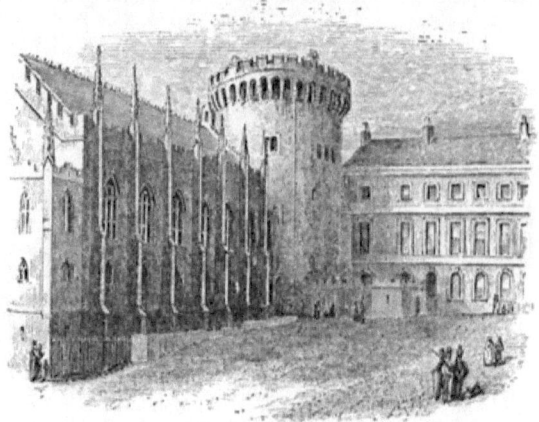

THE BIRMINGHAM TOWER.

But if few of the public structures of Dublin possess "the beauty of age," many of its churches may be classed with "the ancient of days." Chief among them all is the Cathedral of St. Patrick; interesting not alone from its antiquity, but from its association with the several leading events, and remarkable people, by which, and by whom, Ireland has been made "famous." It is situated in a very old part of Dublin, in the midst of low streets and alleys. It was built A.D. 1190, by John Comyn, Archbishop of Dublin, by whom it was dedicated to the patron saint of Ireland; but, it is said, the site on which it stands was formerly occupied by a church erected by the saint himself—A.D. 448.*

Institutions for promoting science, literature, and the arts, are far too limited: first in rank and utility is "the Dublin Society," occupying Kildare House, purchased in 1815 from the Duke of Leinster for £20,000—a noble mansion, "long celebrated as one of the most splendid private residences in Europe." The society received its charter of incorporation as "The Dublin Society for promoting husbandry

---

* Until recently, this venerable edifice was in a ruinous state; happily it has been thoroughly restored, in strict accordance with the original plan. The cost of this work exceeded £150,000. No visitor to Dublin should pass even a day in that city without seeing this most noble and beautiful temple of God, nor without rendering homage to that truly illustrious citizen, BENJAMIN LEE GUINNESS, *who has defrayed the whole of the cost of the restoration*, and under whose personal direction and superintendence it has been effected, from first to last. His name will be held in honour by generations yet to come.

and other useful arts." Next in importance is the Royal Irish Academy, incorporated in 1786, "to promote the study of science, polite literature, and antiquities."

The improved aspect of Dublin will be obvious to all who knew the city even but a few years ago. The streets are cheerful; the shops vie externally with those of London; there is a character of comfort and prosperity in all its highways. Its spacious squares have been always famous; many new buildings have been added to its suburbs; and it is rare to find anywhere a house uninhabited.

Our object, however, is not to describe Dublin. There are guide-books enough to which the Tourist may apply for the information he will need.

The immediate vicinity of Dublin, in all directions round the city, is of great interest and beauty. The beauties of the county of Wicklow are next only to those of Killarney in fame. A railway is now open through Bray and Wicklow town to Enniscorthy and Wexford, through scenery of surpassing loveliness. Our Tour is to the south, by the SOUTH-WESTERN RAILWAY.* This railway commences in one of the suburbs of Dublin, at KINGSBRIDGE—about a mile from the centre of the city, and close to the PHŒNIX PARK, though at the opposite side of the LIFFEY. It is in all respects admirably managed. The line is the middle gauge; the carriages are roomy and comfortable; the attendance at all the stations prompt and active; the several station-houses are models of architectural beauty on a small scale; while the great station at the terminus in Dublin ranks, as a public building, with the many fine structures that have made the city famous.

Here we commence our tour.

The first station out of Dublin is that of CLONDALKIN—a distance of but four miles and a half. At this village there is a round-tower, in a perfect state of preservation. Its height is about ninety feet, and it measures fifteen feet in diameter; its base was, however, about sixty years ago, encased with strong mason-work, in order to protect it from the assaults of time. Immediately adjoining the round-tower are, as usual, the ruins of an ancient church; and it is certain that an abbey was founded here at a very early period.

CLONDALKIN ROUND-TOWER.

Passing the stations of LUCAN, HAZLEHATCH, STRAFFAN, SALLINS, and NEWBRIDGE, places of little note and of no interest, the train stops within sight of KILDARE. The city, although famous for centuries as a "city renowned for saints," has dwindled into comparative insignificance; some remains of its ancient grandeur, however, still exist, the ruined

---

* The Company issues Tourist Tickets, particulars of which will be readily obtained; they are supplied at greatly-reduced rates, being intended as "temptations" to the tour. These tickets have priority of all rights, while the officials pay special attention to those who hold them. They are, indeed, at all stations, and everywhere, letters of recommendation to such courtesies and services as the holder may desire or require.

cathedral retaining marks of its original beauty, extent, and magnificence; and the "round-tower," one of the "tallest" in the kingdom, still attracting the attention of the curious, and the veneration of the antiquary. The bishopric of Kildare is said to have been founded by St. Conloeth, about the middle of the fifth century. The saint, however, was assisted in his labours by the famous St. Bridget, who established a nunnery here, A.D. 484. Her nuns were long celebrated as the guardians of an "inextinguishable fire"—

> "The bright lamp that shone in Kildare's holy fane,
> And burn'd through long ages of darkness and storm,"—

so called, "because," according to Giraldus Cambrensis, "the religious women are so careful and diligent in supplying it with fuel, that, from the time of St. Bridget, it

KILDARE.

hath remained always unextinguished through so many successions of years; and though so vast a quantity of wood has been in such a length of time consumed in it, yet the ashes have never increased."

Within a short distance of the town, between Newtown and Kildare, is the far-famed CURRAGH (through which the railway runs), the principal race-ground in Ireland. It is a fine undulating down, about six miles in length and two in breadth, and is unequalled, perhaps, in the world, for the exceeding softness and elasticity of the turf, the verdure of which is "evergreen," and the occasional irregularities of which are very attractive to the eye. The land is the property of the Crown, and includes about 6,000 acres, where numerous flocks of sheep find rich and abundant pasture.*

The railway next passes through a part of the far-famed Bog of Allen. The Tourist will, however, see little of it in his way. It is of immense extent, containing above 300,000 Irish acres, i.e. about 450,000 English acres.

The next station is MONASTEREVAN, and the next PORTARLINGTON: Portarlington is

---

* A line at the Kildare Junction branches off to Carlow and Kilkenny, and thence to Waterford.

in the Queen's County, and sends a member to Parliament. It is situated on the river Barrow, hence navigable to the sea at Waterford. The county received its title in compliment to Queen Mary, in the fifth year of her reign.

The station next reached is that of MARYBOROUGH. Although the capital town of the Queen's County, it is a place of little note. Distant from it, however, about four miles, and within sight of the railway traveller who looks southward, is the famous Rock of Dunamase, one of the most striking and interesting objects in Ireland. The ruins of a castle stand in the centre of a fertile plain upon a solitary rock, and occupy nearly the whole of it, from the base to the summit. The accompanying print may afford some idea—yet but a limited one, we must confess—of the early strength of the fortress and the exceeding grandeur of the scene. Although from its great natural strength the castle would seem impregnable—except to "the giants," who,

DUNAMASE.

we were told, leaped into it from a far distant hill, leaving the impress of their feet, still shown "in the solid rock"—it was several times taken and retaken by the "ferocious Irish," and the English invaders, their brave but merciless enemies.

The view from the rock summit is to the highest degree magnificent. The spectator stands in the centre of an amphitheatre, gazes over fine and fertile valleys, and notes how bountifully nature has endowed the land. At his feet are huge masses of masonry, scattered in picturesque confusion, which form a strange contrast to the tranquil beauty of the surrounding scene. The fortress seems to have been built for eternity, yet there it is, scarcely one stone upon another.

Passing the stations of MOUNTRATH and CASTLETOWN, ROSCREA, BORRIS, and TEMPLEMORE, we reach the station of THURLES, in the far-famed County of Tipperary.

The station of GOOLD'S CROSS AND CASHEL is next reached.

All the ecclesiastical ruins (of which there are many) in Tipperary, and indeed in Ireland, sink into insignificance compared with those that crown the far-famed "Rock of Cashel." The rock, rising above the adjacent country, is seen from a very long distance, and from every direction by which it is approached—its summit crowned by the venerable remains that have excited the wonder and admiration of ages, and will continue to do for ages yet to come.

The "city"—for the rank belongs to it—has an aspect almost as time-worn as the ruins on the "rock," while infinitely less picturesque. The principal street is wide, and well built; but the lanes and alleys that branch from it, and the suburbs, are mean and wretched.

Let the reader then imagine the beautiful pile of sacred edifices crowning the entire summit of a huge limestone rock, completely isolated and occasionally precipitous, standing in the midst of a luxuriant country, "the Golden Vale," and commanding an extensive prospect—bounded on one side by the lofty range of the Galtee mountains, but permitting, upon all other sides, the eye to wander over miles

ROCK OF CASHEL.

upon miles of a richly cultivated and proverbially productive land; the picturesque effect of which, however, is impaired by the total absence of trees.

The station next reached is DUNDRUM, and the next "the LIMERICK JUNCTION," where, as the name indicates, the branch line to Limerick commences; the city being distant twenty-two miles; and this also is the Waterford Junction: for here the carriages for Waterford join to proceed either to Limerick, Cork, Dublin—or MALLOW, *en route* to Killarney.

The station next, on the Cork line, is KNOCKLONG, and next, that of the ancient and venerable town of KILMALLOCK—the ruins of which are seen to the right. Kilmallock has been termed, not inaptly, the "Baalbec of Ireland." It was the chief seat of "the Desmonds." Their history is akin to romance. Throughout the south of Ireland, and in Limerick county more especially, it will be difficult to travel a dozen miles in any direction without encountering some object that tells of their former greatness.* Kilmallock is now a mass of ruins; miserable hovels are propped up by the walls of stately mansions, and "the ancient and loyal borough"—for so it was styled so recently as 1783, when it retained the privilege of sending two members

---

* The whole central district of Limerick is, indeed, studded with remains, religious and castellated, still emphatically speaking of the former power of the Geraldines—now ruined and decayed. A chain of towers may be traced in continuous succession from the Shannon to Kilmallock, indicating the territorial supremacy of the Fitzgeralds; whilst their numerous and elaborate ecclesiastical structures tell of the wealth, munificence, and taste of that noble race. Kilmallock, Askeaton, and Adare are objects of pilgrimage, to all who love the picturesque and relics of the magnificent.

to Parliament—is as humiliating a picture of fallen grandeur as may be found in any country of the world:—

"The peasant holds the lordly pile,
And cattle fill the roofless aisle."

The ancient houses, or rather the remains of them, are of hewn stone, and appear to have been built on a uniform plan; they were generally of three stories, ornamented with an embattlement, and tasteful stone mouldings; the limestone window frames, stone mullions, and capacious fire-places, are carved in a bold and massive style, and retain nearly their original sharpness. The engraving is a copy of one of the few remaining doors, braced with iron. The abbey and church, being held sacred by the peasantry, are in a better state of preservation than the houses. The former, which stands within the town walls, and adjoins the river, was dedicated to SS. Peter and Paul. It consists of a nave, choir, and south transept.

AT KILMALLOCK.

The Dominican Friary, of which we also give a view, is situate at the north-east side of the town. It is subdivided into a church and convent. The former is again separated into a choir, nave, and transept, a tall steeple standing at their intersection; the west wall of which, as well as the south wall of the steeple, have fallen down.

A distinguished English antiquary, the late Sir Richard Hoare, observes of this Friary, "It surpasses in decoration and good sculpture any I have yet seen in Ireland; but does not," he adds, "seem older than the reign of King Edward the Third." A fragment of the tomb of the White Knights lies on the ground; a small hollow in the middle of which is said to be never without a supply of water. This they call the *Braon shinsher*, i.e. the "drop of the old stock."

RUINS, KILMALLOCK.

The next station is CHARLEVILLE, a poor town, so named by the Earl of Orrery, the Lord President of Munster, as a compliment to Charles II., having been previously called, to use his lordship's expression, by the "heathenish name of Rathgogan."

RUINS, KILMALLOCK.

The next station is BUTTEVANT, described by Borlace as "an old nest of abbots, priests, and friars." Though formerly a place of note, it dwindled into a mere village with the decay of its noble abbey. Buttevant was anciently called Botham; and by the Irish—a name which Spenser has recorded—Kilnemulagh.

Buttevant and its neighbourhood—its hills, its valleys, and its rivers—have been rendered classic by the pen of the immortal poet; for Spenser not only resided at Kilcoleman—the ruined walls of which still remain—but here he composed his "Faëry Queen," making surrounding objects themes of his undying song.

In the neighbourhood of Kilcoleman there are several objects to which Spenser has especially referred; and we are justified in concluding that the country around him excited his imagination, influenced his muse, and gave being to many of his most sublime and beautiful descriptions of scenery—

"Mole, that mountain hore,
And Mulla mine, whose waves I whilome taught to weep!"

The river and the mountain still endure, but the poet's estate long ago passed into the hands of those who have neither his name nor lineage.

The station next reached is MALLOW. Here is the Cork and Killarney Junction; and here the Tourist will be called upon to choose his route; proceeding direct to Killarney—or on to Cork, with a view of taking a route less direct, but more picturesque, and infinitely more instructive.

We shall presently describe the Railway route from Mallow to Killarney Town; briefly, however, for it is of little interest. We advise the Tourist to first visit Cork, distant only twenty miles, returning thence to Mallow; or what, we repeat, will be far better, taking one of the coach routes from Cork; our reasons for tendering such advice will be given in due course.

He will be well repaid, however, if he stay a day at Mallow, especially if he be

KILCOLEMAN CASTLE.

an angler, and will tread the banks of pleasant Blackwater. At Mallow there is now a first-class hotel, well furnished, and in all ways comfortable; moreover, the grounds are laid out with much taste.

Thus far, then, we have conducted the Tourist. The only point of interest between Mallow and Cork—and the only station—is BLARNEY, which we prefer to describe as one of the excursions from "THE BEAUTIFUL CITY OF CORK."

CORK AND ITS HARBOUR.

THE distant appearance of Cork harbour, from the seaward approach, is gloomy, rocky, and inhospitable; but as its entrance between two bold headlands—scarcely half a mile apart, and crowned by fortifications—opens upon the view, its character undergoes a complete change. The town of QUEENSTOWN,* with the island of Spike (forming a sort of natural breakwater), and several smaller islands, give variety and interest to a noble expanse of sea that spreads out, like a luxuriant lake, to welcome and rejoice the visitor; its sparkling billows heaving and tumbling in sportive mimicry of the wild and wide ocean without. The harbour is one of the most secure, capacious, and beautiful of the kingdom, and is said to be large enough to contain the whole navy of Great Britain. Queenstown is seen fronting the mouth of the harbour almost immediately after it is entered. It is built on the side of a steep hill, and rises from the water's edge, terrace above terrace; the more elevated parts commanding a magnificent bird's-eye view of the extensive anchorage. The town has, therefore, natural advantages of a rare order. On all sides the shore is covered with villas—the trees, usually stunted on the coast, grow here gracefully and majestically; the

---

* "Queenstown" will not be found in any of the books older than 1849, although "Cove" has been at all times famous. The name of this port-town was changed from Cove to Queenstown in honour of Her Majesty, who there first landed in Ireland, in the year 1849.

islands, and fortified headlands, are so many imposing objects within view; and the gay yachts, which a Tourist described a century ago as "little vessels, that for painting and gilding exceed those of the king at Greenwich," give animation and variety to the exciting scene.

HAULBOWLIN HARBOUR.

The harbour is diversified by other islands beside that of SPIKE—the largest: one of the most conspicuous, Haulbowlin—the depot for naval stores—is here represented, with fishing-boats waiting for the tide to proceed to sea.

Leaving these islands to the left, the voyager passes up the beautiful river; rounding a wooded promontory, the village and castle of MONKSTOWN come in sight. The castle was built in the year 1636, and, according to popular tradition, at the cost of a groat. To explain the enigma, the following story is told:—Anastatia Goold, who had become the wife of John Archdeken, determined while her husband was abroad, serving in the army of Philip of Spain, to give him evidence of her thrift on his return, by surprising him with a noble residence which he might call his own. Her plan was, to supply the workmen with provisions and other articles they required, for which she charged the ordinary price; but as she had made her purchases wholesale, upon balancing her accounts it appeared that the retail profit had paid all the expenses of the structure, except fourpence! The Archdekens were an Anglo-Irish family, who, "degenerating," became "Hibernices quam Hiberniores"—more Irish than the Irish themselves—and assumed the name of Mac Odo, or Cody. They "forfeited" in 1688, having followed the fortunes of James II.

About a mile nearer the city is the village of PASSAGE, where all large vessels discharge their cargoes, and where an excellent quay has been built to facilitate the embarkation and disembarkation of passengers; and from whence there is a railway to Cork, through Black-rock. On the other side of the Lee there is a railway direct from Cork to Queenstown.

The whole distance to the city from the harbour's mouth, about twelve miles, is one continued scene of varied interest. To do full justice to the exceeding beauty of the river Lee is impossible. On either side, immediately after passing the harbour's mouth, numberless attractive objects in succession greet the eye; and the wild and the cultivated are so happily mingled, that it would seem as if the hand of taste had been everywhere employed, skilfully, to direct and improve nature. Moore, during one of his visits, called it "the noble sea avenue to Cork;" and an Eastern traveller, with whom we journeyed, observed that "a few minarets placed in its hanging gardens would realise the Bosphorus." As we proceed along, the land seems always around us; the river, in its perpetual changes, appears a series of lakes, from which there is no passage except over the encompassing hills. These hills are clad, from the summit to the water's edge, with every variety of foliage; graceful villas and cottages are scattered among them in profusion, and here and there some ancient ruin recalls a story of the past.

ARMS OF THE CITY.

A sail from Cork to Queenstown is one of the rarest and richest treats the island can supply, and might justify a description that would seem akin to hyperbole. Its noble harbour, indeed, originated the motto—"statio bene fida carinis"— so aptly and deservedly applied to it. The city arms, here represented, there can be no doubt, were suggested by the arms of Bristol; similar privileges to those enjoyed by that city having been granted to Cork by charter.

The moment the voyager lands, he is impressed with a conviction that the natural advantages of Cork have been turned to good account. There is bustle on the quays; carriages and carts of all classes are waiting to convey passengers or merchandise to their destination; and an air of prosperity cheers him as he disembarks.

It does not fall within our province to supply the reader with details concerning the city of Cork—the second city of Ireland. According to our present plan, it is of importance chiefly as furnishing to the Tourist the means that enable him to reach Killarney. He will not, however, pass through it, unless speed be very necessary, without pausing to examine its objects of interest, and they are numerous and striking; nor will he pursue his route without taking a day at least to drive about the beautiful scenery by which it is on all sides surrounded. A few of our pages may therefore be advantageously filled with suggestions for turning this portion of the tour to profitable account.

The situation of Cork is low, having been originally built on marshy islands; whence its name—"Corcagh," signifying in Irish, land occasionally overflowed by the tide: but the northern and southern suburbs stand upon high ground. Scarcely a century has passed since the river ran through its principal streets, which are formed by arching over the stream. Spenser has happily described—

"The spreading Lee, that like an island fair
Encloseth Cork with his divided flood."

Cork has a cheerful and prosperous aspect; the leading streets are wide; and though the houses may be described as built with studied irregularity, their character is by no means ungraceful or unpleasing. The quays at either side of the Lee—here of course a river muddied from traffic—are constructed of limestone, and may be said to merit the term so frequently applied to them, "grand and elegant."

DOORWAY, ST. FINN BAR.

Antiquities are rare; the cathedral, dedicated to St. Finn Bar, is built on the site of the early church, a few of the remains of which have been introduced into the modern structure. The tower of the steeple is comparatively ancient. The pointed doorway, recessed and richly moulded, is shown in the annexed cut. A round tower formerly stood in the churchyard; but having been considerably injured by the fire from the fort on Barrack Hill when the great Marlborough stormed Cork, this venerable remain was taken down, and no trace of it at present exists.*

Institutions, charitable, scientific, and literary, abound in Cork; it has been celebrated more than any other city of Ireland for the production and fosterage of genius, and is the birthplace of many persons who have attained eminence in literature, science, and the arts.

The jails of Cork—the "city" and "county"—are models of good management, cleanliness, and order; and the Lunatic Asylum is among the best conducted institutions of the kingdom. The hotels are excellent;† and the city contains many fine buildings; the most recently erected, the College, the Athenæum, and some others, being now its chief architectural ornaments.

Promenades in the immediate neighbourhood of Cork are few; the oldest is the Mardyke, a walk between rows of aged but ungracefully lopped trees. Once it was lonely and retired, but the spirit of building has surrounded it with houses, and its solitary character, its only recommendation—is for ever gone. The new cemetery, however, demands some notice. It was formerly a botanic garden attached to the Cork Institution; but in 1826 was sold to the Very Rev. Theobald Mathew, who converted it to its present use.‡ It is, therefore, perhaps unrivalled in the kingdom,

---

* The Cathedral of St. Finn Bar is, however, about to be rebuilt; although interesting and full of association, it is by no means worthy of the city.

† The best of the hotels is "the Imperial," on the South Mall: it is as well managed as any hotel in the kingdom. Here a table d'hote is fitted up especially for the accommodation of tourists, and the charges are very reasonable. Those who desire to post the tour to Killarney may procure good carriages and horses at the posting establishment of Mr. Cotton, opposite the hotel—in Pembroke Street. His drivers are generally excellent guides; and he sees himself to all the wants and wishes of travellers.

‡ No writer concerning Cork can omit to mention with honour and homage the name of the Rev. Theobald Mathew, who now rests from his labours in this cemetery. In the city of Cork this truly great and good man commenced the temperance movement; it spread rapidly throughout Ireland; millions received from the hands of the estimable Roman Catholic clergyman a pledge "to abstain from all intoxicating drinks, and to discountenance the cause and practice of intemperance." The regeneration of the people thus effected can be understood and estimated only by those who knew Ireland and the Irish in "old times:" it is said, indeed, that the pledge has been frequently broken; and that numbers have gone back to the evil habit of drinking. This may be—we believe is—the case; but hundreds of thousands have

being full of rare trees; its walls are covered with climbing roses and other shrubs; and from the nature of its soil and aspect, everything is growing in luxuriant profusion. The hand of science has laid out its gravelled paths, and the art of the

THE CEMETERY, CORK.

sculptor has been employed to ornament it—occasionally with good taste and effect.

The whole of the immediate outlets of Cork possess considerable interest, and their natural beauties are, perhaps, not exceeded by those of any of the kingdom. The Glanmire road on the one side, and the Black Rock road on the other side of the Lee, are charming walks or drives: villas abound all the way; and the river, with its many objects of interest, is always in view. The most "famous," and certainly the most interesting of the neighbouring localities, is BLARNEY—a village about four miles north-west of Cork. Few places in Ireland are more familiar to English ears. This notoriety is attributable, first to the marvellous qualities of its famous "stone," and next, to the extensive popularity of the song—

"The groves of Blarney, they are so charming."

When or how the stone obtained its singular reputation, it is difficult to determine; the exact position among the ruins of the castle is also a matter of doubt. The peasant-guides humour the visitor according to his capacity for climbing, and direct, either to the summit or the base, the attention of him who desires to "greet it with

---

shared the blessings of temperance; a vast proportion of the people are now sober who were formerly drunkards: drunkenness, at one time considered rather a glory than a shame, has become a reproach; and neither "gentle nor simple" would now-a-days openly exhibit himself intoxicated without the certainty that his society would be shunned by all respectable persons of his class. Let then those who visit Cork honour it as the city of the Rev. Theobald Mathew: for truly his "works do follow him," and his name will be venerated from generation to generation. No man ever bore his honours more meekly, encountered opposition with greater gentleness and forbearance, or disarmed hostility by weapons better suited to a gentleman and a Christian. Recently his fellow citizens have placed a statue of the good and venerable clergyman in one of the leading streets of their city. It is an admirable work of art, from the atelier of the great Irish sculptor, Foley.

a holy kiss." He who has been dipped in the Shannon is presumed to have obtained, in abundance, the gift of that "civil courage" which makes an Irishman at ease and unconstrained in all places and under all circumstances; and he who has kissed the Blarney stone is assumed to be endowed with a fluent and persuasive tongue, although it may be associated with insincerity: the term "Blarney" being generally used to characterise words that are not meant to be either "honest or true."

It is impossible to contemplate the romantic ruins of Blarney Castle without a

BLARNEY CASTLE.

feeling more akin to melancholy than to pleasure; they bear, so perfectly, the aspect of strength utterly subdued, and remind one, so forcibly, that the "glory" of Ireland belongs to days departed.

The stronghold of Blarney was erected about the middle of the fifteenth century by Cormac Mac Carthy, surnamed "Laider," or the Strong; whose ancestors had been chieftains in Munster from a period long antecedent to the English invasion, and whose descendants, as Lords of Muskerry and Clancarty, retained no inconsiderable portion of their power and estates until the year 1689, when their immense possessions were confiscated. The scenery that adjoins the castle is exceedingly beautiful. We visited "The sweet Rock-close"—it well deserves the epithet—during a sunny day in June; and never can we forget the fragrant shade afforded by the luxuriant evergreens that seem rooted in the limestone rock. The little river Comane is guarded by a natural terrace, fringed by noble trees; several of the spaces between are grottos—natural also; some with seats, where many a love-tale has been told, and will be, doubtless, as long as Cork lads and lasses indulge in pic-nic fêtes, while the blackbird whistles, and the wood-pigeon coos in the twisted foliage above their heads: it is indeed a spot of exceeding wildness and singular beauty; at some particular points you catch a glimpse of the castle, the river, and the mysterious entrance to the "Witches' Stairs." We wandered from the shades of the Rock-close across the green pastures that lead to the lake—a fine expanse of water about a quarter of a mile from the castle. The scenery here is rather English than Irish, but every step is hallowed by a legend; it is implicitly believed that the last Earl of Clancarty who inhabited the castle committed the keeping of his plate to the deepest waters, and that it will never be recovered until a Mac Carthy be again Lord of Blarney. Enchanted cows on midsummer nights dispute the pasture with those of the present possessor, and many an earthly bull has been worsted in the contest. As to fairies—their rings are upon the grass from early summer to the last week in harvest.

The road to Blarney is singularly beautiful: it runs along the upper Lee, through Sunday's Well; commanding charming views, near and distant. On a hill side, approaching Blarney, is the famous and prosperous establishment of Dr. Barter—the "cold water cure;" the Turkish baths are under the same roof.

We have devoted as much space as we can well spare to the City of Cork and its vicinity. The subject, however, might supply material for a full volume instead of a few pages. Thus much, at least, appeared necessary in order to suggest hints of the enjoyment the Tourist may derive from a visit to "THE BEAUTIFUL CITY."

THE ROUTES FROM CORK.

BANDON AND THE SEA COAST.

LEAVING Cork for Killarney, the Tourist will, as we have intimated, have a choice of routes: that which takes him from Dublin to Killarney direct by railway we have described. Travellers who have but little time to spare, and study economy, may proceed from Cork to BANDON (by railway) through Dunmanway, and thence to Bantry. From Cork to Bandon, by railway, the distance is twenty miles.* Bandon is situate, according to Spenser, on

"The pleasant Bandon, crown'd by many a wood."

The woods have, however, long since fallen under the axe of the woodman. The town was formerly called Brandon-bridge, and was built by the first Earl of Cork, who in a letter to Mr. Secretary Cook, dated April 13, 1632, describes "the place in which it is situated" as "upon a great district of the country, that was until lately a mere waste of bog and wood, serving for a retreat and harbour to wood-kernes, rebels, thieves, and wolves." His lordship adds, as the strong claim of Bandon to royal favour and protection, that "no Popish recusant, or un-conforming novelist, is admitted to live in all the town;" † and Smith, so late as 1750, states, that "in the town there is not a Popish inhabitant, nor will the townsmen suffer one to dwell in it, nor a piper to play in the place, that being the music formerly used by the Irish in their wars." The old and illiberal system has long since been exploded; the bagpipes are now heard as frequently in Bandon as elsewhere; and among its dealers and chapmen are numerous descendants of the Irish Mac Sweeneys and O'Sullivans, and the Anglo-Irish Coppingers and Fitzgeralds. The town is of considerable size, populous and flourishing, being the great thoroughfare into Carbery. It belongs partly to the Duke of Devonshire, and partly to the Earl of Bandon, whose beautiful seat, Castle Bernard, is in its immediate neighbourhood.

---

* A coach is "put on" during summer to drive to Bantry, through Inchageelah, and the Pass of Keim-an-eigh, thus taking in much of the picturesque route we shall presently describe.

† There is a statement generally credited, but which, we believe, rests on no good authority (for we have vainly searched for and inquired concerning the alleged fact) that the Corporation formerly had carved upon the town gate the illiberal and insulting couplet:—

"Enter here, Jew, Turk, or Atheist,
Anybody but a Papist;"

under which, it is said, upon authority equally apocryphal, an angry wit wrote the following:—

"Whoever wrote this wrote it well—
The same is carved on the gate of H—."

It is more than probable that the author of the latter was also the author of the former couplet; and that neither was ever seen upon the gates of Bandon.

From BANDON to BANTRY there are two roads: the northern and nearest, through BALLYNEEN, DUNMANWAY, and DRIMOLEAGUE; and the southern and most picturesque, along the coast, through CLONAKILTY, ROSS-CARBERY, and SKIBBEREEN. Dunmanway is a poor town, although the only one in a large district. This is the shorter road to "the Lakes," and is therefore preferred by those whose time is limited. The coast road, however, has many attractions; and although, as we shall show, they are yet greater by the inland route, through Macroom, a brief notice of the coast line may be desirable.

The coast-road runs from Bandon almost due south to CLONAKILTY. Although a seaport, Clonakilty carries on but small trade, and is a place of no importance. Ross-CARBERY demands more particular notice. It is one of the oldest towns in Ireland, the ancient name being Ross-Alithri, "the field of pilgrimage;" and, according to Hanmer, "there was here anciently a famous university, whereto resorted all the south-west part of Ireland for learning sake." It was formerly a bishop's see, but was united with that of Cork, and also with that of Cloyne.

Between the towns of Ross-Carbery and SKIBBEREEN, and at the head of GLANDORE harbour, the Tourist passes along a beautiful and picturesque road, where

"Lakes upon lakes interminably gleam,"

and to one point in particular his attention should be directed—the glen called "the Leap," the ancient boundary which divided the civilised from the uncivilised, "Beyond the Leap, beyond the Law," being, even within our memory, an accepted proverb.* Not far from Skibbereen is a singular salt-water lake—Lough Hyne, or Ine (the Deep Lake). In the centre is a long island, upon which are the ruins of one of the castles of the O'Driscolls. It is surrounded by picturesque hills, some rocky and precipitous, others steep and woody, rising from the lake. Our sketch is from a churchyard, peculiar to Ireland, devoted exclusively to the interment of children,† and where there was formerly a chapel dedicated to St. Bridget. In the foreground is one of the singular ring-stones, or pillar-stones, engraven with inscrutable characters. It is

---

* Walking one day in the neighbourhood of his residence, at Glandore, Colonel Hall (to whose mining undertakings we shall have occasion to refer when visiting Ross Island at Killarney) noticed some fish bones of a green hue among turf ashes; his curiosity was excited to inquire by what means they obtained so singular a colour, and on analysing them he found they contained copper. His next object was to ascertain how they acquired this unnatural quality; and he learned that it was received from contact with the ashes of turf, cut in a neighbouring bog, known to the peasantry as the "stinking bog," and that neither dog nor cat would live in the cabin in which the turf was burnt. Having gathered so much, his farther progress was easy. The ashes were strongly impregnated with copper. He first collected from the heaps adjoining the cottages as large a quantity as he could, and shipped it to Swansea, where it brought, if we remember rightly, between eight and nine pounds a ton—a remunerating price. His next step was to take a lease of the bog, build kilns upon it, and burn the turf. This plan he continued until the whole of the bog was consumed, and sent, to the extent of several hundred tons, to the Welsh smelting-houses, the ease with which it was smelted greatly enhancing its value. It was a curious sight—and one we recollect well—to see scores of workmen cutting the turf, conveying it to one kiln to dry, and then to another to be burnt; while the carts were bearing the ashes to the river side to be shipped for Wales. Mr. Croker, in his volume on "the South of Ireland," states that "the particles contained in the turf are supposed to have been conveyed into the bog by a stream from one of the surrounding hills, which, passing through a copper vein, took them up in a state of sulphate; but meeting with some iron ore in its progress, or in the bog, became deposited in the metallic state, though a large proportion contained in the turf was still in a state of sulphate, which was proved by allowing a knife to remain in it a few minutes, when it became incrusted with a coat of copper." Unfortunately for Colonel Hall, however, when the bog was burnt out, he considered his operations as only commenced; his object being to discover the vein of ore by which the bog had been supplied with copper. In a vain search for the source, technically called "the lode," he expended all he had made by sales of the ashes. Shafts were sunk in several of the surrounding hills, and he continued the pursuit until his capital was exhausted.

† These singular and peculiar grave-yards occur frequently in the counties of Cork and Kerry; in the Island of Valentia there are no less than four; their date is very remote. They have been used only occasionally during the present century.

immortalised in traditionary lore, and the country people attach great value to it, affirming that it has been gifted by the patron saint with miraculous power—at least for its own preservation. It has been repeatedly removed, to form lintels for doors,

LOUGH HYNE.

and to answer various other purposes, but always found its way back again to its original station. With this lake there is also connected another legend—but one common to nearly all the deep-bedded and lonely loughs, with "gloomy shores;" for Lough Hyne

"Skylark never warbles o'er."

As at Glendalough, the sweet birds "singing to heaven's gate" having disturbed the saint at her orisons, she prayed to the Virgin to silence their song; and was so far answered, that they were ordered into a solitude less sacred to penitence and prayer. From Skibbereen the Tourist will probably proceed to Bantry: leaving the wild coast with its two village-towns, BALLEDEHOB and SKULL.* To the south-west the coast is dotted with islands—

"Sea-girt isles,
That, like to rich and various gems, inlay
The unadorned bosom of the deep;"

the most famous of which is CAPE CLEAR. INISHERKEN, immediately opposite Baltimore harbour is full of interest; its ruined abbey is pictured in the annexed print.

---

* At Balledehob are the ruins of two copper mines, discovered and worked by Colonel Hall—one of them so extensively, as for a long period to employ between 400 and 500 persons. The copper mine of Kippagh, also discovered and worked by him, is some four or five miles from the sea. It is the famous mine on the Audley estate, to work which a company was formed in London *after* it had been exhausted and abandoned by Colonel Hall; of course the speculation was a total loss to the shareholders.

The O'Driscolls had formerly castles here, which defended the entrance to the harbour. Cape Clear—the well-known landmark for vessels outward or inward bound—is the most southern point of Ireland. On the south side is the lighthouse, which, it is

INISHERKEN.

said, may be distinguished in clear weather from a distance of twenty-eight nautical miles. On the north-west point of the island is the singularly picturesque ruin of the castle of Dunanore, or the Golden Fort. It stands on a rock; a very narrow

DUNANORE CASTLE.

passage leads to it; the path being so steep and high, and the sea dashing and foaming against it on either side, the ascent to it is a somewhat perilous task. Legends enough to make a volume are connected with this ruin; it was formerly a stronghold of the O'Driscolls, some of whom are stated to have mingled the hospitalities of the Irish chieftain with the daring of the buccaneer.

The mail-coach road from Skibbereen to Bantry runs through a wild and uninteresting country; and the traveller who desires to examine the most peculiar and picturesque portion of the Irish coast will have to pursue a route less easy of access, but far more certain of recompense for the expenditure of time and labour. The mountains appear to rise directly from the sea, as if they were but the continuations of mountains underneath the ocean; small villages are thickly scattered at their base. Mount Gabriel, bleak and barren from the foot to the summit, looks down upon the poor village—once a famous collegiate town—of Schull.

Lakes are to be seen in every valley, upon the mountain sides, and on their summits, from whence pour down the streams that now and then break in cataracts over precipices; while opposite is the sea, with its stores of green islands, or black rocks—creeks, and bays, and harbours running into the land; and beyond all, the broad Atlantic, that affords no resting-place for the sea-bird until he closes up his wings and stands on the continent of America.

The ocean with its tales of shipwrecks and piracies, the land with its legends and traditions, afford themes to fill folios of interest and excitement; every castle (of which there remain the ruins of many) has its story of bold adventure. The lakes, too, are fertile of legends: for examples—that on the summit of Mount Gabriel, with its eternal serpent and depth that has never been fathomed; Loughdrine, where on a certain day in every year the islands used to dance merrily, change places, and shift from one side to the other from sunrise to sunset; Ballinlough, where the fairies keep nightly guard, protecting the passage that leads from the ancient rath that borders it to the bottom, where flourishes the Thierna-na-oge—"the land of perpetual youth." The stranger will, in short, find, wherever he travels in this wild and comparatively primitive neighbourhood, a rich abundance to interest, excite, and amuse, and not a little to inform and instruct.

And so, by this Coast Route, the Tourist arrives at Bantry. A brief sojourn here will suffice: it will be recompensed principally by the views to be obtained from the summits of adjacent hills, or by a sail across the bay.

MACROOM, INCHAGEELA, AND GOUGANE BARRA.

THOSE who desire to see the landscape beauties of the South, to form ideas of the peculiar character of the peasantry, and generally as to the condition and prospects of the country—to whom time is not an object—will take the route we are about to describe to them, through Macroom, Inchageela, and Gougane Barra, to Bantry; and from Bantry to Glengariff and Kenmare, and thence to Killarney.

We assume that the Tourist will travel by one of the ordinary "cars" of the country, concerning which he will have heard much; and as it is necessary he should form acquaintance with this peculiar vehicle, we will take advantage of the opportunity to picture for him the several carriages from which he will be called upon to take his choice, premising, however, that in nearly all cases "the outside car" will be preferred.

During the summer months, and for the convenience of Tourists (as we have intimated) stage-coaches ply from Bandon to Macroom, Inchageela, Gougane Barra, and Glengariff; yet we shall advise all who can do so, to travel this wild and beautiful district at leisure, with a "conveyance" of their own. We may begin by advising the traveller in Ireland to lay in a stock of good humour; for petty annoyances will frequently occur, and it is a coin that passes current everywhere, but is of especial value there; and to take also a plentiful supply of water-proof clothing, for sunny June is no more to be trusted than showery April. Some one has said that the only day in which you can be certain to escape a wetting is on the 30th of February—a day that never comes; and it is recorded of Mr. Fox, we believe, that whenever he received a visitor from Ireland, after his own brief tour in the country, his invariable question was, "By the way, is that shower over yet?" This is, undoubtedly, a sad drawback upon pleasure; the humidity of the atmosphere is a continual affliction to those who are not used to it; and is sufficiently compensated for by the fact, that the grass in Ireland is ever green, and the clouds are at all times moving in forms, majestic or fantastic, of infinite variety. Yet the evil is one that can be guarded against; and, inasmuch as prevention is better than cure, heavy showers should always be encountered by anticipation.

Machines for travelling in Ireland are, some of them at least, peculiar to the country. The stage-coaches are precisely similar to those in England, and travel at as rapid a rate. They, of course, run upon all the great roads, and are constructed with due regard to safety and convenience. The public cars of Mr. Bianconi have, however, to a large extent, displaced the regular coaches, and are to be encountered in every district of the south of Ireland. In form they resemble the common outside jaunting-car, but are calculated to hold twelve, fourteen, or sixteen persons; they are well horsed, have cautious and experienced drivers, are generally driven with three horses, and usually travel at the rate of seven Irish miles an hour; the fares for each person averaging about two-pence per mile. They are open cars; but a huge apron affords considerable protection against rain; and they may be described as, in

BIANCONI'S CAR.

all respects, very comfortable and convenient vehicles. It would be difficult for a stranger to conceive the immense influence which this establishment has had upon the character and condition of the country; its introduction, indeed, has been only second to that of steam in promoting the improvement of Ireland, by facilitating intercourse between remote districts, and enabling the farmer to transact his own business at a small expense and with little sacrifice of time.* Mr. Bianconi, a native of Milan, ran his first car—from Clonmel to Cahir—on the 6th of July, 1815. The experiment was at the commencement very discouraging: he was frequently for whole weeks without a passenger. But his energy and perseverance ultimately triumphed, and he has succeeded in obtaining a large fortune, while conferring incalculable benefit on the community; having preserved an irreproachable character, and gained the respect of all classes.†

---

* It would be impossible to exaggerate the importance of opening roads through the less frequented districts of Ireland. The necessity which formerly existed for keeping a large armed force there has had, at least, this one good effect: "military roads" are to be found in all quarters. One of the wildest mountain-tracts of the county of Cork was, a few years ago, dangerous for travellers at all seasons, and a source of considerable annoyance to the Government. The question was asked, "What was to be done?" A shrewd adviser answered, "Make a road through it." The advice was taken, and the Bograh mountains are now peaceable and prosperous.

† Bianconi, at the Social Science in 1861, made these remarks:—"Notwithstanding the inroads made on my establishment by the railways, and which displaced over 1,000 horses, and obliged me to direct my attention to such portions of the country as had not before the benefit of my conveyances, it still employs about 900 horses, travelling over 4,000 miles daily, passing through twenty-three counties, having 137 stations, and working twelve mail and day coaches 672 miles; fifty four-wheel cars, with two and more horses, travelling 1,930 miles; and sixty-six two-wheel one-horse cars, travelling 1,604 miles. And I repeat with pleasure the testimony I gave in 1857—namely, that 'my conveyances have been in existence now forty-six years; many of them carrying very important mails, have been travelling during all hours of the day and the night, often in lonely and unfrequented places, yet the slightest injury has never been done by the people to my property, or that entrusted to my care.'"

Post-chaises are now but seldom used; they are to be had in all the larger towns but, although very different from what they were when the caricature pictured one thatched with straw, from the bottom of which the traveller's legs protruded, they are by no means vehicles that can be strongly recommended. In all the leading towns, however, comfortable carriages for travelling are to be obtained.

The cars are of three kinds; "the covered car," "the inside jaunting car," and "the outside jaunting car;" the latter being the one most generally in use, and the only one employed in posting. The two former, indeed, can seldom be procured except in large towns. The covered car is a comparatively recent introduction, its sole recommendation being that it is weather-proof, for it effectually prevents a view of the country except through the two little peep-hole windows in front, or by tying back the oil-skin curtains behind: yet our longer journeys in Ireland have been made in this machine; it preserved us from many a wetting, and we endeavoured to remedy the evil of confinement by stopping at every promising spot, and either getting out or making the driver turn his vehicle round, so that, from the back, we might command the prospect we desired.

COVERED JAUNTING CAR.

The inside jaunting-car is not often to be hired; it is usually private property, and is, perhaps, the most comfortable, as well as elegant, of the vehicles of the country.

INSIDE JAUNTING-CAR.

The outside jaunting-car is that to which especial reference is made when speaking of the "Irish" car. It is exceedingly light, presses very little upon the horse, and is safe as well as convenient; so easy it is to get on and off, that both are frequently done while the machine is in motion. It is always driven with a single horse; the driver occupies a small seat in front, and the travellers sit back to back,* the space between them being occupied by "the well"—a sort of boot for luggage; but when there is only one passenger, the driver usually places himself on the opposite seat "to balance the car," the motion of which would be awkward if one side was much heavier than the other. The foot "board" is generally of iron, and is made to move on hinges, so that it

---

* This arrangement has been characterised as unsocial; but conversation is easily carried on by leaning across "the well." Its disadvantage is that the eye can take in but the half of a landscape; a caustic friend likened it to the Irish character, which limits the vision to a one-sided view of everything.

may be turned up to protect the cushions during rain. This foot-board projects considerably beyond the wheels, and would seem to be dangerous; but in cases of collision with other vehicles, a matter of no very rare occurrence, the feet are raised, and injury is sustained only by the machine. The private cars of this description are, of course, neatly and carefully made, and have a character of much elegance; but those which are hired are, in general, badly built and uncomfortable.

The cabriolet is, however, now generally used in Dublin and the other leading cities and towns of Ireland: the fares being, as with the outside cars, sixpence a mile.

The car, or rather cart, used by the peasantry, requires some notice. Flat boards are placed across it, and upon these straw is laid, and often a feather-bed. The one

OUTSIDE JAUNTING CAR.

described in the engraving has the old-fashioned wheels, cut out of a solid piece of wood. These vehicles are now, however, nearly obsolete; their unfitness having been understood, they have given way before modern improvements. The "low-back'd-car," which Lover has made famous in song, belongs to this class; they have, like

OLD CAR OF THE PEASANT.

most things Irish, been of late made infinitely more pleasant than they used to be. In Ireland there are few turnpikes; the repairs of the roads usually falling upon the county, money for the purpose being annually voted by the grand juries. The roads are for the most part good; and of late years a better system of surveying, so largely introduced into the country, has led to the formation of "new lines," to nearly every place of importance. The old plan, therefore, of carrying a road "as the bird flies," up and down the steepest hills, through morasses, and along the brinks of frightful precipices, has been entirely abandoned; and, at present, the carriage will generally require springs no stronger than those which are used in England. The lover of the picturesque, indeed, will not unfrequently prefer the rugged pathway of former times, and think himself amply repaid for greater toil and fatigue by the prospect opened to him from the mountain tops, or the refreshment he derives from following the course of the river that rushes through the valley. He will, however, sometimes have to leave the car, and walk through a morass, over a broken bridge, or along a dangerous ravine, which time has deprived of the wall that once guarded it. Our esteemed and valued friend, the late Mr. W. Willes, supplied us with a sketch, that may convey some idea of the "perils that do environ" the traveller who seeks adventure along the neglected or deserted tracks.

Persons who have never travelled in Ireland can have but a very inadequate idea

OLD IRISH ROAD.

of the wit and humour of the Irish car-drivers. They are for the most part a thoughtless and reckless set of men, living upon chances, always "taking the world aisy"—that is to say, having no care for the morrow, and seldom being owners of a more extensive wardrobe than the nondescript mixture they carry about their persons. They are the opposite in all respects of the English postilions: the latter do their duty, but seldom familiarise their "fares" to the sound of their voices. In nine cases out of ten the traveller never exchanges a word with his post-boy; a touch of the hat acknowledges the gratuity when "the stage" is ended; and the driver having consigned his charge to his successor, departs, usually in ignorance whether his chaise has contained man, woman, or child. He neither knows, nor cares for, aught of their concerns, except that he is to advance so many miles upon such a road, according to the instructions of his employer. The Irish driver, on the contrary, will ascertain, during your progress, where you come from, where you are going, and, very often, what you are going about. He has a hundred ways of wiling himself into your confidence, and is sure to put in a word or two upon every available opportunity; yet in such a manner as to render it impossible for you to subject him to the charge of impertinence. Indeed it is a striking peculiarity of the lower classes of the Irish, that they can be familiar without being presuming; tender advice without appearing intrusive; and even command your movements without seeming to interfere in the least with your own free-will. This quality the car-driver enjoys to perfection. Formerly, he rarely took his seat without being half-intoxicated; now-a-days an occurrence of the kind is very rare. It cannot be denied, however, that much of his natural drollery has vanished with the whiskey. The chances now are that the Irish driver will be as commonplace a personage as the English postilion, conveying you safely to your journey's end without causing alarm or exciting laughter. Still you may be lucky in meeting a pleasant fellow, who combines the humour of the old school with the prudence of the new; who can be sober without being stupid; can entertain you with amusing anecdotes along a dull road; describe interesting objects upon a road that supplies them, and communicate information upon all points of importance, without endangering the bones of the passenger.

There are two roads to MACROOM—one on the south, the other on the north bank of the river Lee. We shall conduct the Tourist by the former, although the latter is frequently preferred.

The river Lee, the Luvius of Ptolemy, from the mouth to its source in the romantic lake of Gougane Barra—a distance of fifty-five miles from the city of Cork—is exceedingly picturesque and beautiful. It is less rapid than most of the Irish rivers, and its banks are frequently wooded. The Lee is interesting, however, not alone from its natural advantages: it has associations with the history of the past—numerous castles, now in ruins, look down upon it, and many abbeys skirt its sides.

South of the Lee, the road to Macroom runs upon elevated ground, and, for several miles, commands fine views of the valley, through which the river pursues its tortuous course, and the hills on the opposite side, upon the slopes of which are many beautiful villas. A little to the right, almost on the brink of an overhanging cliff, is the castle of Carrigrohan. Two or three miles farther is the town of BALLINCOLLIG, a Government manufactory of powder, and a barrack for artillery and cavalry. South-west of the town about a mile are the remains of an ancient castle, once a stronghold of the Anglo-Saxon Barretts. Two miles farther is the small village of "the Ovens," famous for its limestone caves. About halfway between Cork and Macroom, are the friary and castle of KILCREA. They were both built by Cormac, lord of Muskerry, the one for the protection of the other, and stand on the banks of the small river Bride, a mile to the south of the mail-coach road. They are highly interesting and picturesque. The approach to both is over a long and narrow bridge, which appears to be as old as the venerable structures to which it leads. The castle is described by Smith as "a strong building, having an excellent staircase of a dark marble from bottom to top, about seventy feet high. The barbicans, platforms, and ditch still

KILCREA CASTLE.

remain. On the east side is a large field called the Bawn, the only appendage for-

KILCREA ABBEY.

merly to great men's castles—places that were used for dancing, goaling, and such diversions; and where they also kept their cattle by night, to prevent their being carried off by wolves or their more rapacious neighbours." Much of this character it still retains, and the hand of time has been less busy with it than with others of its class.

In the friary, or, as it is usually but erroneously called, "the abbey," are interred the bodies of a host of the MacCarthys, and among them that of its founder, who died of wounds received in battle, in 1494. A considerable portion of the edifice still remains. It is divided into two principal parts—the convent and the church—and retains a character of considerable magnificence as well as of great extent. As in all the ancient churches, human bones are piled in every nook and cranny, thrust into corners, or gathered in heaps directly at the entrance—a sight far more revolting than affecting. The tower of the church is still in a good state of preservation, and may be ascended to the top with a little difficulty. Rows of ancient elm-trees lead to the venerable ruin.

Between Kilcrea and Macroom there are several ruins of castles, once the strongholds of the Mac Sweeneys, powerful chieftains, although feudatories to the lords of Muskerry. On the high road, it is stated on the authority of Smith, there was a

MACROOM BRIDGE.

stone set up by one of the family, who were "anciently famous for hospitality, with an Irish inscription, signifying to all passengers to repair to the house of Mr. Edmund Mac Sweeney for entertainment." The historian adds, that, in his time, the stone was still to be seen lying in a ditch, where it had been flung by a degenerate descendant, "who never throve afterwards."

The town of Macroom, twenty-four miles from Cork, is situated on the Sullane—a river that for extent and beauty rivals the Lee. The castle of Macroom is very ancient, or rather parts of it are of very remote antiquity, for it has undergone many of the chances and changes incident to the civil wars. The town is entered by a long and narrow bridge.

From Macroom to INCHAGEELA (*i. e.* "the Island of the Hostage"), a village midway between the town and Gougane Barra, the road becomes gradually wilder and more rugged; huge rocks overhang it, high hills look down upon them, and over these again the mountains tower, each and all clothed with purple heath and golden furze, and other plants that love the arid soil; here and there patches of cultivation have been snatched from them by the hand of industry and toil: while from many a small fissure the smoke arises, giving token that civilisation is astir even in this region of savage grandeur and beauty.

Soon after passing Inchageela, the Lee widens out into a sheet of water, forming the picturesque LOUGH ALLUA. The road winds for about three miles along its northern margin; the rocks on one side, the clear and deep water on the other—a more perfect solitude it is impossible to imagine. Not a tree is to be seen; but the rocks, as if to remedy the defect, have assumed forms the most singular and fantastic; and, every now and then, seem to stay the further progress of the wayfarer by pushing a monstrous base directly across his path. Yet a century and a half ago, these rocks and hills, as well as the valleys, were clothed with forests to the water's edge; in their fastnesses, unfamiliar with the step of man, the red deer roved; and often the labourer delves out, from a patch of mountain bog, some huge trunk that tells of the former occupiers of the soil—existing in decay many feet below the surface. Some three or four miles onwards, and we reach the first bridge that crosses the Lee—a bridge of many arches. We are now about two miles from the source of the noble river, in the singularly romantic lake of Gougane Barra. The car stops suddenly in the midst of remarkably savage scenery; and while the horses rest, a guide is summoned, or rather is sure to be at hand, and the Tourist prepares for a walk across the hill to the Holy Lough.

The approach to GOUGANE BARRA is now sufficiently easy; although, a hundred years ago, a pilgrimage of two miles occupied two hours. Dr. Smith pathetically describes the toil; he calls it "the rudest highway that ever was passed; a well-spirited beast trembles at every step: some parts of the road lie shelving from one side to the other, which often trips up a horse; other places are pointed rocks, standing like so many sugar-loaves, from one to three feet high, between which a horse must take time to place and fix his feet."

A sudden turning in the road brings the Tourist within view, and almost over, the lake of Gougane Barra. A scene of more utter loneliness, stern grandeur, or savage magnificence, it is difficult to conceive; redeemed, however, as all things savage are, by one passage of gentle and inviting beauty, upon which the eye turns as to a spring-well in the desert—the little island with its group of graceful ash-trees and ruined chapel. Down from the surrounding mountains rush numerous streams, tributaries to the lake, that collects and sends them forth in a bountiful river—for here the Lee has its source—until they form the noble harbour of Cork, and lose themselves in the broad Atlantic. In summer these streams are gentle rills, but in winter foaming cataracts; rushing over ridges of projecting rocks, and baring them even of the lichen that strives to cling to their sides. We have literally hopped across the river Lee.

When the traveller stands within this amphitheatre of hills, he feels, as it were, severed from his fellow-beings—as if imprisoned for ever; for on whichever side he looks, escape from the valley seems impossible; "so that if a person," writes the old historian, "were carried into it blindfold, it would seem almost impossible, without the wings of an eagle, to get out—the mountains forming, as it were, a wall of rocks some hundred yards high.

The small island is nearly midway in the lake; a rude artificial causeway leads into it from the mainland. This is the famous hermitage of St. Fin Bar, who is said to have lived here previous to his founding the cathedral of Cork. It is classed among the "holiest" places in Ireland, and has long been a favourite resort of devotees, in the confident expectation that its consecrated waters have power to heal

GOUGANE BARRA.

all kinds of diseases; making the blind to see, the deaf to hear, and the lame to walk. Here, at certain seasons—twice in the year—they assemble in crowds, bringing their sick children and ailing animals to bathe; and upon the neighbouring bushes and wooden crosses hang fragments of clothes, or halters and spancels, in proof that to the various animals, biped and quadruped, the lake has performed the anticipated miracle of making them whole.

These wells are to be found in nearly all the parishes of the kingdom: they are generally, as we have intimated, betokened by rude crosses immediately above them, by fragments of cloth, and bits of rags of all colours hung upon the neighbouring bushes and left as memorials; sometimes the crutches of convalescent visitors are bequeathed as offerings, and not unfrequently small buildings, for prayer and shelter, have been raised above and around them.

The greater portion of the island is covered by the ruins of a chapel with its appurtenant buildings, and a large court or cloister containing eight arched cells. In these arched cells the penance is performed. The penitent proceeds to one, where he repeats five "aves" and five "paters," adding five prayers to each of the cells subsequently visited, making forty to be said at the eighth cell; and the whole, with the addition of five more, are to be repeated at a chapel outside. First, however, five prayers must have been said at "the tomb of Father O'Mahony"—a priest who about the beginning of the last century closed a life of seclusion here. A spot better fitted for gloomy anchorite or stern ascetic, who desired perfect seclusion from

"The cheerful haunt of men and herds,"

it would be hard to find; but here too, undoubtedly study might have prepared the early Christian missionary for the "labour of love" he was called upon to undertake.

The sacred character of Gougane Barra has, it is said, preserved it from the pest of so many Irish lakes—the monster worm or enchanted eel. We have heard stories of them in abundance; and "have seen the man who had seen" the metamorphosed demon that infests the little lough on the top of Mount Gabriel—it is "deeper than did ever plummet sound;" yet not so deep but that it supplies a home to one of these "things horrible." Often, but always at night, the hideous head of the serpent is raised above the surface of the water; and if a cow be missing from some neighbouring herd, there is no difficulty in ascertaining its fate—it has been made "a toothful for the ould enemy." In ancient times, indeed, the blessed isle of St. Fin Bar was subjected to the visits of such an intruder; who having been guilty of the imprudence and impudence of snatching, from the very hand of the officiating priest, the loneen —a vessel for holding holy water—as he was in the act of sprinkling with it a crowd of devotees, witnesses of the sacrilegious act, he was expelled the neighbourhood for his wickedness, and has never since ventured to leave his loathsome slime upon the green banks of the lake.

The Tourist will greatly enjoy a visit to the Holy Lake, not only as introducing him to one of the strongholds of which superstition held possession for centuries; but the stern and sterile grandeur of the place will astonish him, if perchance here his first acquaintance shall have been formed with the wild magnificence of Nature in Ireland. The scene is a fine subject for the poet; and it has been happily treated by one who "died too soon," J. J. Callanan:—

"There is a green island in lone Gougane Barra,
Where Allua of songs rushes forth as an arrow;
In deep-vallied Desmond—a thousand wild fountains
Come down to that lake, from their home in the mountains.
There grows the wild ash, and a time-stricken willow
Looks chidingly down on the mirth of the billow;
As, like some gay child, that sad monitor scorning,
It lightly laughs back to the laugh of the morning.
And its zone of dark hills—oh! to see them all brightening,
When the tempest flings out its red banner of lightning
And the waters rush down, 'mid the thunder's deep rattle,
Like clans from their hills at the voice of the battle;
And brightly the fire-crested billows are gleaming,
And wildly from Mullagh the eagles are screaming.
Oh! where is the dwelling in valley or highland,
So meet for a bard as this lone little island!

> " How oft when the summer sun rested on Clara,
>   And lit the dark heath on the hills of Ivera,
>   Have I sought thee, sweet spot, from my home by the ocean,
>   And trod all thy wilds with a minstrel's devotion,
>   And thought of thy bards, when assembling together,
>   In the cleft of thy rocks, or the depth of thy heather;
>   They fled from the Saxon's dark bondage and slaughter,
>   And waked their last song by the rush of thy water,
>   High sons of the lyre, oh! how proud was the feeling,
>   To think, while alone through that solitude stealing,
>   Though loftier minstrels green Erin can number,
>   I only awoke your wild harp from its slumber,
>   And mingled once more with the voice of those fountains,
>   The songs even Echo forgot on her mountains,
>   And gleam'd each grey legend, that darkly was sleeping,
>   Where the mist and the rain o'er their beauty was creeping."

The journey is resumed, and the far-famed pass of KEIM-AN-EIGH is entered. Perhaps in no part of the kingdom is there to be found a place so utterly desolate and gloomy. A mountain has been divided by some convulsion of nature; and the narrow pass, nearly two miles in length, is overhung, on either side, by perpendicular masses clothed in wild ivy and underwood, with, occasionally, a stunted yew-tree or arbutus growing among them. At every step advance seems impossible—some huge rock jutting out into the path, and, on sweeping round it, seeming to conduct only to some barrier still more insurmountable; while from all sides rush down the "wild fountains," and, forming for themselves a rugged channel, make their way onward—the first tributary offering to the gentle and fruitful Lee:—

KEIM-AN-EIGH.

> " Here amidst heaps
>   Of mountain wrecks, on either side thrown high,
>   The wide-spread traces of its watery might,
>   The tortuous channel wound."

Nowhere has Nature assumed a more appalling aspect, or manifested a more stern resolve to dwell in her own loneliness and grandeur, undisturbed by any living thing —for even the birds seem to shun a solitude so awful; and the hum of bee or chirp of grasshopper is never heard within its precincts. Our print affords but a poor idea of a scene so magnificent.

Protected by these fortresses of rocks, ages ago, the outlawed O'Sullivans and O'Learys kept their freedom, and laughed to scorn the sword and fetter of the Saxon: and from these "mountains inaccessible" they made occasional sallies, avenging themselves upon, and bearing off the flocks and herds of, the stranger. As may be expected, in modern times, these rocky fortresses have given shelter often to bands of lawless or disaffected men: here, in some deep dell, might have been detected the light curl of smoke issuing from the roof of some illicit still-cabin, to disturb the inmates of which would have required a very strong force of the revenue. Among these rocks, too, the smugglers had many a cave, in which they deposited their goods until suspicion had been lulled on the highways, so that they might be conveyed in safety to the neighbouring towns. And here, too, men who had set themselves in battle array against the law, have often met to arrange their plans for carrying destruction into the adjoining valleys.

From "the Pass" to Bantry the road is full of objects that cannot fail to interest the stranger.—First, he will note the source of a river that will accompany him all the way to Bantry Bay—the river Ouvane, issuing from a small crevice in the rock, creeping along among huge stones, at length becoming a brawling and angry stream, and ere long a broad river making its way into the sea. The ruined castle of Carriganass—one of the old fortalices of the O'Sullivans—lies directly in his path; and a little to the left is the picturesque ruin of a venerable church—with its small churchyard in the centre of a group of aged trees. A view of the Bay is soon obtained—a glorious accession to the landscape; and just at the turn where the road branches off— the left leading to Bantry, the right to Glengariff--is the fine waterfall of Dunamare, at times a magnificent sight.

At this spot the Tourist will be called upon to decide whether he will proceed to Bantry, two miles distant, or to Glengariff, distant eight miles. There are many reasons why he should visit Bantry (although he is not compelled to do so, *en route* to Killarney), and therefore to that town we shall first conduct him.

BANTRY, GLENGARIFF, KENMARE.

EITHER by the Coast road, the road through DUNMANWAY, or the road through Gougane Barra, the Tourist arrives at BANTRY. The far-famed "Bay" is, perhaps, unsurpassed by any harbour in the kingdom for natural beauties combined with natural advantages. As we approach it, along the dreary road from Skibbereen, a sudden turn, at the base of a rugged hill, brings us suddenly within view of the most striking objects which make up the glorious scene. Far away, in the distant background, are dimly seen Mangerton and the Reeks; nearer, rise Hungry Hill, the Sugar Loaf, and a long range—the Caha Mountains; among which, it is said, there are no fewer than three hundred and sixty-five lakes—the number having, of course, suggested a legend that some holy saint prayed effectually for one to supply water for each day of the year. Little flat and fertile islands lie at the feet of the spectator; and, nearly facing the town, is WHIDDY ISLAND, with its fierce-looking fortifications, and its fields rich with the promised harvest. It is impossible to do justice to the exceeding grandeur and surpassing loveliness of the scene; the whole of it is taken in by the eye at once. We are not called upon to turn from side to side for new objects to admire—we gaze upon it all; and he must be indeed dead to nature who does not drink in as delicious a draught as Nature, in the fulness of her bounty, ever presented.

The road into the town—a town that has been too truly described as "a seaport without trade, a harbour without shipping, and a coast with a failing fishery"—runs immediately under the fine demesne of the Earl of Bantry—and all the way it is one continued line of beauty: we never for a moment lose sight of the distant mountains, or the foreground of green islands; while the ear is gladdened by the mingled harmony of rippling waves, and birds that sing among the foliage of the thickly and gracefully wooded plantations.

There are not many islands in this vast expanse of water—"Whiddy" is the largest: and there are besides Hog, Horse, Coney, and Chapel islands, flung into the glorious bay—landlocked, as we have said, by gigantic abrupt headlands, beyond which the Killarney mountains seem to tower into the clouds.*

The Bay is memorable in history as having been twice entered by a French force, for the invasion of Ireland—the first in 1689 in aid of James II.; the next in 1796:—some details concerning the latter cannot fail to interest our readers.

---

* Were such a bay lying upon English shores, it would be a world's wonder; perhaps if it were on the Mediterranean, or the Baltic, English travellers would flock to it in hundreds. Why not come and see it in Ireland?—THACKERAY.

The project no doubt originated with Theobald Wolfe Tone, who had visited France, after a residence in America, as agent for the Society of United Irishmen, and had obtained a commission in the French service.*

On the 1st of December, Tone embarked on board the "Indomptable," a ship of the line, and on the 16th of December the fleet "for the invasion of Ireland" set sail in two divisions from the port of Brest. It consisted of 17 ships of the line, 13 frigates, 5 corvettes, 2 gun-boats, and 6 transports; with about 14,000 men, 45,000 stand of arms, and an ample supply of money for the purposes of the expedition. In their passage from the harbour, as if ominous of the disasters they were

BANTRY BAY.

subsequently to encounter, one of their ships, a seventy-four, struck on a rock, and of 550 men on board only thirty were saved; and a few days afterwards another was driven on shore, when 1,000 out of 1,800 perished. After other disastrous accidents—every ship of the line being more or less injured—the main body arrived off the coast of Ireland, and on the 22nd anchored off Bere Island, in Bantry Bay. Intelligence of the event was, as rapidly as possible, communicated to the Irish and English governments. Not the slightest preparation, however, had been made to meet the enemy; and, but for the interposition of Divine Providence, Ireland must have been the seat of a bloody and desolating war.

For several days previous, the weather had been very stormy; and when the wind lulled, a dense fog overspread the sea, so that the French ships were seeking each

---

* Tone afterwards made another attempt to introduce the French into Ireland—in 1798. He was captured in the "Hoche," off Donegal; transmitted to Dublin, tried by court-martial, and sentenced to death. He appeared at his trial in French uniform; and, on hearing the sentence, requested to be shot as a soldier holding a commission in the French service under the name of Smith: the request was refused. On the evening previous to the day fixed for his execution, he wounded himself in the throat so desperately, that he could not be moved without the probability of dying before he reached the scaffold; after lingering in this state for a week, he died in prison, on the 19th November, 1798.

other, in vain, along the ocean. Of the 43 that quitted Brest, 16 only anchored at Bantry; next day a heavy gale once more dispersed them. On the morning of the 26th, others having parted company, the fleet was reduced to seven sail of the line and one frigate. The force in them by this time dwindled to 4,168; it was, therefore, resolved at a council of war "not to attempt a landing, as no demonstration had been made" by the Irish on shore in favour of the French;* and it was determined to put out to sea, and to cruise off the Shannon, in the hope that the dissevered armament might be concentrated there. On the 27th, they weighed anchor and quitted the Bay; but on the 1st of January a portion of them returned, and remained inactive for two or three days. By degrees, ship after ship of the once formidable fleet re-entered the French harbours; and on the 15th, Hoche himself, in the "Fraternité," reached Rochelle, having had several narrow escapes from capture by the English fleet.

Bantry was, thus, soon freed from the presence of invaders; no Frenchmen having trodden upon Irish ground, excepting an officer and seven men, who being sent in a boat to reconnoitre, were taken prisoners.

The storm that scattered the French fleet, and, under Providence, preserved Ireland from civil war, and contamination by the atrocious principles of the republicans of 1793, is still remembered in the vicinity of Bantry Bay, where it is referred to as an epoch to assist memory.

To visit GLENGARIFF, the Tourist may proceed either by land round the Bay, or by sea across it. It will be a pleasant row, introducing to a remarkably beautiful scene; but the road is, perhaps, preferable, inasmuch as a noble view of the Bay will be obtained from the hills above Bantry or Glengariff, or by taking a boat a mile or two from the shore of either. The road—although a "new road" —is exceedingly wild and picturesque. About two miles from the town the Mealugh, "the murmuring river," is crossed by a small bridge, close to which is the Fall of Dunamare.

The traveller should not pass unnoticed a mountain, north-west of Bantry several miles, but seen from all parts of the road he journeys. It is the mountain of the Priest's Leap—formerly the principal line of communication between the two

---

* The French had marvellously miscalculated as to the co-operation they anticipated from the Irish people; who were, in 1796, totally unprepared to receive them as friends, or to adopt the republican principles and government they designed to disseminate and establish. In his memorials to the Directory, Tone had represented the Irish as "fixing their eyes most earnestly on France," as "eager to fly to the standard of the republic;" the Catholics as "ready to join it to a man;" and that "it would be just as easy, in a month, to have an army in Ireland of 200,000 men as 10,000." Whether he had wilfully misstated the fact, or whether his sanguine temperament had led him to believe that his countrymen would join the French en masse, it is difficult to say; but it is certain that the invaders would have been received by the Irish generally, not as friends, but as enemies. Along the coast, the south and west, most distinctly threatened, the peasants were actually in arms—such arms as they could command—to repel them. We have frequently heard Colonel Hall state that on his march to Bantry his men were cheered by the peasantry, supplied with food and drink by them, and received unequivocal demonstrations of their resolve to fight upon their cabin-thresholds against the entrance of a Frenchman. (Colonel Hall commanded the small force of about 500 men, hastily collected, and foolishly sent "to oppose the landing of the French.") In the London Gazette of the 7th of January, 1797, this feeling is particularly adverted to, "The accounts of the disposition of the country where the troops are assembled are as favourable as possible, and the greatest loyalty has manifested itself throughout the kingdom. In the south and west, where the troops have been in motion, they have been met by the country people of all descriptions with provisions and all sorts of accommodation to facilitate their march; and every demonstration has been given of the real and ardour to oppose the enemy in every place where it could be supposed a descent might be attempted." The Gazette of the 17th contains a letter from the lord-lieutenant (Earl Camden), in which, after noticing the good disposition evinced by the troops, his excellency states, "The roads, which in parts were rendered impassable by the snow, were cleared by the peasantry. The poor people often shared their potatoes with the soldiers * * * In short, had the enemy landed, their hope of assistance from the inhabitants would have been totally disappointed." Every account published at the time bears out this statement.

most picturesque portions of Irish scenery, Glengariff and Killarney, but now abandoned for one of the best roads in the kingdom. This old road possesses to perfection the characteristics of the fine old vigorous and uncompromising system of road-making, now exploded, that was observant only of the straightest line of access—following as nearly as possible the flight of the bird—regardless alike of acclivity or declivity, of cliff or crag, of stream or torrent. In this respect the Priest's Leap road offers to every student of the ancient mystery of road-making the fairest subject for inquiry and contemplation; nothing can be more direct than its up-hill flights, or more decided and unswerving than its downward progressions; no mountain elevation, however bristling with crags or formidable the aspect of its precipitous sides, deterred the stern and uncompromising engineer who laid it down. He carried it over the loftiest summits, the wildest moors, at the bottom of the most desolate glens, and along the most dizzy steeps overlooking the deepest dells. A savage-looking defile is sometimes made available as a conduit for every ferocious breeze that loves to howl and sweep along such localities; and the loneliness of many of the scenes is emphatically marked by the significant "leacht," or stone-heap, that points out the spot where, in other times, some solitary traveller met his fate from the way-side plunderer. Such alarming "hints" are now, indeed, rare; and, of later years, the record of acts of violence, committed in the security of these seldom-trodden paths, is a barren one. The heaps of stones, to indicate where deeds of murder have been done, still remain, however; and to the present day the peasant discharges what he considers his solemn duty by flinging, as he walks or rides by, a contribution to the mass.

To the lover of the wild, the picturesque, and the romantic, this road may be recommended. Glorious is its scenery over mountain and through glen. The broad bay of Bantry is glistening far beneath, and the blue shores of Iveragh and Bere in the distance are noble features in the majestic panorama. Nor has the voice of tradition failed, or become silent, among these hills; many a wild legend and whimsical fiction may be gathered, by a little kindness, from their imaginative inhabitants.

Nearly midway in the course of the mountain road stand the ruins of one of those small, ancient churches, whose era, from their style—the Romanesque—must be placed between the fifth and eleventh centuries. A portion of the walls only remains. The stones are large and Cyclopean, curiously jointed, and well-fashioned. We were told that it is "one of the first churches called at Rome"—a traditional record of its high antiquity. Outside the burial-ground is a curiosity;—a natural rock of a tabular form with five basin-like hollows on the surface, of four or five inches in depth, and about a foot in diameter. These are filled with water, and in each is a stone of a long oval form fitting the space fully.

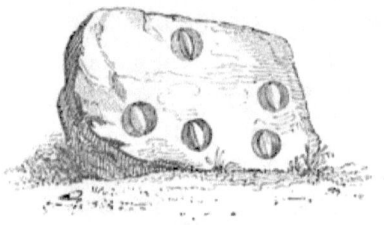

THE LEGEND-STONE.

Language utterly fails to convey even a limited idea of the exceeding beauty of

GLENGARIFF—"the rough glen"—which merits to the full the enthusiastic praise that has been lavished upon it by every traveller by whom it has been visited. It is a deep alpine valley, enclosed by precipitous hills, about three miles in length, and seldom exceeding a quarter of a mile in breadth. Black and savage rocks embosom, as it were, a scene of surpassing loveliness—endowed by nature with the richest gifts of wood and water; for the trees are graceful in form, luxuriant in foliage, and varied in character; and the rippling stream, the strong river, and the foaming cataract, are supplied from a thousand rills collected in the mountains. Beyond all, is the magnificent bay, with its numerous islands—by one of which it is so guarded and sheltered as to receive the aspect of a serene lake. The artist cannot do it justice; and the pen must be laid aside in despair! Our memories, indeed, recall every portion of the magic spot—but only to convince us how weak and inefficient must be our efforts to describe it. We are again wandering through the glen—among majestic trees, fantastic rocks, and bubbling rivulets which every now and then rush by huge masses of stone, and, finding a declivity, roar along their rapid way, until, encountering some new obstruction, they creep awhile, and anon force a passage onwards, breaking into masses of foam—for there the mountain torrents creep or gallop to mingle with the broad Atlantic. The song of birds is either hushed or unheard; and but for the ripple, or the roar of waters, there is no sound to disturb a solitude perfect and profound. We look up to the mountains; they are of all forms, altitudes, and outlines. The most prominent among them is the Sugar-loaf, Slieve-na-goil, "the mountain of the wild people," with its conical head, soaring into the clouds; and, to the rear, Hungry Hill, with its naked and meagre sides, down which runs a stream from the lake upon its summit, until, gathering as it goes, it breaks in a tremendous cataract of eight hundred feet, expanding as it falls, and flinging a spray around it, that seems to cover with a thick mist a third part of the hill.

> "Now a blue wat'ry sheet; anon dispersed,
> A hoary mist; then gathered in again,
> A darted stream along the hollow rock;
> This way and that tormented, dashing thick
> From steep to steep, with wild refracted course
> And restless roaring, to the humble vale."

We turn from the mountains but a step, and gaze over the broad bay; the foreground is dotted with islands of various shapes and sizes;* and we stand in the midst of cultivation, as if nature had resolved upon mingling as much grandeur and beauty as the eye could take in at once. We turn again and look inland; enormous rocks are scattered in all directions, without order or arrangement, but picturesque from their very confusion; seeming as if the giants of old had done battle here, and fought with huge masses they had wrenched from the adjacent mountains.

But one of the grandest views is from the height of the hill-road that leads to Killarney. Before we ascend it, however, we must visit Lord Bantry's pretty cottage. It is sheltered like a wren's nest in its little island. We cross a foot-bridge, made it is said, from the planks drifted on shore after the wrecks of 1796 in the Bay, and are in the grounds. Crossing another little bridge, we are invited to ascend a soft and

---

* Of these islands there is only one of size—Garnish Island, which contains thirty-six acres. It is crowned by a Martello Tower. The other islands are, Bramly Island, Ship Island, Rough Island, Back Island, &c., &c.

gentle-looking hill, and to our delight find it commands a scene fit to illustrate "the Happy Valley." Nothing can be more delicious, more varied, more enchanting, than the panoramic view that surrounds you on all sides; mountain, rock, river, and ocean—trees of the most picturesque growth, and shrubby underwood, of such luxuriance that painters there may study nature under every shade and form. We could have lingered on that hill until night shut out the landscape, but we had much to do; and, recrossing the fairy-like bridges, we proceeded to drive through the demesne. We do not know whether others may feel as we did the deep silence of Glengariff: we

AT GLENGARIFF.

heard neither bleat of sheep nor song of bird. The weather, when we visited it last, was warm—the very sea-breeze blew hot; and the sun, reflected by the white and grey rocks, rendered the heat still more oppressive. When we complained of this, our guide smiled. "Ah! then it's just proud the weather is to see ye; and it's the other thing, the wet, and the rain, and the storm, we do have to complain of, just changing from one bad luck to the other—as Molly Malone said when she married her third husband. It's seldom we're too much of the sunshine, glory be to God! The birds are silent, through the heat—they're not used to it either; nor the cattle, poor things!—there isn't a bleat left in them hardy goats." This was certainly true, for every creature seemed oppressed by the unusual and continued sunshine. The drive through the demesne is one of a peculiar kind; for though art and cultivation have done a great deal, the wild, rugged, abrupt character of the glen is admirably retained. Patches of rich brown bog produce the most luxuriant vegetation—marsh weeds of every hue flourish—rocks of various sizes form the bases of now sloping, now abrupt hills; while above them are the mountains; and above them again, canopied by the clear blue sky, the eagle floats calmly, now rising, now falling, and then soaring away, away, until he becomes to our pained and restricted vision a speck, an atom.* Sometimes the drive is arched over by trees; then you cross a bridge feathered with ferns and wild heaths, beneath whose arches a bright glittering river steals along, as if half asleep; then you turn away from the cultivation, and are by the borders of mimic morasses, with hoar mountains on the one side, and such peeps and glances of the bay on the other, that you are fairly bewildered; then again you are plunged into thickets of stunted oak and birch—and sunbeams creep through the branches, and freckle the long dark grass; and after thanking Heaven for the cool green shade, you open upon a bit of fresh prairie, watered by countless little shy, sly brooks, crawling listlessly from their "home in the mountains;" while above them float an absolute host of sparkling insects. It was Midsummer-day, and the previous evening we had watched for nearly two hours "the bone-fires," or, properly speaking, the Baal fires, kindling on the most prominent headlands, and brightly reflected in the glorious bay beneath.

But to enjoy the adjacent scenery to perfection, the Tourist should ascend the "SUGAR LOAF" mountain. This will be hard labour—amply recompensed.

The village of Glengariff consists of but a few houses. The only "antiquity" in the immediate neighbourhood is the old bridge, now a picturesque ruin, which, in ancient times, was on the high road to Berehaven; it is called "Cromwell's Bridge." History being silent as to the origin of the name, we must have recourse to tradition. When Oliver was passing through the glen to visit the O'Sullivans, he had so much trouble in getting across the narrow but rushing river, that he told the inhabitants if they did not build him a bridge by the time he returned, he would

---

* The "Eagle's Nest—" the cliff where the lordly bird has for centuries made this dwelling—rises five hundred feet above the valley. Cæsar Otway relates a story connected with it—so beautifully, that we recommend it to all who love a well-told legend, merely offering a brief outline of what, entire, would here occupy too much space.

At the time when the O'Sullivan had real right to the territory of which he was despoiled, he took refuge, with his wife, children, and a remnant of his people, in Glengariff. Here he maintained a guerilla warfare against his foes, who were unfortunately almost as good guerillas as himself. At last, driven to the last extremity of despair and starvation, he resolved to join his friends in Ulster and Breffny, leaving his wife and children to the care of his follower and fosterer, Gorrane M'Swiney. All honour be to his inharmonious name! Gorrane conveyed his precious charge to the foot of the Eagle's Cliff, and sheltered the Princess of Bere and Bantry beneath a hut so cunningly contrived as to seem but a rise in the furze, or a swell in the heather. It is true, he had neither sheep, nor cow, nor goat; he had one salt salmon wrapped in a rough skin; but he had, like all his countrymen, a stout heart and an inventive brain; and though the country was reeved and rent by cruel Saxons, Gorrane put his trust in the saints, and kept a clear look-out, hoping something would turn up "for good." But still he suffered bitter trouble, because of his noble mistress, not knowing how he would procure her food; and one morning, as he was wondering what he should do, he observed one of the eagles sailing with a leveret in its talons to its eyrie, and then he heard the joyful screams of the young birds as they divided their prey. A sudden thought struck Gorrane, and, without communicating it to any one, he busied himself all day long in twisting a rope made from the fibres of the bog fir; and, long before the dawn of the next day, accompanied by his son, he climbed the mountain, and, as twilight opened to the morning, saw the old eagle soar away to meet the sun. He then told his boy his project, which was, that he was to let him down by his woody rope to the eagles' nest—that he should tie a strap round their necks, not so tight as to injure them, but sufficiently tight to prevent their swallowing— that he would then draw him up, and await the eagles' return, who would leave, as usual, their prey in the nest, and then soar away to seek for more. During their absence, the boy was again to descend, loosen the eaglets' throats, and, leaving them the offal, ascend with the game, which the birds intended as a banquet for their own young. The youth managed as cleverly as his father desired—the eagles provided liberally for the sustenance of the lady and her children, until the English abandoned the glen; when the Princess sought and found a more secure and fitting refuge.

hang up a man for every hour's delay he met with. "So the bridge was ready agin he came back," quoth our informant; "for they knew the ould villain to be a man of his word." From every part of the glen some attractive object may be discovered;

CROMWELL'S BRIDGE.

one of the best views, perhaps, is to be obtained from a small hill—small in comparison with its stupendous neighbours—in the immediate vicinity of a chapel west of the village: it places the spectator in the very centre of a glorious panorama, absolutely bewildering from its profusion of beauties. But as we have intimated, it is from the road to Kenmare that the surpassing loveliness of the valley and the full glory of the bay will be seen to perfection.* For three or four miles the traveller winds round the side of a mountain. Suddenly he arrives on the brow of the hill. He is over the glen, many hundred feet over the ocean, which he beholds stretching out into space, while the islands appear as dots upon it; the river that runs through the valley has dwindled to a white thread; the trees have gathered into masses; and the hill upon which he stood, so lately, seems no bigger than a fairy mound. Midway down are scattered cottages, the pale smoke from which alone distinguishes them from mole-heaps. Thin and narrow streams, like snow-wreaths, are running from the mountains; and every now and then his eye falls upon the lakes that send them forth to fertilise the valley. The whole scene is within his ken—its sublime beauty and its transcendent grandeur—ocean, mountain, glen, and river. He is in the midst of solitude; the clouds are on a level with him; at times they hide for a moment every object from his sight. There is no song of bird to break the perfect loneliness; but if he look upward he will see the eagle winging his way homewards in solitary grandeur. We were startled by the scream of one of them flying over our heads, so near to us that we could almost count the feathers in his wing.†

We have described the view of Glengariff and Bantry Bay from the summit of the hill-road that leads to Killarney. There is another view, however, from another height, scarcely less grand. Upon this height is the division between the counties of

---

* "The twenty miles from Kenmare to Glengariff form the grandest road, barring the Alpine passes, that I know. An ascent of four English miles brings you to a tunnel six hundred feet long; on emerging from which, the head of Glengariff opens upon you. Thence, at every step you descend, the scenery becomes more and more beautiful, every turn of the road revealing some hitherto unseen charm, with Bantry Bay and the Atlantic ever bounding the view."— LORD JOHN MANNERS.

† There are reasonably good inns at Bantry, and at Glengariff there are two inns that profess to be for the accommodation of Tourists. Neither of them, however, can be described as of first class; and must be regarded only as places that will give comfortable shelter en route. But in "the season" even that is not always sure. Tourists will do well to order rooms, either from Mr. Roche, at the "Royal Hotel," or from Mr. Eccles, at the "Bantry Arms." At Kenmare there is a good hotel kept by "Tom Macarthy." Tourists, who post from Cork, usually take the same horses on to Killarney, having rested a night and a day at Glengariff. Glengariff is 42 (English) miles from Killarney; Kenmare being exactly midway, i.e., 21 miles. It is, however, common to order carriages and horses from Killarney to meet parties at Glengariff. Those who visit Glengariff, after visiting Killarney, take the same horses and carriage on to Cork, having obtained rest at Glengariff.

Cork and Kerry. The entrance to the county of Kerry ("the kingdom of Kerry," as it was anciently called), from that of Cork, is through a tunnel of about two hundred yards in length; a very short distance from which there are two others of much more limited extent. They have been cut through rocks, peaks to the Esk mountain. As the traveller emerges from comparative darkness, a scene of striking magnificence bursts upon him, very opposite in character from that which he leaves immediately behind; for while his eye retains the rich and cultivated beauty of the wooded and watered "glen," he is startled by the contrast of barren and frightful precipices along the brinks of which he is driving, and gazes with a shudder down into the far-off valley, where a broad and angry stream is diminished by distance into a mere line of white. Nothing can exceed the wild grandeur of the prospect; it extends miles upon miles: scattered through the vale and among the hill slopes are many cottages, white always, and generally slated; while to several of them are attached the picturesque limekilns so numerous in all parts of the country. The road, of which there is a view almost the whole way to Kenmare Harbour, is a gradual descent, and has been so admirably constructed, and is kept so carefully in repair, that it is smooth and finished enough to be the entry to a demesne, and is classed by universal consent among the best roads of the kingdom; such was not always the case; at one period it was proverbial for the poverty of the land and the wretchedness of its inhabitants. The misery of the soil has been illustrated by a saying, that "a Kerry cow never looks up at a passing stranger, *for fear it would lose the bite;*" and it was asserted that, long ago, at stated seasons, the agents of the lord of the land stationed themselves at the old entrance into the county to meet the beggars as they were returning homewards from Cork to Kerry, and received the rents of their cabins by taking from them the half-pence they had collected.

And so we reach the town of Kenmare, concerning which, or rather the scenery to which it leads, we shall have more to say before we close our book.

LIMERICK AND THE SHANNON.

NO doubt many tourists will visit *en route* the city of LIMERICK, inasmuch as it is not distant more than twenty-two miles from the Limerick Junction, and also inasmuch as it may be taken *en route* to Killarney, partly by railway to FOYNES (twenty-six miles), or by voyaging the "mighty Shannon." Limerick is distinguished in history as "the city of the violated treaty;" and THE SHANNON, on which it stands, has been aptly termed "the King of Island Rivers." Few of the Irish counties possess so many attractions as that of Limerick for the antiquarian and the lover of the picturesque; and, with one exception, no city of Ireland has contributed so largely to maintain the honour and glory of the country. The brave defenders of Limerick and Londonderry have received—the former from the Protestant, and the latter from the Catholic historian—the praise that party spirit cannot weaken; the heroic gallantry, the indomitable perseverance, and the patient and resolute endurance under suffering of both, having deprived political partisans of their asperity—compelling them, for once at least, to render justice to their opponents; all having readily subscribed to the opinion that "Derry and Limerick will ever grace the historic page, as rival companions and monuments of Irish bravery, generosity, and integrity."

The charter of Limerick is as old as Richard the First; and King John, according to Stanihurst, "was so pleased with the agreeableness of the city that he caused a very fine castle and bridge to be built there." The castle has endured for above six centuries; in all the "battles, sieges, fortunes," that have since occurred, it has been the object most coveted perhaps in Ireland by the contending parties; and it still frowns a dark mass, upon the waters of the mighty Shannon.

CASTLE OF LIMERICK.

Recently, improvements that have taken place in the

city have opened it to view; and an idea of its strength and magnitude may be obtained from the accompanying print.

The city is, indeed, very famous in history. Before it, in 1651, Ireton "sate down;" there he continued to "sit" for six months; and underneath its walls the fierce republican died of plague. Greater celebrity and higher honour were, however, obtained by Limerick in 1690. Early in August, William summoned it to surrender: the French general, Boileau, who commanded the garrison—"rather for the king of France than the king of England"—returned for answer that "he was surprised at the summons, and thought the best way to gain the good opinion of the Prince of Orange was to defend the place for his master King James." The siege was at once commenced. It was raised on the 30th of August. But in the autumn of 1691 it endured a second, which occupied about six months, when the garrison wearied of a struggle from which they could derive nothing but glory; on the 23rd of September a cessation of hostilities took place; an amicable intercourse was opened between the two armies; and articles of capitulation were, after a few brief delays, agreed upon. The treaty was signed on the 3rd of October, 1691; it consisted of two parts, civil and military. It is said to have been signed by the several contracting parties on a large stone, near to Thomond Bridge, on the county of Clare side of the river. The stone remains in the position it occupied at the period, and is an object of curiosity to strangers, as well as of interest to the citizens of Limerick. We therefore thought it desirable to procure a drawing of the relic, which retains its name of "the Treaty Stone."

THE TREATY STONE.

Although the statement depends on tradition, it is not unlikely to be true.

The city of Limerick, situated in an extensive plain watered by the mighty Shannon, about sixty Irish miles from the sea, is divided, like all the towns of note in Ireland, into English town and Irish town; but a third division, called Newtown Pery, was added to it during the last century—the work being commenced in 1769, by the Right Hon. Edmond Sexton Pery. The English town stands on "the King's Island," an island formed by the Shannon, which divides, about half a mile above the city, into two streams; the narrowest of which is named the Abbey River. There is also an extensive and populous suburb on the opposite side of the river, in the county of Clare. The more modern parts are remarkably handsome, the streets being wide and the houses evenly built: the ancient portions, on the contrary, are narrow and confined, and dirty to a proverb. Limerick may be classed among the best cities of Ireland; and it is rapidly improving. The most remarkable of the ancient structures of Limerick, with the exception of "King John's Castle," is the cathedral, dedicated to "St. Mary;" a large and heavy-looking structure, built on the site of the palace of O'Brien, king of Limerick. Its tower is remarkably high; and from the summit there is a magnificent prospect of the various objects of attraction in the immediate neighbourhood: it is, indeed, the only place from which a view can be obtained, for there are no adjacent hills—a circumstance to which the city is considerably indebted for its natural strength.

The city has been long unrivalled in Ireland for some peculiar advantages; the world is familiar with the fame of Limerick lasses, Limerick gloves, Limerick hooks, and Limerick lace—the latter, however, is a distinction of more recent growth.

The great attraction of Limerick—although by no means the only one—is, however, its majestic and beautiful river; "the king of island rivers"—the "principalest of all in Ireland," writes the quaint old naturalist, Dr. Gerrard Boate. It takes its

ST. MARY'S CHURCH.

rise among the mountains of Leitrim, and, running for a few miles as an inconsiderable stream, diffuses itself into a spacious lake, called Lough Allen. Issuing thence it pursues its course for several miles, and forms another small lake, Lough Eike; again spreads itself out into Lough Ree—a lake fifteen miles in length and four in breadth; and thence proceeds as a broad and rapid river, passing by Athlone; then narrowing again until it reaches Shannon Harbour; then widening into far-famed Lough Derg, eighteen miles long and four broad; then progressing until it arrives at Killaloe, where it ceases to be navigable until it waters Limerick city; from whence it flows in a broad and majestic volume to the ocean for about sixty miles: running a distance of upwards of two hundred miles from its source to its mouth—between Loop Head and Kerry Head (the space between them being about eight miles), watering ten counties in its progress, and affording facilities for commerce and internal intercourse such as are unparalleled in any other portion of the United Kingdom. Yet, unhappily, up to the present time, its natural advantages have been too much neglected; its munificent wealth having been suffered to lie as utterly waste as if its blessings were offered only to an unpeopled desert.

LIMERICK.

"The spacious Shenan spreading like a sea," thus answers to the description of Spenser. For a long space its course is so gentle that ancient writers supposed its name to have been derived from "Seen-awn," the slow river; and for many miles, between O'Brien's Bridge and Limerick, it rolls so rapidly along as almost to be characterised as a series of cataracts. At the Falls of Killaloe it descends twenty-one feet in a mile, and above 100 feet from Killaloe to Limerick; yet there is scarcely a single mill at work all that way. Its banks too are, nearly all along its course, of surpassing beauty. As it nears Limerick, the adjacent hills are crowned with villas; and upon its sides are the ruins of many ancient castles. Castle Connell, a village about six miles from the city, is perhaps unrivalled in the kingdom for natural graces; and immediately below it are the Falls of Doonas, where the river rushes over huge mountain-rocks, affording a passage which the more daring only will make, for the current, narrowed to a boat's breadth, rushes along with such frightful rapidity that the deviation of a few inches would be inevitable destruction.* This, although the most remarkable of the falls, is succeeded by several others, between Castle Connell and Limerick—the whole scene, however discouraging to the political economist, as presenting a picture of wasted strength, being delicious in the highest degree to the lover of natural beauty.

The immediate environs of Limerick are not picturesque; the city lies, as we have said, in a spacious plain, the greater portion of which is scarcely above the level of the water; at short distances, however, there are some of the most interesting ruins in the kingdom, in the midst of scenery of surpassing loveliness. As we have said, there is a railway to Foynes, a port on the Shannon, whence there is a good road to Tarbert, and so on to Tralee.

We shall describe this route at the close of our book, when we are taking note of the sea-coast accessible from Killarney. We need only now observe that there are reasonably good inns at both places, and that cars are readily obtained at either.

* We cannot easily forget our sensations of mingled alarm and enjoyment, while rushing along this course—at night, but by the light of a brilliant moon; it was exciting to the highest degree. We had confidence in our helmsman (if so we must term the man with the paddle-rudder he held in his hand); yet every now and then the voyage was a startling one, and the danger quite sufficient to shake stronger nerves than ours. He had nothing to do but to keep a keen eye upon the rocks at either side, and guide his "cot" by pushing aside a wave with a strong arm, so as to keep in the centre of the current; and he did so with wonderful accuracy. We were afterwards convinced that there was in reality no more peril than there would have been upon the Thames; for the boatmen are so skilful and so well practised, that they govern their boats with absolute certainty. The boats are flat-bottomed (for often the stream is not above a few inches

deep), narrowed, and squared at the stern and stern. The paddle is a piece of flat wood, about three feet long, increasing from the handle to the breadth of about ten inches; only one is used, which the man changes from side to side, according to the direction in which he desires to proceed—using it alternately to advance the boat, and as a helm to steer its course. We refer more especially to the boats used by the fishermen, in which the oars are seldom resorted to; for they are pushed up the stream by a long pole, and the current takes them down it without an effort.

WATERFORD AND ITS HARBOUR.

AMONG the cities of Ireland WATERFORD city holds high rank. Its harbour is reached by steam-boats—large, commodious, and very comfortable, which ply daily from MILFORD HAVEN.* The voyage across usually occupies, from port to port, nine hours; but two hours are occupied within the harbours. There is consequently sufficient time, before the vessel reaches the open sea, for all pleasant or needful preparations on the part of those to whom a sea-trip under the best circumstances is an affliction: the steam-boats are admirably regulated. The times of sailing and arrival are so arranged as to enable visitors to see both harbours to advantage, and to have night only when the open sea is traversed. Among the other advantages of this route, it should be stated that on both sides—at Milford Haven and at Waterford—voyagers "walk on board" from the quays: at Waterford passengers are landed near to a good and well-conducted hotel—and at Milford Haven, close to the terminus, the Company have built an hotel, with all modern improvements, supplying all requisite comforts. The usual "Tourists' tickets" are of course issued by the South Wales Company.

WATERFORD HARBOUR is exceedingly beautiful; not so richly planted or ornamented by villas as that of Cork, yet scarcely inferior to it in the grace of its foreground, and the grandeur of the mountains that look down upon it. But Waterford has one great advantage over its neighbour—the river Suir is navigable for very large ships; having sufficient depth of water to allow vessels of from 800 to 1,000 tons burden to discharge their cargoes at the quay. The Malcolmsons, famous merchants of the city, have indeed built there vessels of large size, which trade to all parts of the world; and their steam-boats, built also in Waterford, are among the largest and best of the trading ships of the kingdom. The quay is unrivalled in Ireland, and, perhaps, in England. It is a mile in length, and in a continuous line. At its western extremity, connecting the city with the county of Kilkenny, is a wooden bridge across the Suir; it is 832 feet in length and forty in breadth; supported on stone abutments and forty sets of piers of oak.

---

* The South Wales Railway—which joins the Great Western at Gloucester—conveys passengers to Milford Haven through a very delightful and highly picturesque district. It leads also to the beautiful sea-bathing place, Tenby, where there are attractions as large and as numerous as can be found in any of the sea-side towns of the kingdom, frequently passing through delicious scenery—especially the Vale of Neath and Chepstow on the Wye, and for a very long distance by the side of "rapid Severn."

Waterford Harbour, from the sea to the quay, is in length eighteen miles; but seldom more than a quarter of a mile in breadth. The two places most famous on the coast, in Waterford county, are DUNMORE and TRAMORE—the former being immediately within the harbour, while to the latter there is a railway from the city. Both are favourite bathing-places; but Dunmore long enjoyed the advantage of being a government packet station, and possesses both a lighthouse and a pier. The village is

DUNMORE LIGHTHOUSE.

beautifully situated; the coast is bold and rocky, and it is immediately upon the sea. The pier is 600 feet in length, and the cost of the works is believed to have exceeded £100,000, a sum immensely disproportionate to their value to the public. "A Druid's' altar" stands on a wild and rocky eminence near Dunmore. It commands a view, on one side of the estuary, of the Suir with Cremla Island and Hook Tower, and on the other the great bay of Tramore, with the rugged precipices of the Cuma rocks in the distance.

On the Waterford side of the bay, the only other object that will attract notice is the village of PASSAGE; now a ruinous place, having succumbed to steam, and the several harbour improvements which prevent a necessity for vessels resting there.

To the opposite—the northern—side of the harbour, the attention of the voyager will be directed: from its commencement in the county of WEXFORD to its continuation into the county of KILKENNY.

On entering, the eye will be at once directed to the famous tower of HOOK, standing at the extremity of the peninsula which divides the harbour from the BAY OF BANNOW; it has been converted into a lighthouse, and occupies a point of land high above the ocean; one of the many marks to mariners with which Wexford county abounds. From its summit there is a magnificent view of the coast, with its numerous creeks and bays, and miniature harbours; its bold barrier of rocks, and the small islands that dot the surface of the ocean. First in interest and importance is the small promontory of BAG-AN-BUN, where, according to the ancient couplet—

"Irelonde was lost and won,"

and where the first hostile Englishman trode upon Irish soil. Farther inland is the castle and village of FETHARD—a corruption of "Fought hard"—where the Irish made their earliest stand against the onward march of the Anglo-Norman invaders,* under Strongbow. At the extremity of its broad bay is the ancient abbey of TINTERN; and, at the termination of a narrow creek, are the seven castles of Clonmines. On the land opposite, the old church of Bannow crowns the summit of a small hill that looks down upon "the Irish Herculaneum"—a town buried long ago in the sand. Looking seaward again, the eye falls upon the two small islands called "the Keeroes"—then upon a narrow neck of land, that, stretching across from one peninsula until it almost touches another, forms the lough of BALLYTEAGUE; due south of which are the far-famed SALTEES, famous in the sea-calendar; for to mariners the sound was, for a long period, one of fear. Farther west, again, and passing Carnsore Point, is the TUSKAR rock, beside which many a gallant vessel went down, the calamity being briefly noticed with the melancholy postscript, "All hands perished." But Wexford county is now far less perilous than of yore; for from the very spot—the Tower of Hook—on which we have placed the reader, we may count at least half a score of "lights;" and wrecks are now comparatively rare upon this once merciless coast.

THE SALTEES.

The object that will next claim attention is Duncannon Fort, occupying a small promontory nearly midway in the harbour; it is still a fortification, as it was so far back as the reign of Henry VI.: but is maintained more for show than defence.

Passing the village of BALLYHACK, immediately opposite Passage, and famous for its old castle and "dirty butter," we come in view of the ruins of DUNBRODY ABBEY, just where the Suir, the Nore, and the Barrow meet, in the harbour of Waterford. The abbey was founded, according to Ware, by Hervey de Montmarisco, for Cistercian monks, in 1182. The remains are very extensive, and in a good state of preservation.

---

* The first invading army was headed by Robert Fitzstephen, who preceded Strongbow by about two years. Tradition states that Fitzstephen embarked his forces in two ships, called the Bagg and the Bunn, and hence the name of the promontory. Redinhed, in his notes on Giraldus Cambrensis, favours this opinion. "There were," he says, "certain monuments made in memorie thereof, and were named the Banner and the Boenne, which were the names (as common fame is) of the two greatest ships in which the English arrived." When the ships of Strongbow were entering Waterford Harbour, he perceived on the one shore a tower, and on the other a church; and inquiring their names was answered, "The tower of Hook, and the church of Crook." "Then," said he, "we must enter and take the town by Hook or by Crook." Hence originated a proverb now in common use.

The scene here is charming; the voyager will see with delight the union of the " goodlie Barrow," the " stubborn Nore," and the " gentle Suire."

Hence, and indeed long previously, both sides of the bay are dotted with good houses or fine mansions in the midst of pleasant woods; and if we find the harbour of Waterford less grand and spacious than that of Dublin, and less picturesque, beautiful, and richly cultivated than that of Cork, we shall, at all events, consider it very attractive, and feel assured that no bay of the United Kingdom has been gifted with more or greater capabilities.

The city of Waterford ranks among the oldest and most famous of the cities of Ireland. It was anciently called " Cuan-na-Grioth"—the Harbour of the Sun; and its existence is said to be dated so far back as A.D. 155. Certain it is, however, that it was a place of some note in the ninth century, when it was a colony of the Danes, who retained possession of it until the invasion of Ireland in 1171. A singular round castle still stands on the quay, and bears an inscription, signed by Sir John Newport, Bart., as mayor, which records that it was erected by Reginald the Dane, in the year 1003; was held as a fortress by Strongbow, in 1171; was used as a mint, by statute 3rd Edward IV. in 1463; and that in the year 1819 it was converted into a jail for refractory boys and sturdy beggars. From the Danes the city is said to have derived its name—Waterford being considered a corruption of " Vader Fiord," the Ford of the Father, or the Great Haven, for it has received both

DUNBRODY ABBEY.

translations. In the various contests of which Ireland has been the arena, Waterford has played a conspicuous part; having endured sieges from Strongbow, Cromwell, and William III., to say nothing of Perkin Warbeck, against whom the citizens fought lustily for eleven days, bringing many prisoners into the city, " who had their heads chopped off in the market-place." For their gallantry they received, among other honours, the motto they still retain—

" URBS INTACTA MANET WATERFORDIA."

The Cathedral of Waterford is reported to have been originally built by the Danes in 1096, when they first embraced Christianity; and, before it was " improved," is said to have been a stately and venerable edifice; its character is now very incongruous. Perhaps no city of Ireland presents a more imposing view than that obtained from the square, at which passengers land, immediately fronting Reginald's Tower; high steeps on the other side of the river, in the county of Kilkenny, are crowned with villas, embowered in pleasant woods; the quays are full of bustle, where many ships are unloading, and the long, yet picturesque bridge is seen at their extremity. We cross the bridge to the railway terminus; having sojourned awhile at one of the hotels, of which the city of course has several—none of them of a high class, but all sufficiently comfortable, and we are *en route* to Killarney.

The railway to the Limerick Junction was constructed in 1850-4, by the eminent engineer George Willoughby Hemans, Esq. (a son of the poetess), and is among the most successful railway achievements of the kingdom. Its extent to the Limerick Junction is 55 miles: all the way through the counties of Kilkenny and Tipperary; the county of Waterford being on the southern side of the Suir. We briefly describe this route, premising that neither in England nor in Ireland is there a line which affords a larger amount of pictorial beauty than we find here during its first thirty miles.*

The river Suir—the "gentle Suire" of Spenser—

"that, making way
By sweet Clonmel, adorns rich Waterford"—

ranks among the noblest rivers of Ireland; it is broad, deep, not too rapid, and its character is highly picturesque, both above and below the city. It is by the side of this river the railway goes a long way. The first station is GRANGE, the next PORTLAW. Portlaw is now a flourishing town, made so by the "Malcolmsons." A few years ago it was a wretched village, among the most wretched of Ireland. It now, we understand, contains 5,000 inhabitants; for here is the cotton factory of this enterprising family; here it is manufactured; and hence it is sent in their own vessels, built in Waterford, to all parts of the world. The Messrs. Malcolmson have made—deservedly and most honourably made—large fortunes by this concern; and they have set an example we may hope to see extensively followed.

It has, indeed, been for a long time obvious that Ireland, with its immense water-power and its superabundant population, living cheaply, and therefore able to work cheaply, was peculiarly calculated to manufacture articles in cotton; but, unhappily, there has been so entire a want of confidence in the steadiness and sobriety of the people, that few were found willing to risk a property which might be destroyed by the evil passions or caprice of a single individual, influencing other individuals. Happily, all difficulties of this kind are now removed; capital is rapidly finding its way into Ireland, and there can be no doubt of its being at no distant period "a great manufacturing country," in which there will be many places flourishing like Portlaw, under the auspices of other such men as the Malcolmsons.

All the way, after leaving Waterford, we have views of ranges of mountains. But the COMMERAGH mountains, which occupy the centre of the county, and are seen from all parts of it, as well as from a considerable portion of Tipperary, are those

---

* The traveller should take the left-hand seat in the railway going from Waterford.

which merit especial notice. They present a varied and picturesque outline from every point of view; and from the sea, or southern side, are well known to mariners, by whom they are called "the high lands of Dungarvon." But the greatest natural curiosity in these mountains is the appearance and site of a nearly circular lake, by name Coom-shinawin, *i.e.* "The Valley of Ants."

Nearing Portlaw, we have views of the grounds of CURRAGHMORE, the seat of the Marquis of Waterford, and of the exquisitely beautiful demesne of Coolnamuch, the residence of his brother. Curraghmore Park is extensive, containing nearly 5,000 statute acres of land, planted with the rarest trees. "The character of Curraghmore" (we copy from the Rev. Mr. Ryland's excellent history of the county) "is grandeur; not that arising from the costly and laborious exertions of man, but rather the magnificence of nature. The beauty of the situation consists in the lofty hills, rich vales, and almost impenetrable woods, which deceive the eye, and give the idea of boundless forests. The variety of the scenery is calculated to please in the highest degree, and to gratify every taste; from the lofty mountain to the quiet and sequestered walk on the bank of the river, every gradation of rural beauty may be enjoyed."

LOUGH COOM-SHINAWIN.

Not far from the grounds, and adjoining the Suir towards Clonmel, is the picturesque well of Tubber Grieve, a holy well in high repute with the peasantry. We introduce it here; for, although it is not likely to be visited by the passing stranger, he will see many like it in various parts of the country; peasants kneeling about the place, or drinking of its "healing waters;" the thornbush hung with bits of rags being almost invariably close by, containing the votive offerings of devotees. These holy wells, however, are far less numerous than they used to be, and are gradually losing their influence.

We next arrive at CARRICK-ON-SUIR, a prosperous town, with its picturesque castle jutting out into the stream. Near to Carrick is the ancient residence of the Osbornes; but here, unhappily, occurs an awkward *détour*, which carries the line away from the river. It is, however, soon regained, and we journey by its side into Clonmel, the capital town of the county of Tipperary.

The origin of CLONMEL is very ancient, and the traditional account of it is fanciful. The Tuatha-de-danaans, a primitive people of Ireland, who have been identified with the Pelasgi and Titans of the continent, wishing to select a site for a settlement, and being skilled in augury, were guided in their choice by the following omen:—They let off a swarm of bees, and observing where it settled, there erected their baile, or circular fort, and gave the spot the significant name of Cluain-mealla, *i.e.*, "The plain of honey." This very spot is still pointed out. A castle was erected on it in later times in place of the aboriginal fort; and it was before this castle that Cromwell sustained the severest repulse he received in Ireland, losing about 2,000 men; nor would it have surrendered but for the failure of ammunition, the garrison having, it is said, fired away even their buttons. It is also recorded that Cromwell had actually ordered his army to retreat, and as they were marching off he spied something glittering in the grass, which he took up, and found to be a silver bullet. This incident

TUBBER GRIEVE.

suggested the straits to which the garrison was reduced; he accordingly renewed the siege, and the castle was surrendered, but on very favourable terms. The town has a very "business air;" and is indeed conspicuous for its prosperity, being the great outlet for the produce of the county, the Suir being navigable for vessels of size to within a short distance of its quays. Its population exceeds 20,000, and the number of houses is above 1,500. The surrounding scenery is remarkably beautiful, combining every variety of landscape, from the alpine to the pastoral; the Commera mountains which rise to the south, appearing to terminate the streets. There are several agreeable walks in the immediate vicinity of the town, the principal of which are the Wilderness, which for solemn gloom and wild grandeur might convey no inadequate idea of that in which the Baptist preached; the Round of Heywood, a charming sylvan walk; the Green, commanding a delightful prospect of the river; Fairy-hill Road, the fashionable promenade; and the Quay, from which there is another pleasing view of the river.

The principal church at Clonmel, St. Mary's, is picturesque in character, and of great antiquity. The steeple is unique in structure, being an embattled octagon tower rising from a square base. Close to the summit of the steeple, and in each of the eight sides, is a large opening in the form of a Gothic window, to allow free transmission to the sound of a chime of bells placed in the tower. The east window is extremely beautiful: it assumes the form of a double Gothic tracery window, having the space between the two arches filled by a rich cinquefoil, or rather septemfoil, and is perhaps as old as the twelfth century. A stained-glass window has lately been put in. At the east corner of the church (and nearly opposite to the steeple, which is at the north), are the remains of a strong square tower, similar to the one forming the base of the octagon steeple. The principal entrance to the church is from the graveyard,

ST. MARY'S, CLONMEL.

through a stone Gothic portico, which, though well built, does not harmonise at all with the general tone and character of the building. Surrounding three sides of the graveyard are the remains of the old town wall, on which, with a view more effectually to protect it, are small square towers at stated intervals; at the north-west angle of the wall is a massive bomb-proof tower, called "the Magazine;" about 120 yards south of this tower, there is a portion of the wall wanting, which tradition points out as being the breach made by Cromwell when he besieged and took Clonmel.

Clonmel is remarkable as the birthplace of Lawrence Sterne; and of this town the accomplished Countess of Blessington was also a native.

The station next to Clonmel is CAHIR. Passing by the prosperous and well-managed estate of Lord Glengall, we come in view of "the Castle," which stands on the river Suir, and was, as well as the town it protected, very famous in former times. It is said, however, to occupy the site of a structure of the remotest antiquity—its ancient name being "*Cahirdunaascaigh*, or, 'The circular stone fortress of the fish-abounding Dun, or fort;' a name which appears to be tautological, and which can only be accounted for by the supposition that an earthen *Dun*, or fort, had originally occupied

CAHIR CASTLE.

the site on which a *Cahir*, or stone fort, was erected subsequently." It is of considerable extent, but irregular outline, consequent upon its adaptation to the form and broken surface of its insular site, and consists of a great square keep, surrounded by extensive outworks, forming an outer and an inner ballium, with a small court-yard between the two; these outworks being flanked by seven towers, four of which are circular, and three of larger size, square. Its general character, even now, closely assimilates to that which it presented in 1599 (when it was taken by the Earl of Essex), as it is pictured in the Pacata Hibernia. Very recently it has been put into thorough repair; but so judiciously, that its picturesque effect is in no degree injured. At a short distance up the river are the ruins of an ancient monastery, built, it is said in the reign of King John, for canons regular of the order of St. Augustin.

The town of Cahir has a remarkably cheerful aspect, and its prosperity is not alone upon the surface; it is derived principally from the extensive flour-mills, actively and continually at work, in the immediate neighbourhood, and conducted almost exclusively by the "people called Quakers." There are, in several parts of the south of Ireland, towns universally known and distinguished as "Quaker Towns"—they are remarkable for neatness and cleanliness, for the industry and sobriety of the inhabitants, and an air of comfort and good order in their dwellings—so surely does a good example influence all within its reach. The railway bridge which here crosses the

Suir—built in 1852, by the engineer, Mr. Willoughby Hemans, is one of the most graceful works of the kind in the kingdom.

The Tourist may, soon after leaving Cahir, see the hill of KNOCKGRAFFON, with its time-honoured moat; and also a picturesque stone bridge of great antiquity, upon which William the Third is said to have signed the charter of Cashel. The remains of an old circular round tower, which in former times protected the pass, continue in a tolerable state of preservation.

GOLDEN BRIDGE.

The moat of Knockgraffon is the scene of several of Croker's fairy legends. It is indeed a treasury of legendary lore; we gathered from some of the aged women in the neighbourhood a store of traditions of the ancient Irish kings, and of the fairies who still continue to guard their hereditary dominions, to which they are expected, at some future period, to lay claim, and again govern "in the flesh." The wild fictions of Dr. Keating (a native of, and long a resident in, the neighbourhood) are rife among the peasantry; in many instances we found precisely the incidents and events, which the doctor dignified by the term "history," preserved by the memories of old and young in this remarkable locality.

Leaving this district, we come in view of the famous GLEN OF AHERLOE—long notorious in the sad records of agrarian disturbances for which Tipperary county has been "renowned;" but which happily is now but a theme of history: there are at present few more tranquil and well-ordered shires in Ireland.

After Bansha station, the station next reached is that of TIPPERARY. The town, which gave name to the county, although very ancient, has yielded in rank, population, and importance to that of Clonmel. Tipperary is said to be a corruption of the Irish Tobar-a-neidth, which signifies "The well of the plains," from its situation at the base of the Slieve-na-muck hills—a portion of the Galtee mountains. Other etymologists derive it from Teobred-aruin, *i. e.*, "The fountain of Ara"—an ancient chief, whose name, in conjunction with that of another chief (Owny), is now given to one of the baronial divisions of the county. Two and a half miles farther, and the LIMERICK JUNCTION is reached: "the Great Southern and Western" is then entered on; by this line the journey is continued to MALLOW. The several objects of interest between the Limerick Junction and Mallow we have described, *en route* from Dublin; and those from Mallow to Killarney we shall note presently. We have said that at the Junction there is an excellent hotel—and we have given some idea of the exceeding interest and beauty of the road between it and Waterford city.

MALLOW TO KILLARNEY.

FROM Mallow to the Lakes, the railway, although forty-one miles in length, has little to interest the traveller. The scenery immediately adjacent to Mallow is picturesque: although tame by comparison with that he has passed through, and especially that upon which he is about to enter; but it decreases in value as he proceeds: a circumstance by no means disadvantageous, inasmuch as it heightens the effect of Killarney when he is there: the lakes being "rare gems in coarse setting." Between Mallow and Killarney there are five stations—LOMBARDS-TOWN, KANTURK, MILLSTREET, SHINNAGH, and HEADFORD. All the mountains between Mallow and Killarney lie to the south of the line. The first, about six miles from Mallow, is Mount Hilary, along the base of which the line runs, and to the west of which flows the Glen River—a very good trout stream. The range of the Boggeragh Mountain next comes in sight; and about two miles beyond Millstreet we encounter "the Paps," two mountains of singular formation. Hence, all the way into Killarney, the mountain scenery is very fine. Six miles beyond Millstreet we cross a mountain stream—the Annaskertawn River—the boundary between the counties of Cork and Kerry. The Paps are in Kerry. After passing this river, we obtain a good view of Mangerton and the Reeks. In the rugged-looking glen, among the mountains east of Mangerton, is Lough Kittane. As we approach "Killarney," the great feature of its scenery, the perpetual variety of its mountain ridges, will be seen and estimated.

It is, indeed, as we have intimated elsewhere, to their perpetual changes that these lakes are indebted for much of their beauty. Every passing or hovering cloud, every gust of wind, every sunbeam and every shade, every shower and every mist, produces some new effect; insomuch as that even while you look upon it, it shall assume a character so different, that you will scarcely believe your eyes have not been unconsciously removed to another spot. This is especially observable in reference to the mountains, seen either near or distant: and even by rapid railway travelling, the observer will be struck by this remarkable character of the locality: as he looks to the left upon rugged Mangerton, or to the right upon Carran Tuel and the other Reeks—which he will not fail to do from the carriage as he nears the Lakes.

Arrived at the neat and well-managed Terminus,* he will, of course—"as in all such cases made and provided"—be greeted and welcomed by "squires" from the several hotels. The traveller, however, had best judge for himself, having arranged

---

* The railway company have made a very judicious arrangement, by which only one attendant from each of the hotels is permitted to enter the station on the arrival of a train. Cars and omnibuses from each hotel are in attendance at the gates; and of course porters to take charge of luggage.

K

his intended resting-place beforehand, and thus becoming independent of such disinterested counsellors.

During "the season," he will have acted wisely who has ordered his apartments in due time to be ready on his arrival; for, although such is the accommodation at Killarney that perhaps five hundred persons might find beds of one sort or other, it is by no means certain that "the last comer" may have other rest than that afforded by "a stretcher."

Elsewhere we have laid some stress on the necessity of being always prepared for rain. Rain in this district is not altogether a misfortune; for it enhances the beauty of the scenery, filling the mountain streams, and adding power to the waterfalls; but, undoubtedly, the Tourist should be warned against trusting entirely to summer clothing, even on the hottest summer-day.

Probably many Tourists will supply themselves with "Tourists' Tickets." It may be, therefore, well to repeat, that these are always considered—at the stations, the hotels, and, indeed, everywhere—as letters of introduction; they give assurance of "a stranger," who is proverbially, in Ireland, secure of kind and courteous treatment; moreover, the ticket is a contract to avoid delays on all routes—the first places upon occasions of difficulty of right belonging to their holders. Independent, therefore, of the very great saving of expense, all tourists in Ireland should obtain "Tourists' Tickets."

Posting is 1s. a mile, by post-chaise; and by car 6d. a mile for one person, 8d. for two persons, and 10d. for three persons. The rule is pretty nearly established throughout Ireland; but in some places 8d. will be required in all cases, whether for one person or four; about Killarney, however, the charge is 6d. a mile for two persons. The post-boys expect 3d. a mile for post-chaises, and 2d. a mile for cars. It is necessary to bear in mind that the relative proportions of English and Irish miles are eleven to fourteen, eleven Irish miles being equal to fourteen English.

Distances are calculated as English miles on all roads in the south.

And with these remarks we commend the Tourist to a district perhaps more fertile of interest and true enjoyment than any other district of the world, at so small a cost of time and money, with so little risk of annoyance.

KILLARNEY.

The town of Killarney* is distant about a mile from the north-east shore of the Lower Lake. It is a poor town; and although surrounded by resident gentry, can scarcely be described as prosperous. Some tokens of recent improvement may, however, be discerned: the railway terminus exhibits bustle and business; the shops have a gayer look and character than they used to have; those for the sale of arbutus and bog-oak specimens are aiming at "decorative excellence;" and though there is no bookseller's shop, the Railway Station has always an ample supply, under the admirable management of Messrs. Smith and their agents, who have done so much to circulate good and pure literature into places that were not long ago inaccessible to knowledge conveyed in that form.

---

* " Hibernice, CILL-AIRNE, or the Church near the Sloe-trees." (WINDELE.) The legend is, that three sister saints established themselves in this neighbourhood, and built churches here—AHA, whence Kill-aha; AGI, whence Kill-agi; and AIRNE, whence Kill-airne.

The Roman Catholic Cathedral, now finished, was designed by the eminent architect, Pugin, who personally superintended its erection. It is a fine building, constructed of course after the most approved models, and occupies a commanding site, being seen from all parts of the adjacent country. A structure, however, even more elevated in position, is the Lunatic Asylum—a gigantic mass, made, apparently, to "accommodate" half the county. The Workhouse is also a good and "sightly" building: large—happily, now-a-days, too large. The Church is a poor edifice, that has been long gradually, and is now rapidly, falling to decay; exertions are making to supply its place by a structure that shall, at all events, be no blot on the picturesque of the locality—which assuredly the present Church of the Protestants is; an evil that is greatly enhanced by the comparison that cannot fail to be instituted between it and its stately neighbour of the other faith.*

The population of Killarney is about 7,000; and the number of houses may be about 1,000. The proprietor of the town and a large portion of the adjoining district is the Earl of Kenmare, a Roman Catholic peer,† whose family first entered Ireland A.D. 1555, and whose ancestor, Sir Valentine Browne, received, as an English "undertaker,"‡ a grant of 6,560 acres of the estates forfeited in the Desmond rebellion, temp. Elizabeth. The property so acquired he increased by purchase, and it was subsequently augmented by intermarriages with the princely families of the Fitzgeralds, MacCarthys, and O'Sullivans.

When the Down survey was completed, about the year 1656, there was no such town as Killarney in existence. Sir William Petty then surveyed the parish of Killarney; but neither in his general map, nor in his barony maps, is there any notice of a town or village of the name. When Thomas, the fourth Lord Kenmare, came of age in 1747, the town consisted of only his lordship's house, and not more than three or four slated houses and 100 thatched cabins, and the whole population could not have exceeded 500. Before the revolution Lord Kenmare's family resided at Ross, in the castle, and in a contiguous fortified house, and did not reside at Killarney till 1721. Smith, in 1756, says, "A new street with a large commodious

---

* The plan of the proposed Church has been lithographed; it will be an elegant as well as a commodious edifice: and be a credit in lieu of a reproach to the neighbourhood. A printed circular requests assistance from "visitors and tourists;" we hope it may be, as it certainly ought to be, liberally and considerately rendered, by all "strangers"—who will give thought to the good they may do while sojourning in this charming locality, "where the scenery around so strikingly displays the beauty of God's works!" They are fairly and rightly reminded that while the present church is "unsafe and incapable of repair," a larger building for their accommodation is required than would be necessary for the resident congregation; and while an appeal is made to their sense of justice, it will be obvious there are other—and very strong—reasons why they should contribute to this high, holy, and most important work. [This passage was written some four or five years ago; we regret to say that the building is not yet commenced—principally, however, we believe, in consequence of the difficulty of obtaining a satisfactory site.]

† It is only justice to the noble Earl, however, to state that he is not responsible for the dilapidated condition of Killarney, over which he has in reality very little influence, chiefly arising out of the old wretched system of granting long leases for heavy fines. His lordship and his estimable lady have ever been much respected in their town; they do not, however, now reside there; but are well represented by their eldest son, Viscount Castlerosse and his lady, who are doing much to improve the property and the locality also.

‡ The estates confiscated in the Desmond Rebellion contained nearly 600,000 acres, in the counties of Cork, Limerick, Kerry, and Waterford; more than one half were restored to the "pardoned traitors;" the remainder was divided into seigniories of 12,000, 8,000, 6,000, and 4,000 acres. The English undertaker was to have an estate in fee-farm, yielding for each seigniory of 12,000 acres, for the first three years, £33 6s. 8d. sterling, and after that period double the amount. The undertaker was to have for his own demesne 2,100 acres; for six farmers, 400 acres each; six freeholders, 300 acres each; and the residue was to be divided into smaller tenures, on which thirty-six families at least were to be established. The lesser seigniories were to be laid out and peopled in the same manner, in proportion to their extent. Each undertaker was to people his seigniory in seven years; he was to have licence to export all commodities duty free to England for five years—the planters were to be English, and no English planter was permitted to convey to any mere Irish. Each undertaker was bound to furnish the State with three horsemen and six footmen armed—the lesser seigniories in the same proportion; and each copyholder was to find one footman armed; but they were not compelled to serve out of Munster for seven years, and then to be paid by the crown.

inn are designed to be built here; for the curiosities of the neighbouring lake have of late drawn great numbers of curious travellers to visit it." The town lies in a valley; from which the lake is hidden by the well-wooded demesne of Lord Kenmare.

The workhouse at Killarney should be inspected by every visitor: it is at once a most painful and a most gratifying sight. The whole of the arrangements seem to be as near perfection as they can be: the wards, the dormitories especially, are clean and neat and well provided; the ventilation is admirable, the clothing good, the food wholesome and abundant, and a sufficiency of employment is found in grinding flour, and in manufacturing the various articles used in the house. Our only marvel is that any of the destitute poor remain out of it to endure the want and misery of their own wretched hovels.

THE RAILWAY HOTEL.

Entering Killarney, the first question of the Tourist will naturally concern the hotel at which he is to be located.* The first in rank is unquestionably THE RAILWAY HOTEL, close to the station, from which there is a covered way, lined with shrubs and

---

* Mr. Webb states that so late as the year 1808, neither of the inns of Killarney "afforded a coach-house." He adds — writing in 1812 — "it is much to be regretted that there is no place of public accommodation, not even a single house, on the confines of the lake, where apartments can be procured; for, independent of the inconvenience of going and returning, some disgust is liable to be felt at the sudden transition from the rural and sequestered scenery of the lake to the hurry and bustle of a noisy town, which is always crowded with idle people, and among whom beggars, as in every place of public resort in Ireland, bear a very conspicuous proportion." Mr. Webb's "Illustration of the Scenery of Killarney," were published in 1812. It was the first work that drew attention to the Lakes and — allowing for the numerous changes induced by time — it may even now be received as authority upon matters connected with the subject. The book is valuable and interesting — the production of a highly accomplished mind. Mr. Webb was a close observer, a ripe scholar, and a traveller who had learned from travel not to decry, but to appreciate the beauties of his native land. Honour to his memory!

flowers, to the entrance door. It is a building of much architectural elegance; a reasonably good idea of which may be formed from the appended woodcut. It was built by the South-Western Railway Company, expressly for the accommodation of tourists, and contains all modern improvements: a very spacious coffee-room (upwards of seventy feet long); a public drawing-room; hot and cold baths, of large size; and all the appliances that can minister to comfort, including "the kitchen." It may be well to observe that ladies freely use both the coffee-room and the public drawing-room; but there are many private sitting rooms, and upwards of one hundred bedrooms. The manager is Mr. Goodman, who personally attends to every part of his huge establishment, directing the several servants, from the waiter to the guide, and being always present at the liberal Table d'Hôte. It is indeed impossible to overpraise the management of this hotel.* We speak less from our own experience than from the reports of all with whom we have conversed on the subject. Its drawback is that it does not command views of the lake, that is to say, *from the grounds:* for from any of the windows of the second floor, there are fine and extensive views of the waters and the mountains. Some will consider the absence of perpetual views a disadvantage, others will hold an opposite opinion; for from morning till after dusk, tourists will have seen so much of the beauties of the district that perhaps repose will be a relief. The grounds around the hotel are laid out with much taste; the walks are among choice ferns and flowers; fountains are judiciously placed; garden seats are scattered here and there; and all available means have been adopted that can supply enjoyment when the day's tour has been done. The hotel is opposite the entrance to the beautiful grounds of Lord Kenmare.

Much that we have said in praise of this hotel will apply with equal force to the ROYAL VICTORIA LAKE HOTEL, the proprietor and manager of which is Mr. O'Leary. Here are also excellent public rooms and "private apartments," with all the other advantages that make a "home" of an "inn." It is about two miles from the town, on the road to the Gap of Dunloe, and the site it occupies is peculiarly auspicious. It stands on the northern bank of the Lower Lake. Immediately fronting the windows are the Toomies, Purple Mountain, and beautiful Glena; while midway, in a direct line, is fair Inisfallen. To the right are seen the gigantic Reeks—with the entrance to Dunloe Gap; to the left is rugged and lofty Mangerton; behind is the hill, topped by the ruins of Aghadoe, and fringed by the beautiful woods of Lord Headley's demesne; so that, look where we will over the noble expanse of water, or towards the land, some object of interest meets our view. We prefer to a view of the Hotel an engraving of the scenery presented from the windows of either of the front rooms.

"THE LAKE HOTEL" was formerly a private residence, famous for its beauty of situation, the fine growth of trees, and the little island that forms part of the demesne, on which stand the picturesque remains of an ancient castle—Castle Lough. The whole of this demesne, with all its advantages, now forms a part of the hotel grounds. The hotel is surrounded by the most beautiful of the scenery of Killarney: it is bounded on the southern side by Mucross, on the north by the woods of Caher-

---

* We direct special attention to the "airing room" which effectually prevents the possibility of danger from damp sheets or beds; every article of linen is kept in this heated chamber until ordered for use. We inspected with much pleasure the posting establishment, superintended by Mr. JOHN DONOVAN, and attached to the Railway Hotel. There are rarely less than forty horses in the stables; and these horses are of the best. There is no better managed concern than this of Mr. Donovan in any part of Ireland.

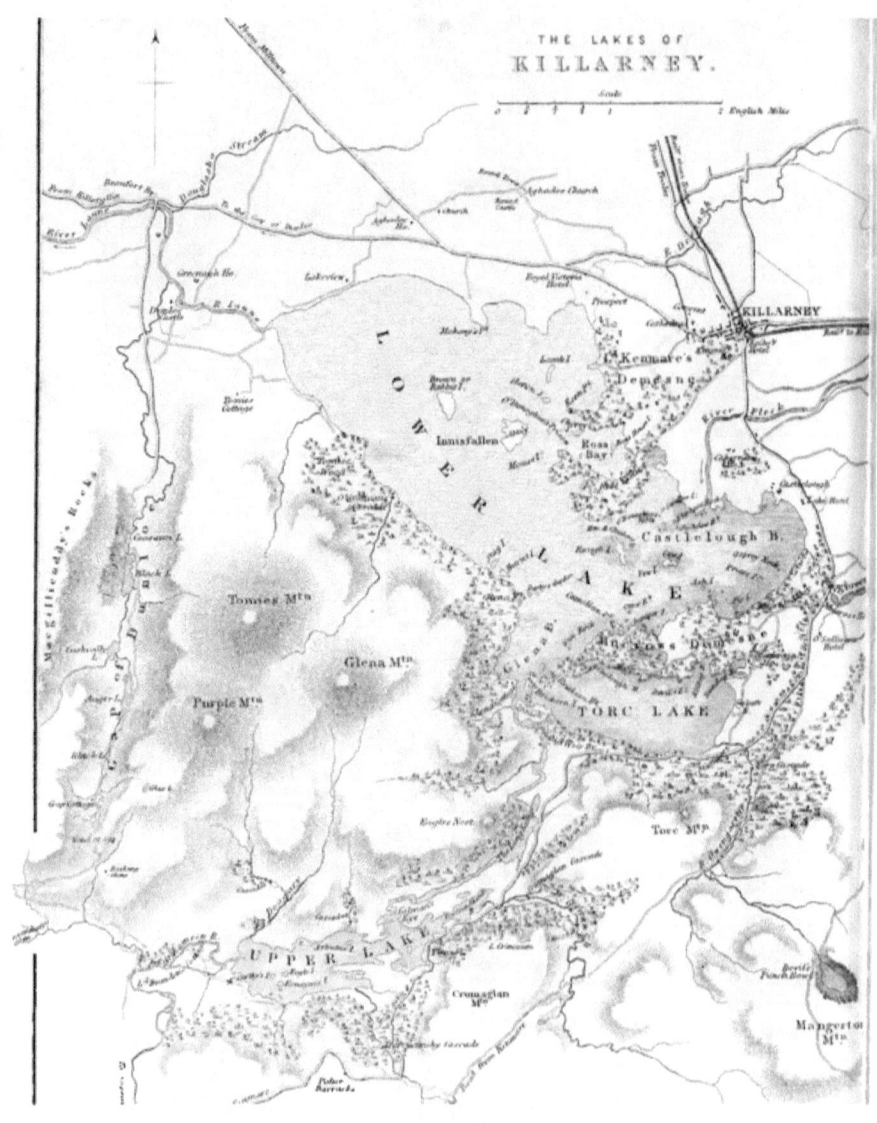

name, and, in front, views are commanded of several of the islands—with Glena Bay. Views are hence also obtained of Mangerton, Tore Waterfall, and Derricunnihy Cascade, and the summits of the several mountains which look down upon the lakes.

VIEW FROM VICTORIA HOTEL.

At Cloghreen, close to Mucross Abbey, there are two good hotels; they do not vie with the three we have named, but they are comfortable and somewhat extensive, and the charges are less than those of their rivals. "THE MUCROSS HOTEL." is close to the Abbey, and near to it is O'SULLIVAN'S HOTEL. They are both near the foot of Mangerton, within half a mile of the Tore Waterfall—the most beautiful of the Killarney Falls—and on the direct route to the Upper Lake, and the "new line" to Kenmare. Their situation therefore is highly advantageous, being equally "convenient" to the three lakes; but "the view" is excluded by the tall trees of Mr. Herbert's demesne.

In the town there are two hotels; they will be occupied when the other hotels are full. These are "THE KENMARE ARMS" and "THE INISFALLEN." In the town also there are several lodging-houses, some of which are boarding-houses.

Each of the hotels issue cards of the charges: rooms, dinners, &c.; boats, carriages, ponies, and guides; noting, indeed, every item, so that the Tourist may calculate his expenses to a shilling.

But the Tourist, no matter where he sojourns, will be sure to find much to content and little to displease. The purpose is, and the continual study is, to give enjoyment—to "earn a good name;" and managers, waiters, "boys about the place," drivers, boatmen, and guides, are zealous in ministering to the comforts of guests.

Guides are essentials at Killarney; and, indeed, in all places *en route;* they add much to the traveller's information and enjoyment. The payment they expect is little, and the comfort they give great. Let no Tourist think he can do "well enough" without a guide. We have more to say on this subject, and our remarks will be found at the end of this chapter.

Each hotel has its boat's crew and its "commodore." The Railway Hotel has a crew of twenty-four, all smart and intelligent young men, dressed alike in blue and white. Their commodore is Jeremiah Clifford, a somewhat more aged denizen of the locality; a most pleasant companion, full of knowledge, who can tell a legend with admirable effect, and dance an Irish jig as vigorously as the best youth in Kerry. The commodore at the Victoria is Miles MacSweeny, to whose skill as an angler we have borne testimony. There are several excellent aids to anglers also at the Railway Hotel—Callaghan, Macarthy, Robert Roberts, Tom Murphy, and especially Jerry Clifford. They will supply all requisite tackle and flies to suit the season; such flies as laugh to scorn the gaily fill'd "book" the Tourist frequently takes with him—to find useless.

Much of the pleasure and information of the visitor will be derived from the driver of the car in which he is seated. The two with whom we have had most intercourse, during our eight visits to the lakes, Jerry Sullivan and Michael Sullivan, are now both at the Railway Hotel. Frequent references are made to them in the course of this book. The Tourist will be fortunate who falls into the hands of either. They know every inch of the locality: Glengariff, Kenmare, Dingle, Valentia, all round the coast, and every spot about the lakes. They are in all ways to be depended upon—obliging, careful, and intelligent. No doubt there are others as good; but it so happens that one of the brothers has always been with us when we have visited Killarney, and we have reason to know that if there be drivers as good, there are none better, in the district—such are Pat McCarthy and James Shee.

It will be seen, therefore, that by hotels and lodging-houses there is ample accommodation for an "influx" of visitors, such as any season may bring;—there will be no great difficulty in giving "sleeping-rooms" to five hundred persons, if so many should be in Killarney at one time.

Let us now imagine the Tourist taking "his ease at his inn," called upon to determine how his time may be most pleasantly and most profitably expended. We shall endeavour to guide him; first supplying him with some information respecting the wonderful and beautiful district in which he is for a time located.

The Lakes of Killarney are three in number; the LOWER LAKE, the UPPER LAKE, and the MIDDLE, or TORC LAKE. In reality, however, the three must be considered as one; for they are divided only by narrow channels, the passage between the lower and middle lakes being, indeed, only of a bridge's breadth.* They are situated in the centre of a range of lofty mountains, among which are Carran Tuel and Mangerton,

---

* "The Lake consists of three distinct bodies of water; of these, the first, which is called the Upper Lake, lies embosomed amidst the mountains; the others, situated at the exterior base of the chain, are bounded at one side alone by mountains; and in the opposite direction they open to a cultivated country, whose surface is diversified by innumerable hills. The last two divisions are nearly upon the same level, and lie contiguous to each other, being separated merely by a narrow peninsula (MUCKROSS) and some small islands (BRICKEEN and DINIS), between which there are channels passable for boats; but the Upper Lake stands three miles distant, at the head of a navigable river, which flows through a romantic valley or defile (THE LONG RANGE). Near the termination of its course this river divides into two branches, one of which flows peaceably into the Bay of Glenn, on the Great or Lower Lake; the other, forcing its way through a rocky channel, issues with considerable impetuosity into the Middle Lake, under the woods of Dinis Island." (WELD.) This river separates after passing the "Old Weir Bridge."

THE ARBUTUS.

the former the highest in Ireland.* The mountains, that run directly from the water, are dotted with evergreen tree-shrubs and magnificently grown forest trees, reaching from the base almost to the summit. This, indeed, forms one of the leading peculiarities of Killarney.†

The Tourist, on approaching the Lakes, is at once struck by the singularity and the variety of the foliage in the woods that clothe the hills by which on all sides they are surrounded. The effect produced is novel, striking, and beautiful; and is caused chiefly by the abundant mixture of the tree shrub *Arbutus Unedo*‡ with the forest trees. The Arbutus grows in nearly all parts of Ireland; but nowhere is it found of so large a size, or in such rich luxuriance, as at Killarney, excepting, perhaps, at Glengariff. The extreme western position, the mild and humid atmosphere (for, in Ireland, there is fact as well as fancy in the poet's image—

THE ARBUTUS.

"Thy suns with doubtful gleam
Weep while they rise"),

and the rarity of frosts, contribute to its propagation, and nurture it to an enormous growth, far surpassing that which it attains in any part of Great Britain; although, even at Killarney, it is never of so great a size as it is found clothing the sides of Mount Athos. In Dinis Island there was a tree seven feet in circumference, and its height in proportion,§ being equal to that of an ash-tree of the same girth which grew near it. There are several others nearly as large. Alone, its character is not picturesque: the branches are bare, long, gnarled, and crooked; presenting in its wild state a remarkable contrast to its trim, formal, and bush-like figure in our cultivated gardens. Mingled with other trees, however, it is exceedingly beautiful; its bright green leaves happily mixing with the light or dark drapery of

---

* Heights of the principal mountains surrounding the Lakes:—

Carran Tual	3,414 feet
Mangerton	2,756
Tore Mountain	1,764
Eagle's Nest	1,100
Purple Mountain	2,739
Toomies	2,500

The only mountains that actually rise from the Lake are Tore, Glena, and Toomies,—the Purple Mountain ascends behind the latter. Between Toomies and the water's edge, there is a tract of fertile ground under cultivation.

† The autumn months are generally recommended for visiting Killarney, chiefly because the tints of foliage are then more varied; but to our minds this attraction ill compensates for the shortness of the days. We have visited the Lakes at three different seasons—in April, in June, and in September. The Lakes may be seen to great advantage so early as May or June; when, according to a common saying, Inisfallen is covered with snow—i.e. the hawthorns are in full bloom. This tree blooms most luxuriantly at Killarney, and grows to an amazing size. In the demesne of Lord Kenmare there is one tree of such prodigious growth, that we imagine four hundred men might stand under its branches.

‡ Pliny says it is called "Unedo," because, having eaten one, you will never desire to eat another. It is said, however, that an agreeable wine is made from the berry in the south of Europe.

§ This arbutus-tree was not long ago blown down; its trunk, however, remains to show its size.

its neighbours—the elm and the ash, or the holly and the yew, with which it is almost always intermixed. It strikes its roots apparently into the very rocks—thus filling up spaces that would otherwise be barren spots in the scenery. Its beautiful berries, when arrived at maturity, are no doubt conveyed by the birds, who feed upon them, to the heights of inaccessible mountains, where they readily vegetate in situations nearly destitute of soil.* Its most remarkable peculiarity is, that the flower (not unlike the lily of the valley) and the fruit—ripe and unripe—are found at the same time, together, on the same tree. The berry has an insipid though not an unpleasant taste, is nearly round, and resembles in colour the wood-strawberry; whence its common name—the Strawberry-tree. It appears to the greatest advantage in October, when it is covered with a profusion of flowers in drooping clusters, and scarlet berries of the last year: and when its gay green is strongly contrasted with the brown and yellow tints which autumn has given to its neighbours. It is said that, although now found universally in Ireland, and more especially in the counties of Cork and Kerry, it is not a native of the soil, but was introduced into the country by Spanish monks.†

Of the Arbutus wood a variety of toys are made at Killarney, for which there is considerable sale to visitors anxious to retain some palpable reminiscence of the beautiful place. The Tourist will not have passed many minutes at his inn before a fair messenger from one of the "arbutus factories" makes her appearance, and with winning looks and wiling words endeavours to effect sales from the full basket she carries with her. The Arbutus wood—and, very surely, the wood of other trees, such as the yew, the holly, and, above all, the bog-oak—has been converted by the craftsman into a vast variety of items—card-cases, needle-boxes, paper-cutters, silk-winders, and so forth; and sometimes into objects of magnitude—such as tables, writing-desks, and work-boxes. They are manufactured with considerable skill and neatness, and are very pretty specimens of the various woods produced in the neighbourhood—which it would be a serious reproach to any Tourist to leave without having procured a few of these indubitable proofs that he has been where Nature has made a garden of her own for her own self. There are, in the town, four or five manufacturers of these articles, and visitors are invited to inspect the workshops, and see the artisans at work.

Of course there are plenty of photographs of the Lake scenery to be obtained in Dublin. But visitors will do well to postpone purchases until they are at Killarney, where they will find a skilful and intelligent artist—Mr. Hudson—who has a large stock of views, taken by himself, which exhibit nearly all the places of interest and beauty in the locality.

The charm of Killarney lakes, however, does not consist in the varied graces of foliage, the grandeur of encompassing mountains, the number of green or rocky

---

* A worthy gentleman with whom we conversed, in reference to this peculiarity, committed a genuine bull: "If you go to Killarney, 'tis there you'll see NATURE—*the trees growing out of the solid rock.*"

† On this point, however, botanists are much divided in opinion. We have had opportunities of consulting two of the most eminent in Ireland. By one we are told, "There is not the least doubt of its being truly indigenous; for it is found growing on the wild declivities of Glengariff, and bordering many of the little mountain loughs in the remote parts of Kerry, which still remain in a state of almost primitive nature." By the other we are informed, "Touching the Arbutus, although now growing spontaneously around Killarney, particularly on limestone, and what is termed red talcose slate, yet I am inclined to think it not strictly a native, but introduced from Spain by the monks. Inisfallen in the sixth century was a place of great wealth; numerous and valuable presents were constantly contributed to it; and the stranger monks procured from their own countries whatever would prove useful, either medicinally, culinary, or ornamental. Consequently, some of our rarest plants are found in the vicinity of these religious buildings."

islands, the singularly fantastic character of the island-rocks, the delicate elegance of the shores, the perpetual occurrence of bays; but in the wonderful variety produced by the combination of their attractions, which, together, give to the scenery a character inconceivably fascinating—such as the pen and pencil are utterly incompetent to describe.* The shadows from the mountains, perpetually changing, produce a variety of which there can be no adequate conception; insomuch that the very same spot shall present a different aspect twenty times within a day. Assuredly, they far surpass in natural beauty aught that nature has supplied elsewhere in Great Britain; for, with scarcely an exception, the devoted worshippers of Loch Katrine, and the fervid admirers of the northern English lakes, have yielded the palm to those of Killarney; some, however, having qualified the praise they bestow upon "the pride of Ireland," by admitting only that "the three lakes considered as one—which they may naturally be, lying so close to each other—are, *together*, more important than any *one* of the lakes of Cumberland and Westmoreland."† A glance at the map will show, as we have intimated, that the three are separated but by very narrow channels; and that two of them have scarcely any perceptible division. They have, nevertheless, very distinctive characteristics: the Lower Lake is studded with islands, nearly all being richly clothed with evergreens; the Upper Lake is remarkable for its wild magnificence, the mountains completely enclosing it; and the Middle Lake is conspicuous for a happy mingling of both—not inferior to the one in grace and beauty, or to the other in majestic grandeur.

The romantic beauties of the Killarney lakes were celebrated ages ago; in a very ancient poem they are classed as "the tenth wonder" of Ireland. The Irish name is Loch Lene—"the Lake of Learning," according to some authorities—a name by which it is still recognised among the peasantry, and which it is presumed to have derived from the number of "bookish monks," by whom its monasteries of Inisfallen, Mucross, and Aghadoe were at one time crowded.‡ The lakes are formed and supplied by numerous minor lakes that exist in the surrounding mountains, and may be described as an immense reservoir for the several rivers that also flow into them, having received on their way the waters of innumerable tributary streams. The only outlet for the waters thus collected is the narrow and rapid river Laune—a channel along which they proceed to the Atlantic through the beautiful bay of Dingle. The origin of these lakes—covering an extensive valley—is, therefore, self-evident; but fiction has assigned to them one of a far less obvious nature; for, as will be readily

---

* "The whole scene exquisite. Loveliness is the word that suits it best. The grand is less grand than what may be found among the Alps, but the softness, the luxuriance, the variety of colouring, the little gardens that every small rock exhibits, the romantic disposition of the islands, and graceful sweep of the shores—all this is unequalled anywhere else."—MOORE, *Diary*.

† Such is the admission of Mr. Wordsworth in a letter we had the honour to receive from him on the subject; and he adds, "I have more than once expressed an opinion that the county of Kerry, so nobly indented with bays of the Atlantic Ocean, and possessing a climate so favourable for vegetation, along with its mountains and inland waters, might without injustice be pronounced in point of scenery, the finest portion of the British Islands." Sir David Wilkie, writing in 1825, the year of his visit, refers to "the three lakes, that for beauty and grandeur I have never seen surpassed;" and we have the authority of Miss Edgeworth for saying that Sir Walter Scott "considered the Upper Lake the grandest sight he had ever seen—except" Loch Lomond." Spillane, senior (the bugler), who was in the boat with the memorable party, told us that Sir Walter Scott appeared ill; scarcely made a remark the whole day; and expressed his admiration only once—when the boat was close to Innis Island, where the waters of the three lakes meet; then he exclaimed, "Ah, this is beautiful!"

‡ Concerning the signification of the word "Lene," etymologists are far from agreeing. By many it is conjectured to refer to the ancient learned repute of the religious house at Inisfallen; but Sir William Betham thinks the word "Lean" signifies a swampy plain, and that the lake was so called as being on the borders of a swamp, which a large portion of the north shore undoubtedly is.—WINDELE.

supposed, the place is full of wild legends and marvellous traditions, harmonising with the poetical character of the locality.

The legends which account for the existence of the lakes vary in some respects; but all have one common source—the neglecting to close the entrance to an enchanted fountain, which caused an inundation, and covered in a single night, fair and fertile fields, and houses, and palaces with water. One of them attributes the misfortune to the daring impiety of an O'Donoghue, who, full of scepticism and wine, scorned the tradition which doomed to destruction the person who should displace the stone over the well-head, and resolved to expose its falsity by removing it to his castle: his subjects, with whom his word was law, awaited the result in fear and trembling—all but his favourite jester, who fled to the summit of a neighbouring mountain. When the morning sun broke, he looked down into the valley, and saw nothing but a broad sheet of water. Another legend throws the responsibility of the awful event on a fair young peasant girl, who was wont to meet her lover—a stranger ignorant of the mystic spell—by the fountain-side: one night they were lulled to sleep by the music of its flow: at daybreak the girl awoke screaming "The well! the well!" It was too late; the water was rushing forth, and overtook them as they ran. They were drowned, and involved in their fate the inhabitants of the whole district.

The legends all agree, however, that the men and women who then peopled the lovely valley did not perish, but still exist beneath the lake; where the O'Donoghue continues to lord it over his people, living in his gorgeous palace, surrounded by faithful friends and devoted followers, and enjoying the delights of feasting, dancing, and music, as fully as he did upon dry land. Many a time and oft as by the banks of the lake

> "The fisherman strays
> When the clear cold eve's declining,
> He sees the round towers of other days
> In the wave beneath him shining."

The lakes are understood to be thirty miles in circumference; the distance between the two extreme points—the entrance to the river LAUNE and the extreme end of the Upper Lake—being about eleven miles (including the "Long Range," about three miles), the greatest width being about two miles and a half.* In the Upper Lake there are several islands, but none of large size: in Tore Lake there are only two, and they are small; while the Lower Lake contains, of islands and island-rocks, upwards of thirty.

The principal river which supplies the lakes—THE FLESK—rises in the mountain, and enters the Lower Lake at Cahirnane: contributions to its waters are made also by the Deenagh and several tributary mountain streams; the principal of which are those from the Devil's Punch-bowl in Mangerton, forming in its progress the Tore Waterfall; that from the summit of Glena, which forms O'Sullivan's Cascade; and

---

* The exact length and breadth of the three lakes are as follows:—

Length of Lower Lake	5¼	miles English
Greatest Breadth	2¼	" "
Length of Tore Lake	1¼	" "
Greatest Breadth	2	" "
Length of Upper Lake	2¼	" "
Greatest Breadth	¾	" "

This statement, although it differs much from former estimates, and very largely from the popular notion, may be relied upon as accurate.

that from the mountain, which forms the Cascade of Derricunnihy. The Flesk, as it enters the Lower Lake, flows under a picturesque old bridge, covered with ivy.

THE FLESK BRIDGE.

A huge supply to the Lakes is also contributed by the river Garameen, that runs through the Black Valley, and enters at the extreme end of the Upper Lake.

These points we merely glance at in commencing our tour; but each and all of them, being leading objects of interest and attraction, we shall be called upon more minutely to describe, when under the "heads" to which they properly belong.

Let us, then, arrange the mode in which the Tourist can best divide his time, so as to see all he ought to see, and that to the best advantage. We shall first express a hope that his visit to Killarney will not be a hurried one,—to see, merely that he may "say he has seen," the greatest of the many natural beauties of Ireland. He may, indeed, have a vague notion that it is a very wonderful and a very beautiful place, by rushing through Dunloe Gap, and rowing from point to point of the Lakes, Upper and Lower; and there are tourists in abundance who have given themselves no longer time to do the subject justice.* But if he desire to receive enjoyment incon-

---

* Unhappily, Sir Walter Scott was one of these. His stay in Killarney was not extended beyond a day, consequently he could have had no conception of the vast store of grandeur and beauty which a sojourn of a week might have opened to him. The lakes, therefore, have profited very little by his rapid row over their surface. There is a rumour that Sir Walter left Killarney suddenly, in consequence of the uncourteous refusal of a gentleman in the neighbourhood to entertain him with a "stag hunt"—on the ground of political differences. Mr. Lockhart, indeed, in his "Memoirs of Scott," by some singular mistake, gives currency to the opinion—so discreditable to Irish courtesy, and so opposed to the almost constitutional bias of Irish gentlemen. We felt convinced that so humiliating a circumstance never occurred, and took some pains to be enabled to set the matter right. The rumour, although very general, is without the slightest foundation. Miss Edgeworth, who accompanied Sir Walter to Killarney, writes us, that "their party did not visit

ceivably fresh and powerful, and to estimate really and truly the vast beauty and mighty magnificence of the locality, his stay must be prolonged to at least a week. A week will enable him to examine the whole scene fully and justly; but it is necessary to add, that time much more prolonged may be profitably expended; that every day will exhibit some new feature; and it is certain that the more the Lakes are examined, the more they will gratify and the more they will astonish.

The plan we propose is to devote FIVE DAYS TO THE LAKES; and we shall draw out what we conceive to be the best order of proceeding—premising, however, that much may be seen in ONE DAY, a good deal in TWO DAYS, nearly every prime object of interest in THREE DAYS, the whole in FOUR DAYS; and the whole, with the addition of several striking matters in the neighbourhood, in FIVE DAYS.

This five days' tour, then, we shall take the visitor, appending such hints as may be requisite for the benefit of those who can dedicate to the purpose only days one, two, three, or four.*

FIRST DAY.—THE KENMARE ROAD; LOUGH-LUIS-CA-NAGH; UPPER LAKE; DERRICUNNIHY WATERFALL; TORC WATERFALL; DEMESNE OF MUCROSS; DINIS ISLAND; MUCROSS ABBEY.
SECOND DAY.—THE ASCENT OF CARRAN TUEL, OR MANGERTON.
THIRD DAY.—AGHADOE; GAP OF DUNLOE; BRANDON'S COTTAGE; THE UPPER LAKE; LONG RANGE; EAGLE'S NEST; WEIR BRIDGE; TORC LAKE; LOWER LAKE; GLENA.
FOURTH DAY.—THE ISLANDS AND THE SHORES OF THE LOWER LAKE.
FIFTH DAY.—OBJECTS OF MINOR IMPORTANCE IN THE VICINITY OF THE LAKES; VARIOUS VIEWS, ETC. ETC.

Our plan is to visit and examine the beautiful and interesting objects around the lakes; to point out those which ought to be seen, and to indicate those that *may* be seen if time will sanction a proper scrutiny.

We shall, then, endeavour to induce the Tourist to visit the singularly wild and beautiful sea-coast; through either of the magnificent harbours of Bantry, Kenmare, Dingle, or Tralee, and so round to the Shannon—for we may hope that visitors to Killarney will be induced to make there, or in the neighbourhood, a longer stay than will barely suffice to see the "Lakes:" as we shall show, it will be impossible to examine scenery more lovely or more sublime than that which a day will bring within their reach while in this enchanting district.

A primary and a very necessary step, however, as we have intimated, for those who desire to see the lakes in perfection, and to comprehend their beauties thoroughly,

---

Killarney expecting a stag hunt; on the contrary, before they arrived there, they heard on their progress that the master of the hounds had just died. And," she adds, "before any one knew we had arrived, we were gone; 'for Sir Walter was so tied to time, that we could not remain another day.'" Miss Edgeworth's memory of the circumstance is borne out by that of her sister, who writes us, "I remember being told, as we drove into Killarney, that we should have no stag hunt, as the master of the hounds had died that morning." We hope this slander against Irish hospitality will not again occur.

* It will be obvious, however, that to lay down a route that will answer in all cases, is quite out of the question; it must be so continually influenced by circumstances, especially by the state of the weather. Our own plan satisfies us better than any other,—and we obtained several from competent guides. When the Tourist has determined the length of time he will give to pleasure, he will do well to consult the landlord of the hotel, and arrange with the guide how that time may be best turned to account. It is obvious that much may be done from sunrise to twilight of a summer day. And if the weather seems unsettled, it will be wise to make our plan for the third day the arrangement for the first day; as the whole of the objects on such visits *must* be seen at any rate.

will be the selection of A GUIDE ;—up Mangerton or Carran Tuel, and through Dunloe Gap, indeed, his aid is absolutely essential; for without it, the Tourist would not only be in danger of losing his way, but would be subjected to many annoyances from which the forethought of a guide will relieve him. Upon this subject we ask awhile the patience of our readers.

Irish guides are the most amusing fellows in the world; always ready to do anything, explain any matter, go anywhere; for if the Tourist proposes a trip to the moon, the guide will undertake to lead the way—" Bedad he will, wid all de pleasure in life." They are invariably heart-anxious to please; sparing no personal exertion; enduring willingly the extreme of fatigue; carrying as much luggage a pack-horse; familiar, but not intrusive; never out of temper; never wearied of either walking or talking; and generally full of humour. They enliven the dreariest road by their wit, and are, of course, rich in old stories; some they hear, others they coin, and, occasionally, make a strange hodge-podge of history—working a volume of wonders out of a solitary fact.*

But our especial business, now, is with the Killarney guides, and truly their name is " Legion ;" every child, boy or girl, from the time it is able to crawl over the door-step, seems to have a strong natural instinct to become a guide.

Our pleasantest memories of Killarney are associated with those of a guide—*Sir Richard Courtenay*†—who now sleeps in the mid-aisle of Mucross. His picture, although that of a hero gone by, may be worth retaining, for it is a picture of a class in the old times; his successors being far less " Irish," and much more refined. Note his peculiar hat—not quite a " caubeen," although the mountain blasts have materially changed its shape since it was "a bran-new baaver;" his small keen grey eyes; his loose good-natured mouth, that pours forth in abundance courteous, if not courtly phrases, and pronounces scraps of French with the true pronunciation of an actual native—of Kerry; for Sir Richard, having mixed in good society, " parley-voos " as well as bows with the grace of a travelled gentleman. His coat was certainly not made by a Stulz, nor his brogue by a Hoby; but the frieze suits well with his healthy and sunburnt countenance, and the shoes are a fitting match for limbs that have borne him a thousand times up the steep and high mountain of Mangerton.

Alas! the Tourist who has experienced his courtesy will miss him now from his

---

* It is not to be questioned that they sometimes "make" as well as "tell." Once at Glendalough, when George Winder was relating to us " a legend," we said, " Now, Winder, tell us truly, is that a veritable legend?" "Well," he replied, "I'll tell truth to your honors; *it is not*, for ye see I make as many laagends over night as will do for the quality next day."

† By what means he obtained his dignity we could never learn; but the knight had once the honour of conducting a Viceroy to the top of Mangerton, where the peer and the peasant being both literally "in the clouds," the latter, at least, descended to mid-earth a much more important personage than he was when he commenced the ascent—and ever afterwards with plain Richard Courtenay it was

" Good den, SIR Richard."

A merchant of Cork invited him to dinner, told his wife a gentleman was to dine with him—Sir Richard Courtenay, of Killarney. The lady got out her best plate, and prepared a more than usually sumptuous entertainment for her guest; after waiting for him half an hour beyond the time fixed, she got impatient, and expressed as much to her servant. " Oh, ma'am," said he, " he's below." " Indeed! what's he doing?" " He's in the kitchen, ma'am, drying his stockings at the fire." Question Jerry Sullivan concerning this and other stories of Sir Richard.

It will interest and amuse those who have visited the Giant's Causeway, to compare and contrast the guides there with those at Killarney. In the north, they are singularly matter of fact; all their " discoorse " is learned. They tell you what Doctors This and That said of That and This, and school you with science upon some learned " authority." In Killarney, on the contrary, they are all imaginative; full of rich fancies, and fruitful in the inventive faculty. They are lively and merry withal, and infinitely more pleasant companions than their fellows of the north.

accustomed places; they will not fail to pay him a tribute of remembrance as they stand beside the gravestone —as yet, we regret to say, unmarked by his name— that covers his remains, in holy Mucross, every spot of which knew his footsteps well.

Honour, then, to the memory of pleasant "Sir Richard;" and if now enlisted in the troop of O'Donoghue, the "good people" themselves may listen with delight to the "laagends" with which he was familiar, and follow him, without dread, through every

"Glen and bosky dell."

THE OLD GUIDE.

of their delicious dominions. We owe him much, and recall with gratitude the information he gave us, the stories he told us, and the wit and genuine humour that sparkled in so much he said and did. It has been difficult for us to visit any of the "ould places" during our recent visits, without bringing him to mind; and we are happy in the knowledge that we lessened somewhat his poverty during his closing days, and helped to lay him decently in his grave.

There is, of course, a guide— or, rather, there are guides— attached to each hotel; and it is not etiquette to retain the services of "strangers to the house." An exception, however, seems to be universally made, and by common consent, in favour of one of them, to whom we shall refer presently, who is sent for when any of his old acquaintances desire his attendance—or when important guests arrive—no matter at what house they may be located.

There is Gandsey, son of the famous piper, himself a good musician, plays an excellent bugle, and is a very intelligent man, having travelled also in America and mingled much with "the quality." Miles Mac Sweeny, a most attentive and obliging person, who knows the locality, and can describe it well. He throws a fly, too, can aid the craftsman, and teach the neophyte, and makes the flies he uses. He is *par excellence* the angler of the lakes. Both these "good men and true" are now retained at the Victoria. Thomas Murphy, a good guide, a careful boatman, and an excellent fisherman—as we know by experience, for he contrived, although the wind was cast, that we should transfer a dish of trout from the lake to the kitchen of the Victoria. The O'Connors, father and son, will be found excellent guides in all respects. Edward Dumas is a kind and care-taking fellow, and a useful ally, notwithstanding he has but one arm, a defect for which he amply compensates by thought and consideration; he is located at Cloghreen. Jack Lowney is an acquisition of much value. John Duggan, Jerry Clifford, James Cronan, and others, "too numerous to mention," will be found desirable companions and councillors to mountains and lakes. You must take your chance as to which of these will be your attendant, for it will depend on the hotel at which you are located.

By many degrees, the best guides at the lakes and all through the district, are the brothers Spillane, sons of a worthy and venerable man, who was guide there before the present century was born, and who was the companion of all the "celebrities" by whom Killarney has been visited during the last sixty or seventy years. Both the brothers are attached to the Railway Hotel; and the chances of retaining the services of either will, no doubt, often sway the visitor in determining where he will reside.

The guide for whom all parties inquire—and ought to inquire—is Stephen Spillane. Stephen is, perhaps, better fitted for the new, than he would have been for the old, order of things; for he is of new, rather than of old, Ireland; a young man of good education, a teetotaller, and, although quite as courteous and actively obliging as his predecessors, he is acquainted with none of the "tricks" which, it must be confessed, have given their renown to Irish guides. He is a good angler, plays a bugle second only to his father, and in addition to being exceedingly well read in the history of the district, he is familiar with all the legends concerning which the Tourist should be anxious to hear. We consider, indeed, that Stephen Spillane is an acquisition to Killarney; and rejoice that, if the fun, and frolic, and "rollicking" of the guide are daily becoming more and more matters of history, in their successors we find greater intelligence supplying the place of wit; and at least as much civility, attention, and zeal.* Stephen had, in the spring of 1858, the honour to act as guide to his Royal Highness the Prince of Wales, during his Royal Highness's sojourn of eight days at "The Royal Victoria Lake Hotel," accompanying him also to Valentia and the wild sea-coast; Micky Sullivan having had the honour to be his driver—the Prince using, on that occasion, the common car of the country. Stephen does not by any means appear to have been "puffed up" by the privilege he enjoyed of so long and so often sitting beside the heir-apparent; but he speaks, in terms it was very gratifying to hear, of the Prince's condescending and unaffected goodness to all who came within his reach. So also it may be said of the "charioteer," Micky Sullivan. His Royal Highness is a pleasant and happy "memory" at Killarney.

John Spillane, the brother of Stephen, is also one upon whom dependence may be placed for courtesy, and general knowledge of the several matters concerning which Tourists will desire to be informed. He is also well acquainted with "the legends," and tells a story with point and effect. He inherits the family quality of musical

---

* Stephen Spillane is also a somewhat extensive dealer in "Kerry cattle;" and every year, when the "season" is over at Killarney, he visits England to deliver the "orders" he has received from visitors to the Lakes. His integrity and general good conduct have made him the confidant of all who have dealings in this way. He is indeed carrying on a thriving trade in Kerry cows; having had large experience in their good qualities—selecting "choice specimens" wherever he meets them on his journeys about the district; and being deservedly trusted.

taste, and is of course a master of the bugle. John superintends the fishery at Glena, and all the fishery rights belonging to Lord Kenmare.

Michael Clifford, son of Jeremiah Clifford, the "commodore" at the Railway Hotel, and husband of a gentle woman, who sells the bog-wood ornaments there, is also one of its guides. He is a very intelligent young man, who collects ferns for visitors; knows all the varieties of the district and their habitats: how to prepare and pack them; and may enrich many a city conservatory with "things of beauty," such as may be always pleasant memories of beautiful places—happy associations of happy days.

In "the town," visitors must take their chance for guides; but, as we have intimated, they will never be at a loss for one. Those, however, will be fortunate at Killarney who are lucky enough to obtain a good "body-guard." Candidates for the anticipated honour and emolument will present themselves at every turn, chattering eagerly—of all sizes and ages, prompt to display their accomplishments, and set themselves off to the best advantage.*

---

* Notices at the several hotels inform the Tourist that no fees or gratuities are to be given to drivers, boatmen, or guides, who are charged for in the bill. Assuredly they will ask for none, they will be quite content to have done their day's work for their day's hire. But who is there that does not feel how much he may add to his own happiness by making happy those from whom so much of his enjoyment is derived? Who is there that when pleasure is a sole purpose, will not like to give pleasure? Notwithstanding these requisitions to give nothing, we believe few Tourists will act upon the warning. They will contrive some means by which a gratuity may be bestowed - especially if there be a large party — upon the boat's crew, for instance, who will have toiled hard in the midst of much loveliness; upon the driver, whose "top coat" may have been wet through for hours; upon the guide, upon whose active zeal, good humour, and natural politeness, so much of a day's delight has depended; under the very best circumstances the money earned by boatmen, drivers, and guides, is money hardly earned, and but for a brief season!

THE FIRST DAY'S TOUR.

LOUGH LUIS-CA-NAGH; UPPER LAKE; DERRICUNNIHY
WATERFALL; TORC WATERFALL; MUCROSS DEMESNE;
MUCROSS ABBEY.

Our First Day's Tour will be to the Upper Lake, commencing at Lough Luis-ca-nagh, thence to Derricunnihy Waterfall; thence to the Torc Waterfall; and thence to Mucross Demesne and Abbey.

We adopt this course, because those who visit Killarney *via* Glengariff will take all these objects in their route, and so occupy one of the allotted days to be given to the Lakes; that is, however, assuming they leave Glengariff early in the morning of a summer's day. It is obvious that those who arrive by railroad will have to "begin backwards;" but many who arrive at Killarney by railroad, return to Cork by Glengariff and Bantry; and there are many who recommend this route as the best, obtaining horses at the hotel in Killarney, and carrying them on until a railway is reached.

The Lakes may be said to commence midway between Kenmare and Killarney. Midway, therefore—that is to say, just ten miles from either town—we shall now place the Tourist.

Just at the point we refer to is a small lake—LOUGH LUIS-CA-NAGH. It lies in a little valley, through which the road runs. It is without trees, and almost without underwood; denuded even of the broom, the bramble, and the furze; indeed, all the minor lakes about Kerry have the same barren and naked character. Scarcely is it passed, however, and a small steep ascended, when the glory of the Upper Lake bursts upon us. The spectator is startled by the sudden prospect to which a few steps introduce him; he is totally unprepared for the wonderful sublimity of the scene—taken in almost at a glance. He stands on the summit of a lofty hill—yet a

VIEW FROM THE POLICE BARRACKS.

molehill compared to the mountains that surround him; below, winding about the valley, is "the Upper Lake," so narrow and tortuous, and so diminished by distance, that at first sight it seems nothing more than one of its tributary rivers. Far away, between Tore and Glena mountains, which from this point appear to jut out and assume the aspect of supporters to vast, but ever open, gates, a glimpse is caught of the Lower Lake, and of the hill crowned by a modern castle that looks down upon its eastern border. Immediately pushing out, as it were, before us, on our path, is "the drooping mountain"—Cromagloun—the most rough and rugged of all the guardians of the Lakes. To the left are the mountains—outskirts of the eternal Reeks—that shut in Dunloe Gap. The whole of the Upper Lake is fully and amply seen; the eye traces the twisting channel—"the Long Range"—that connects it with its sister lakes; numbers of small islets are scattered about its surface;* and in the far-off glimpse of a broad sheet of water—the Lower Lake—we obtain the foretaste of a banquet—abundant, healthful, and delicious. But if the Upper Lake—considered as a Lake, merely—is calculated, as we think it is, to disappoint at first, it is grand beyond conception, and certainly far surpasses its more beautiful sisters in the wild magnificence and stern sublimity of Nature. From the point we are describing, this peculiar characteristic is not perhaps so striking as it will be when we descend more into the valley. And let us descend:—presently we reach "the Constabulary Barrack," from a spot adjacent to which there is another glorious view. It is called "THE VIEW ROCK." The eye stretches along over the several islands—the Lake Hotel bounding the distance, behind which is a range of hills. We have been watching, from the height, the road that runs past it, and have marvelled how it can convey us down the steep: tracing it closely, however, we perceive that it travels round two or three jutting rocks, covered with the richest foliage; a peep at it may be had every now and then; at length it is seen, deeply below, skirting the borders of the Lough. We shall reach it anon, and be on level ground; but not until we have made at least a score of pauses, sprung as often off and on the car, and mounted some tiny hillock to feast upon the prospect once again. We reach the Tunnel at length; we pass through it, and the mountain is at our back. We shall have to climb no other while the day lasts. Here we are in the centre of Beauty's attractions only; the road is overhung by huge rocks; but each of them is richly clothed—some with huge forest trees, others with the lighter and gayer arbutus; while, at the bases of all, spring up gigantic weeds in marvellous luxuriance, fed perpetually by the clear water that oozes through every crevice, forming here and there miniature cataracts, bearing down tiny pebbles to deposit by the road side. So, on we go—now and then peeping, through breaks in the foliage, at the bleak hills opposite, and occasionally crossing a bridge, under which pushes a rapid river. One of them, on its way into the lake, forms the CASCADE OF DERRICUNNIHY; and this the Tourist must delay to visit. A by-road of about a quarter of a mile leads to it. We soon hear its roar, and ere long mark its foam ascending above the trees. It is beautiful—very beautiful—and its beauty is enhanced by the charming character of the locality in which it is placed. A little rustic bridge crosses the narrow river, and leads to a cultivated garden, where a cottage—Hyde's Cottage—formerly stood. The old cottage is gone, but the liberality of Lord Castlerosse has given to travellers another in its place, where they may "rest and be thankful;" but the garden remains; and never have we seen shrubs of finer growth. The rhododendrons have mounted almost into forest trees, and were literally covered with giant blossoms. A tangled path, overshadowed by the arbutus, holly, yew and hazel, leads to the cascade. It is inferior to that of Tore, which we are now approaching; and we leave it, therefore, undescribed.†

---

* These islets we shall notice more particularly when rowing through the Upper Lake. It may be proper here to mention that the advantage of a guide at this spot is incalculable. During our first visit we were without one, and passed within a few yards of the most magnificent views presented by the locality without seeing one of them. Indeed, there is one particular spot—a mile or so from Lais ca-ragh—where a small rock pushes up a little above the road; unhappy will be the tourist who does not stop here! Just at the other side of this rock, turning a mere corner, perhaps the finest view in the whole district is to be obtained.

† While resting underneath the Waterfall, and close beside a pretty rustic bridge, we encountered an entomologist with whom we fell into discourse. He was in the seventh heaven of delight, for he had just discovered and filled his box

A short distance farther, and we reach the entrance to the long and narrow promontory, called "COLEMAN'S EYE,"—a promontory which, stretching out into the lake, compresses it, and produces the channel known as THE LONG RANGE. At some

THE TUNNEL.

convenient place in this vicinity, let the traveller stop and look back. A rude diagram (introduced on the succeeding page) may convey some idea of the locality in which it stands.

No fewer than twelve of the mountains are within ken—he may see the summits of them all by merely looking right and left, over his shoulder. Perhaps it would be difficult to find, in the whole district, a single spot that can furnish so grand and accurate an idea of the peculiarities of Killarney.

The road is continued just above the lake; but the lake is hidden, now and then, by intervening trees, and thick masses of underwood; at length we are opposite the "EAGLE'S NEST"—a craggy rock from this point of view; we shall see it better when rowing through the Long Range.

A mile or so, and we reach a small mountain rivulet, trickling down the sides of the natural wall, that makes the land boundary of the road; the lakes and their con-

with many specimens of "the Hydrilla Banksiana"—a small moth, beautifully marked, that had not, he informed us, been found in the British islands for forty years. It was discovered by Sir Joseph Banks, after whom it was named. Our acquaintance had gone forth to seek for it; expecting he might meet it in some place where "the sweet gale" was growing abundantly; and he did so find it—in a little bog in this vicinity. Eureka!

necting river form it on the other side. This streamlet is "THE LENE," said (upon what evidence we cannot tell) to have given, in days of old, a name to the Great Lake. To point out all the scenic beauties that occur along this course is out of the question. That must be the task of the guide. He will not hurry you, if you let him have his own way—as you will do, if you are wise. Once at least in every furlong you will have to stop, and gaze either upon some distant object or some beauty close within your ken; noting where the ancient denizens of the woods and forests—the oak, and yew, and holly of centuries old—are mingled with the young growths of

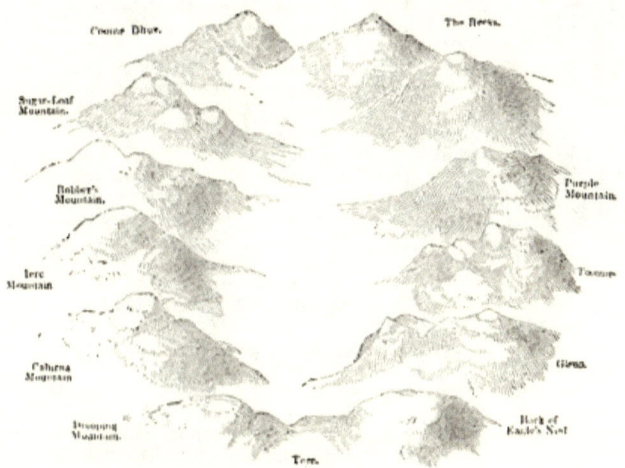

KILLARNEY MOUNTAINS.

yesterday. Moreover, it is not improbable that if you ascend one of the heights, you will see a group of red-deer in the valley underneath.

At length we arrive at the TORC WATERFALL.—the most famous, and beyond comparison the most grand and beautiful of all the cascades about the Lakes. The path that leads to it is entered through a gate (close to which is a small lodge) and over a bridge which crosses the stream that runs into the lake.

The cascade is a chasm between the mountains of Torc and Mangerton: the fall is between sixty and seventy feet. The path that leads to it by the side of the rushing and brawling current, which conducts it to the lake, has been judiciously curved, so as to conceal a full view of the fall until the visitor is immediately under it; but the opposite hill has been beautifully planted—Art having been summoned to the aid of Nature—and the tall young trees are blended with the evergreen arbutus, the holly, and a vast variety of shrubs. As we advance, the rush of waters gradually breaks upon the car, and at a sudden turning the cataract is beheld in all its glory. And most glorious, in truth, it is, seen under any circumstances;—even in the most arid season it is beautiful—the white foam breaking over huge rocks, casting the spray to inconceivable distances; rushing and brawling along its course into the valley; scattering its influences among the long green ferns, and giving such prodigious vigour to the wild vegetation it nourishes, that giant weeds thicken into underwood along its banks, and here and there meet and join across the stream.

TORC WATERFALL.

In the hot summer time this waterfall is indeed beautiful; but in winter—or in winter weather—its magnificence can scarcely be pictured by the imagination. Let not the reader think this poor print can do it. It conveys about as much idea of the grace and grandeur of the Torc Waterfall as a single feather can do of the form and plumage of a bird of paradise. The water descends in a broad sheet, and the first fall is of considerable width. The passage is then narrowed, and another fall occurs; then follows a succession of falls—all rushing and foaming against the mountain sides; and, indeed, almost from the base of the great fall until it reaches Torc Lake, the river goes leaping from one rock to another. Sitting by its side, it requires no great stretch of fancy to believe it a living thing.*

Leaving the waterfall we resume our journey, and soon reach the pretty village of CLOGHREEN. Mr. Weld described it, in 1812, as "a decayed village." It has, we are happy to say, got rid of that character. A very elegant little building—the village school—has been placed here, at the expense of the Herbert family; and a pretty church, of recent erection, gives an aspect of cheerfulness and comfort to the locality. The shops and cottages about are neatly built and well ordered. Behind it is a pretty lough, out of which a clear stream runs, and flows into the Lower Lake. On a height immediately above the village is the little church of KILLAGHIE—we believe the smallest church in the kingdom. In its construction it is very simple, and is obviously, with the exception of its tower, of remote antiquity. Wild flowers, of various hues, grow from the walls, and adorn its roof of stone. From this spot an extensive and most attractive view may be obtained; indeed, it is one of the favoured places from which to gain a prospect of the Torc and Lower Lakes.

At the village of Cloghreen, then, we rest awhile—if our home, for a season, is to be either Hurley's (formerly Roche's) or O'Sullivan's Hotel. The entrance-gate to Mr. Herbert's demesne is near at hand. Through this gate we must pass.

---

* Close to the Torc Waterfall has been found the rarest of British ferns—the Bristle Fern (*Trichomanes speciosum*). It is, we believe, peculiar to Ireland, and has not hitherto been discovered either in England, Scotland, or Wales.

THE DEMESNE AT MUCROSS.

But before we visit "the Abbey," let us take a ramble through the demesne, half riding and half walking; for the tourist will have little notion of the distance he has yet to travel before the day's work is done; a very long distance it will be; although, being within the demesne, he does not again leave it.*

A visit to the Abbey may be postponed for an hour or two. It will be improved when the evening shades are over it; the sunlight is in ill-keeping with its sombre

KILLAGHIE CHURCH.

character. On, then, we go, leaving Mucross to the left, driving nearly in the middle of the narrow promontory that separates the Lower Lake from Tore Lake,† and making our way over BRICKEEN BRIDGE into DINIS ISLAND.

The tourist, then, will enter at Mucross gate—open to visitors every day, and on Sundays after two o'clock—and proceed along "the drive," by which Mr. Herbert, with admirable taste, has girdled his beautiful lake. A poet might liken it to a huge diamond encircled by emeralds; and surely, in the three kingdoms, for its extent (ten English miles), there is nothing to surpass it. Immediately after entering, the Abbey to the left, and the deep woodland, are so close and sheltered, that you are unprepared for the alternating views of mountain and water presented at every turn.

The peninsula, which runs out in a line with the Abbey, divides the two lakes. On the right, glimpses are perpetually caught of the Lower Lake; while on the left the prettiest parts of Tore have been skilfully brought into view—the mountains, distant and near, overhanging all. Passing the "old mines" (marked on the map)

---

* From the gate at Mucross through the demesne, passing over Brickeen Bridge, through Dinis Island, out again upon the main road, by Tore Waterfall—during which the demesne has not been quitted—is exactly ten English miles. But, as we shall show, if the tourist examines—as surely he ought to do—the beauties of two most beautiful "walks," the distance will be increased by at least three miles.

† Tore Lake derives its name from the Irish Tore, "a wild boar;" and Mucross from "the pleasant place of wild swine." Dinis is derived from Dine-iske, "the beginning of the water," and Brickeen from Bric-in, "the place of small trout."

and the little Lough Doolagh, the road runs over Brickeen Bridge—a bridge of a single arch, connecting the peninsula with Brickeen Island; continuing through this island, another bridge connects it with Dinis Island. Here Mr. Herbert has built a pretty, picturesque, and commodious cottage, for the gratuitous use of visitors. It is furnished with every requisite for their entertainment, and proper persons are there who render willing service to such as may require attendance—a turf fire being always prepared for that necessary portion of an Irish feast—the potatoes; and moreover, with "arbutus skewers," to aid in producing a luxury that may give a new pleasure to the most refined epicure—the salmon sliced and roasted, within a few minutes after he has been a free denizen of the lake.

BRICKEEN BRIDGE.

Once more a bridge is crossed—a bridge from DINIS ISLAND across the channel that runs from the Long Range into Torc Lake—and the visitor is again on the mainland. Here a small by-road conducts to the high road, and he is again on what is technically

COTTAGE IN DINIS ISLAND.

termed "the new line"—*i.e.* the line between Kenmare and Killarney. But still the drive is continued through the demesne, for parts of it lie on the other side of the public road, and run up the sides of old Torc mountain, farther than the most enterprising pedestrian will be willing to explore; for the underwood is so thickly matted, that it presents an effectual barrier. The rocks jut out so as to form continual lines of inaccessible precipices, and the red deer are not to be disturbed with impunity among their fastnesses, into which entrance is very rarely effected without considerable peril. By the time he returns to the entrance-gate near Cloghreen, the Tourist will thus have driven ten miles—encircling a demesne that assuredly cannot have its equal in the dominions of the Queen. But let him not imagine that this drive will show him all he has to see—very far from it. To the most charming of its beauties neither car nor horse can conduct him. Immediately under the Abbey graveyard is a walk called "the Lady's Walk," which leads just above the borders of the Lower Lake. You may follow it on for two or three miles, and you cannot be wearied; for seats are placed at proper intervals, and the mind will be perpetually refreshed. Above the borders of Tore Lake, also, there is another walk—"the Rock Walk"—of even greater beauty. It extends for nearly two miles, and may indeed be continued to Brickeen Bridge, and so into the island of Dinis. These walks are absolutely delicious. It is impossible for any description to do them justice. Nature formed them; but Art and Taste have combined to render them perfect. Let the Tourist take especial care that the guide under whose guardianship he visits Mucross leads him to them.*

At one particular turn we paused; and as we did so, as if by magic, a glowing rainbow suddenly spanned the lake. It seemed to rise from the slope of a distant hill, and we fancied we could trace its course.

"You'll have the gratest of luck, my lady," said our charioteer; "it isn't every one that sees the 'rainbow's rest.' There's them would give all they have in the world—be it much or little—to see the foot of the rainbow on the mines we past not five minutes agone! It's well known that there's a goold mine somewhere close; and if the foot of the rainbow rested on a spot hereabouts, we'd know what it meant —it would be a tell-truth, and no mistake—the goold would be there!"

"But the foot of the rainbow is lost among those royal ferns yonder," was our reply; "so we do not perceive the luck—if it was on the mine, indeed!"

"Yes, my lady, that would be money-luck; and I often prayed I might catch the rainbow at it. And a poor fellow, laid long ago in holy Mucross, was, I heard tell, known by the name of 'Showery Jack;' for the minute a shower came, he was off to see where the rainbow rested. It's fine exercise he had, I'm thinking, during his lifetime, dancing after the Killarney showers!"

"But," we persisted, "we do not see the luck you talked of that is to come to us from only seeing the foot of the rainbow among those royal ferns."

"The memory of it, my lady, whin you're far away! Is it no luck to have the memory of such a beauty as THAT, whenever you plaze to want it? Sure, King Solomon in all his glory couldn't make the likes of it; no, nor all earth's kings and queens! It's not one party in a hundred that comes this road in sunshine-shower that has the luck of such a sight; and see, now, how it's fading! My grandmother used to say these rainbows were made of O'Donaghoo's tears, that his daughter gathered up on Curanthuel, and dropt into this lake betimes to increase its beauty. It's as gone now, my lady, as if it had never been; but sure, you're in luck to have seen it."

---

* The reader will—by this time—have some idea that, though Mucross, Tore, and the half-score of other places named in this day's tour, may be looked at in a day, the demesne of Mucross alone will demand a full day, and give ample occupation and abundant enjoyment between sunrise and sunset.

And now let us visit the ABBEY, for the shades of night will, no doubt, be setting in—and that is the time to visit it. Lucky, indeed, will you be if the moon is up; for it is quite as true of Mucross as of Melrose—to see it

"Aright,
Go visit it by the pale moonlight!"

The site was chosen with the usual judgment and taste of "the monks of old," who invariably selected the pleasantest of all pleasant places. The original name was IRRELOUGH; and it appears that long prior to the erection of this now ruined structure a church existed in the same spot, which was consumed by fire in 1192. The Abbey

MUCROSS ABBEY.

was built for Franciscan monks, according to Archdall, in 1440; but the Annals of the Four Masters give its date a century earlier. Both, however, ascribe its foundation to one of the Mac Carthys, princes of Desmond. It was several times repaired, and once subsequently to the Reformation, as we learn from the following inscription on a stone let into the north wall of the choir:—

"Orate p felici statu fris Thade Holeni qui hunc sacra conbetu de nobo reparare curabit Anno Domini millesimo sexcentisimo bigesimo sexto."

The building consists of two principal parts—the convent and the church. The church is about one hundred feet in length and twenty-four in breadth; the steeple, which stands between the nave and the chancel, rests on four high and slender-pointed arches. The principal entrance is by a handsome pointed doorway, luxuriantly overgrown with ivy, through which is seen the great eastern window. The intermediate space, as, indeed, every part of the ruined edifice, is filled with tombs, the greater number distinguished only by a slight elevation from the mould around them;

but some containing inscriptions to direct the stranger where especial honour should be paid. A large modern tomb, in the centre of the choir, covers the vault, in which in ancient times were interred the Mac Carthy Mor, and more recently the O'Donoghue Mor of the Glens, whose descendants were buried here so late as the year 1833.* Close to this tomb, but on a level with the earth, is the slab which formerly covered the vault. It is without inscription, but bears the arms of the Earl of Clancare. The convent as well as the church is in very tolerable preservation; and Mr. Herbert has taken care, as far as he can, to baulk the consumer, Time, of the remnants of his glorious feast.

The dormitories, the kitchen, the refectory, the cellars, the infirmary, and other chambers, are still in a state of comparative preservation: the upper rooms are unroofed; and the coarse grass grows abundantly among them. The great fire-place of the refectory is curious and interesting—affording evidence that the good monks were not forgetful of the duty they owed themselves, or of the bond they had entered

ENTRANCE TO MUCROSS.

THE FIRE-PLACE AT MUCROSS.

into, to act upon the advice of St. Paul, "And be given to hospitality." This recess is pointed out as the bed of John Drake—a pilgrim who about a century ago took up his abode in the Abbey, and continued its inmate during a period of several years.

* The descendant and representative of this ancient family is still happily "to the fore" a prosperous and accomplished gentleman; whose title, "The O'Donoghue," is among the most honourable titles of the kingdom.

As will be supposed, his singular choice of residence has given rise to abundant stories; and the mention of his name to any of the guides or boatmen will at once produce a volume of the marvellous.

The cloister, which consists of twenty-two arches, ten of them semicircular and twelve pointed, is the best preserved portion of the Abbey. In the centre grows a magnificent yew-tree, which covers, as a roof, the whole area; its circumference is thirteen feet, and its height in proportion. It is more than probable that the tree is coeval with the Abbey; that it was planted by the hands of the monk who built the sacred edifice centuries ago.

Although for a very long period the monks must have lived and died in the abbey of Mucross, posterity has been puzzled to find out the places where they are interred. Time has mingled their remains with those of the tens of thousands of nameless men who have here found their homes; but the peasantry still point out

A TOMB AT MUCROSS.

an ancient, singular, and rudely-constructed vault on the outside of the church, and immediately under the east window, where the bones of the holy fathers have become dust.

Having arrived at the close of his first day's tour—no doubt prolonged until the twilight has deepened into night—perhaps before the Tourist retires to rest he will have no objection to receive some information on a subject to which a visit to Mucross may naturally turn his attention—the funeral ceremonies of the Irish, which are peculiar, remarkable, and interesting.

The formalities of "THE WAKE" commence almost immediately after life has ceased. The corpse is at once laid out, and the wake begins; the priest having been first summoned to say mass for the repose of the departed soul, which he generally does in the apartment in which the body reposes.

The ceremonies differ somewhat in various districts, but only in a few minor and unimportant particulars. The body, decently laid out on a table or bed, is covered with white linen, and, not unfrequently, adorned with black ribbons, if an adult; white,

THE KEENS, OR DEATH SONGS.

if the party be unmarried; and flowers, if a child. Close by it, or upon it, are plates of tobacco and snuff; around it are lighted candles. Usually a quantity of salt is laid upon it also. The women of the household range themselves at either side, and the keen (*caoine*) at once commences. They rise with one accord, and, moving their bodies with a slow motion to and fro, their arms apart, they continue to keep up a heart-rending cry. This cry is interrupted for a while to give the *ban caointhe* (the leading keener) an opportunity of commencing. At the close of every stanza of the dirge the cry is repeated, to fill up, as it were, the pause, and then dropped; the woman then again proceeds with the dirge, and so on to the close.

The keener is usually paid for her services; the charge varying from a crown to a pound, according to the circumstances of the employer. They—

KEENERS.

"live upon the dead,
By letting out their persons by the hour
To mimic sorrow when the heart's not sad."

It often happens, however, that the family has some friend or relation rich in the gift of poetry, and who will, for love of her kin, give the unbought eulogy to the memory of the deceased. The Irish language, bold, forcible, and comprehensive, full of the most striking epithets and idiomatic beauties, is peculiarly adapted for either praise or satire; its blessings are singularly touching and expressive, and its curses wonderfully strong, bitter, and biting. The rapidity and ease with which both are uttered, and the epigrammatic force of each concluding stanza of the keen, generally bring tears to the eyes of the most indifferent spectator, or produce a state of terrible excitement. The dramatic effect of the scene is very powerful: the darkness of the death chamber, illumined only by candles that glare upon the corpse, the manner of repetition or acknowledgment that runs round when the keener gives out a sentence, the deep, yet suppressed sobs of the nearer relatives, and the stormy uncontrollable cry of the widow or bereaved husband when allusion is made to the domestic virtues of the deceased—all heighten the effect of the keen; but in the open air, winding round some mountain-pass, when a priest, or person greatly beloved and respected, is carried to the grave, and the keen, swelled by a thousand voices, is borne upon the mountain echoes—it is then absolutely magnificent.*

---

* The "keen" is not often heard now-a-days, and the ceremonies connected with death have of late lost much of their earlier—more picturesque, but more barbarous—accompaniments. We followed, in 1858, a funeral to Aghadoe; there were attendant keeners, who chanted the death-song nearly all the way. The funeral was a very large one; a young woman much respected and beloved at Killarney, was going to her last home; it was followed by between two and three hundred men, walking or in cars. We watched them closely, and observed, with exceeding pleasure, that there was not one of the party who gave evidence of having taken "drink." Such a circumstance would have been impossible in old times: it was then a matter of course, if not of positive duty, that every individual of the party should have been drunk on such an occasion. We rejoice, therefore, to supply this conclusive proof that "temperance" has not vanished—if it be in a degree lessened—from Ireland since the labours of Father Mathew ceased.

The following affords an idea of the air to which it is usually chanted:—

The keener is almost invariably an aged woman; or if she be comparatively young, the habits of her life make her look old. We remember one, whom the artist has pictured from our description; we never can forget a scene in which she played a conspicuous part. A young man had been shot by the police as he was

resisting a warrant for his arrest. He was of "decent people," and had "a fine wake." The woman, when we entered the apartment, was sitting on a low stool by the side of the corpse. Her long black uncombed locks were hanging about her shoulders; her eyes were the deep-set greys, peculiar to the country, and which are capable of every expression, from the bitterest hatred and the direst revenge to the softest and warmest affection. Her large blue cloak was confined at her throat; but not so closely as to conceal the outline of her figure, thin and gaunt, but exceedingly lithesome. When she arose, as if by sudden inspiration, first holding out her hands over the body, and then tossing them wildly over her head, she continued her chant in a low monotonous tone, occasionally breaking into a style earnest and animated; and using every variety of attitude to give emphasis to her words, and enforce her description of the virtues and good qualities of the deceased. "Swift and sure was his foot," she said, "on hill and valley. His shadow struck terror to his foes; he could look the sun in the face like an eagle; the whirl of his weapon through the air was fast and terrible as the lightning. There had been full and plenty in his father's house, and the traveller never left it empty; but the tyrants had taken all except his heart's blood—and that they took at last. The girls of the mountain may cry by the running streams, and weep for the flower of the country—but he would return no more. He was the last of his father's house; but his people were many both on hill and valley: and they would revenge his death!" Then, kneeling, she clenched her hands together, and cursed bitter curses against whoever had aimed the fatal bullet—curses which illustrate but too forcibly the fervour of Irish hatred. "May the light fade from your eyes, so that you may never see what you love! May the grass grow at your door! May you fade into nothing like snow in summer! May your own blood rise against ye, and the sweetest drink ye take be the bitterest cup of sorrow." To each of her curses there was a deep "Amen," which the *ban caointhe* paused to hear, and then resumed her maledictions.

THE SECOND DAY'S TOUR.

CARRAN TUEL—MANGERTON.

AWAKEN at daybreak; look up to the Mountains, and see if they, like you, have the nightcap on; for, if the clouds be hovering above with an apparent will to settle there, your plan must be changed, and you may prepare to roam among the Islands, postponing the business of "strong climbers" to a more favourable time. If you have slept at Clogreen, question gentle Tore or rugged Mangerton as to the day's promise. The answer, be sure, will be a true one. If your home be the Victoria, open your window, and you will have, suddenly, a full sight of half a score of Mountains—from either or all of whom you may take counsel. To Glena and Toomies a whisper will be audible; Mangerton himself will hear you without asking you to raise your voice; and the loftiest of the Giant Rocks—even mighty Carran Tuel—is within hearing, if your call be but moderately loud. Let us anticipate the reply—a welcome and a reward! The mountain tops are clear; prepare for the ascent. Bear in mind that you are about to undertake no child's play.

The labour is a severe one, although it may be "thought little of" by those who have performed harder feats; but—

> "Though steep the track.
> The mountain-top, when climb'd, will well o'erpay
> The scaler's toil. The prospect thence——!"

Probably your choice of mountains will be determined by the hotel at which you are located. At the Railway Hotel you are about four miles from Mangerton and twelve from Carran Tuel; at the Victoria, seven from the former, and ten from the latter; at Cloghreen, you are a mile or so from the foot of Mangerton, and fifteen from that of Carran Tuel. The greater feat is to ascend the latter; the easier task to mount the former. In either case be astir early. As we have intimated, a dozen or two of rugged mountaineers, of all ages and sizes, will gather about your car as soon as you arrive at the mountain foot. The ponies, sent on before, have announced your coming; and a rare group will be submitted from which to choose a guide, if you have not been wise enough to take one with you. As the safest way of showing the Tourist what he will have to say, do, and see, let us picture our own proceedings. We begin with CARRAN TUEL.*

A wild and dreary, yet not uninteresting or unpleasing, road leads to the mountain, running through a rude district, where Nature is left for the most part with no other restraint than her own will. Every now and then noble prospects are had—of wide and rich valleys, from the heights of barren hills, and, twice or thrice, glimpses may be caught of the pretty bay of Castlemaine. From Killarney to Carran Tuel, however, there are few objects that will tempt the Tourist to leave his car.

On arriving at the base of the mountain, or rather by the side of a small and rapid river which runs from one of its lakes, the Tourist is invited to repose in a small hunting-lodge,† built by some of the neighbouring gentry chiefly for the accommodation of strangers. It was a good deed. The visitor will bless the architect when seated there after the descent, and to the contents of his basket have been added fresh eggs, milk, and mealy potatoes, with which the care-taker is amply provided. Here the car remains, and the ponies are called into requisition. Half a dozen of "the boys" were about us; but Sir Richard was there as commanding officer, and Jerry Sullivan, as acting adjutant, brought up the rear to see that all was right.

A goatherd joined our group, and, taking the bridle of a pony, commenced the actual duties of a guide. He had become necessary, for the path had grown so rugged that a passage over it seemed impossible. The herd was a stout-limbed fellow, with the expressive face of a savage; he could not speak a word of English; but there was not a stone, a stream, scarcely a tuft of heather in the glen, with which he was unacquainted.

We may pause a moment in our details to relate an anecdote of this herd, as related to us by Jerry Sullivan.

"Well?" exclaimed Jerry, "surely I ought to remember dat stone; for I was

---

* Carran Tuel—"the inverted sickle;" so called from the peculiar form of its top. When Mr. Weld visited it in 1812, the labour of the ascent must have been more serious than it is now, for many ladies contrive to ascend it; nor is it indeed very difficult. The ponies bear them until within two miles of the top; and if the day is begun early, and a couple of hours can be given to these two miles, the feat is easily accomplished. Until Mr. Weld ascended, "no stranger," he was told, "had ever attempted it."

† We noticed the following couplet scrawled in pencil on the wall,—

> "What to the desert is the fountain
> This pleasant lodge is to the mountain."

going up de mountain one fine day wid a party, and dere was one lady of de party got very tired. 'I'll go no farder,' she says: 'only sit and wait here till down you come.' Well, she sat down quite contint; and dere was a lot of dose mountain cattle and sheep grazing—or, I may say, picking de bits o' grass out o' de mountain : and I said to meeself, well, I hope none of de wild mountainy cattle will go and stare at de lady; for, as she is English, she mightn't understand 'em; but dere was no use in saying any ting about it den, for we were far enough from her before I fancied at all about her. We got to de top, and had a most beautiful view—such a view as ne'er a kingdom but Kerry could lay before any gentleman—dere it was, just as stretched out by de ALMIGHTY's word : and to say de trute, it's little any of us tought about de lady below. Her husband told her after, he was tinking of her all de time; but I'd take my oat he never said so. At last we scrambled down, and when we came in sight of de poor lady, I saw dat one of de wild mountain herds, one of de poor boys dat do be herding de cows and sheep night and day on de mountain, was standin opposite to her; and sure I was very glad of it, for I says to meeself, de herd will keep de cattle from her, and not let her feel lonesome. Well ! as we got nearer, I saw de lady every now and den poke someting, which I took to be a long stick wid a little bag at de end of it, to de herd, and once he took de little bag off of it, and looked at it; and den he shook his shaggy red head, and gave it back to her. When she saw us, she seemed going mad wid joy; and de herd began jumping, and trowing up his arms, and capering. By de time we got to de lady she was a'most in a faint; and pointing to de herd, she said, 'he had come to murder her; and she had offered him her purse on de top of her parasol not to do her any harm; and he looked at de money tro' de net-work, but would not keep it.' And den she turned on her husband, and gave it to him for laving her (as she said) to be devoured by wild Irishmen ; and he coaxed her up, and told her how she would stay, and how she was never out of his toughts a minit. And den de poor herd told us, in Irish, how 'seeing a lady alone in de mountain, he was fearsome de cattle might do her some harm; and he came over to her for company, to keep dem off; and how she had done noting but make faces at him, and wouldn't answer anyting he said; and he doing his best for her, and didn't know what she meant by giving him a little bag to look at ;—and sure it couldn't be dat such a fine lady could be fearsome of such as he.' And when de lady gave time to herself to get her senses togeder, she was grately amused at her own fright, and gave de poor fellow five shillings : and, indeed, I've often tought dat she is not de only English person dat is afeerd of us, just because dey don't understand us." *

We resume the ascent up Carran Tuel. "THE HAG'S GLEN" is now reached. The glen is, in reality, the base of the mountain. For, although we have been ascending for above three miles since we left the lodge, the ascent is so gradual as to be scarcely perceptible. Here, however, we come to a dead stop. We stand between two small but singularly leaden and dead-looking mountain loughs. They are the baths of "the Hag"—the ruling demon of the glen; in one of them is her bed; among the overhanging cliffs are her chair, her crutch, and her cap; while "her tooth" is a crag, as hideous-looking as if it really belonged of right to the jaw of the foul fiend.

---

* In this anecdote we have transcribed the Kerry pronunciation ; for English Tourists cannot fail to perceive how seldom they hear "th" properly sounded. The English language, however, was for a long time, to the peasant a *foreign one*, and frequently those who cannot sound the diphthong can quote Latin verses.

We look up—the mountain seems absolutely perpendicular: to climb it appears an impossibility. The ponies are left to browse the stunted herbage round; and those who have strong limbs and sound lungs must commence a task of labour, for which, however, there is a huge reward. On we go—up we go—resting every now and then, to take breath, to receive the encouraging cheers of the guide, and to look about us. After a couple of hours' most severe labour, the two miles—thereabouts— from the Hag's Glen to the summit, are passed over. We stand on the peak of Carran Tuel—the highest mountain in Ireland, exactly 3,414 feet from the level of the sea.

Here the London Pride grows in rich luxuriance; and a small stream of pure water issuing from the crevice of a rock, and oozing through the soil, makes the surrounding herbage of the richest and brightest green. Frightful are the precipices all about us; but we have no business, as yet, to look down. North, south, east, and west, the view is open. How weak is language to picture memory!

The prospect is indeed inconceivably grand—past counting are the Lakes—seen everywhere among the minor Reeks, the lesser hills, and the valleys near and distant.* Within immediate ken are the Bays of Tralee, Kenmare, Dingle, and Bantry; farther off is Cape Clear on the one side, and on the other the mighty Shannon; while, beyond all, is the broad Atlantic. A glorious day—a day never to be forgotten—a day full of profitable and most rich enjoyment—will he have spent who spends it ascending Carran Tuel.

From this description and these details, good reader, you will know that the task of ascending Carran Tuel is no light one. If you be old, or plethoric, or scant of breath, do not attempt it; for if you be either, you will "give in" when half-way up, or be so thoroughly overworked, that the remainder of your tour will be a trouble. Yet it is pleasant to state that in May, 1858, this work was undertaken and carried through by a youth aged but sixteen; bred, it is supposed, in the lap of luxurious ease; who might have been excused if he had been either unwilling or unable to perform a task so assured of toil and difficulty. He did it manfully and well; stepping out boldly—help being neither asked for nor available here: climbing from cliff to cliff, leaping from morass to morass, and pacing through acres of wet and heavy bog; breasting the rude blasts that came through every gulley on his way, and encountering the fierce wind that triumphs ever on the mountain top. It is, we say, pleasant to know that a youth did all this—which a man in the vigour of life might have hesitated to go through—and that the youth was the Prince of Wales. We are thus happy in having evidence of his strength of lung and limb; seeing with no common joy the track he took in ascending, and especially that by which he descended into the Black Valley, so making his way—and still a long way for a stout walker—to the boat that awaited him at Brandon's Lodge—a boat placed at his disposal by Mr. Herbert, and manned by four as fine fellows as Her Majesty could find in her dominions.†

And now for the ascent up MANGERTON.

Here let us remark that Carran Tuel has fewer pilgrims than Mangerton—obviously

---

* But a small portion of the Lower Lake is, however, visible from this point. It is shut from the sight by intervening Toomies.

† Spillane has marked the spot upon the highest point on Carran Tuel by a few stones, of which his Royal Highness placed the first. It is probable that all after visitors will add to it, and that in time it will become a large cairn with a happy memory.

because Mangerton is more accessible, while the ascent is easier; and perhaps it would be unjust to say that the recompense is much less. To those, indeed, whose grand object is to form acquaintance with "*The Lakes*," Mangerton has attractions greater even than those of Carran Tuel—as we shall show presently.

If the ascent up Carran Tuel be a serious labour, neither is the journey to the summit of Mangerton to be thought of lightly; although mighty efforts at mounting both may excite a smile in those who have climbed the "Monarch of Mountains." For a very long period, until within the present century, indeed, Mangerton had usurped the honour of ranking as the highest of the Irish mountains: so Dr. Smith describes it, although he admits that the Reeks "*look* more lofty." Since the inquiries of Mr. Nimmo, and the improvements in surveying, Mangerton has, however, been compelled to resign its throne, and "hide its diminished head." Still, to dwellers in the valley, and more especially those of the city, its height is sufficient to afford a pretty correct idea of what a veritable mountain actually is. We commenced our

VENDOR OF GOAT'S MILK.

excursion on a morning that gave promise of a fine day; mounted on the sure-footed ponies whom "practice had made perfect," and who are never known to stumble. Indeed, a trip would not unfrequently prove fatal to the rider. A road leads from Cloghreen to the base of the mountain. As this portion of his service seemed to be that upon which Sir Richard chiefly prided himself, he had assumed an additional degree of importance; and issued orders "in good set terms" to his subordinates.

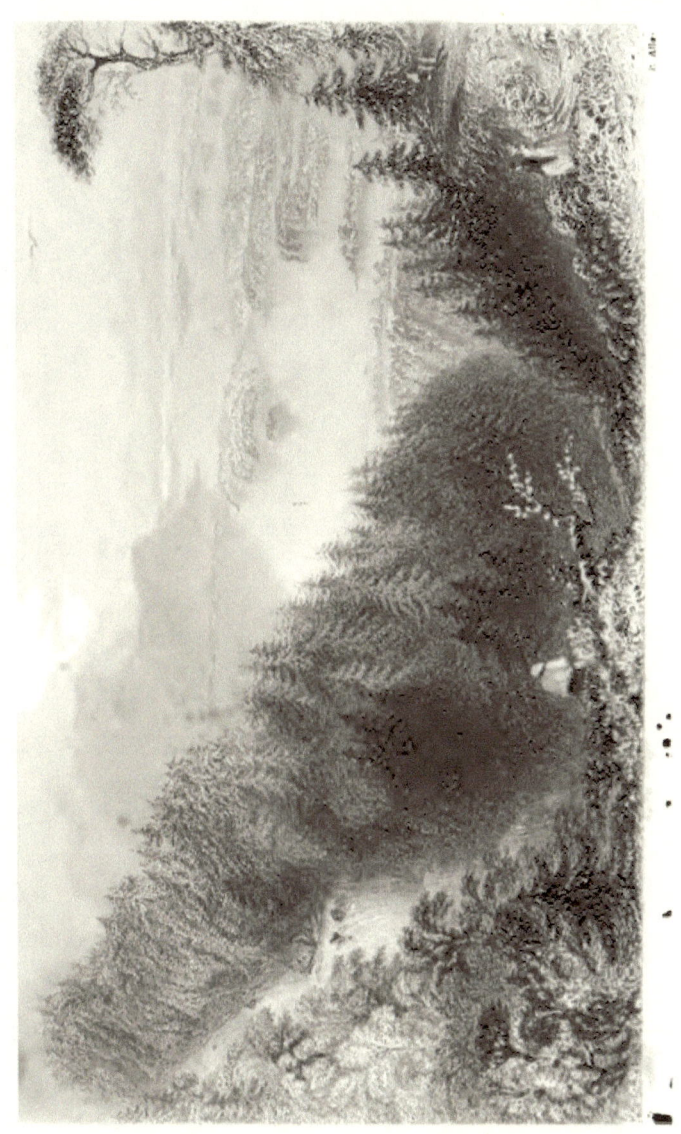

THE ASCENT OF MANGERTON.

A crowd soon gathered about us, men, women, girls, and boys, with vial-bottles of potheen and cans of goat-milk: each with a greeting—"Yer honour's welcome to Mangerton." About a score of them were in attendance as we reached a group of wretched hovels at the foot of the mountain; and the crowd grew like a snow-ball as it moved onwards.* Take a portrait of one of them—a fine hale and healthy mountain maid; as buoyant as the breeze, and as hardy as the heath that blossoms on its summit. The sure feet of our horses were soon tried; the little rough-coated animals had to make their way over rocks, bogs, and huge stones, through rushing and brawling streams, and along the brinks of precipices—places where it would be very difficult for persons unaccustomed to mountain travelling to move along on foot. At length we reached "the Devil's Punch-bowl," a small lake in the midst of rocks almost perpendicular. Our rude sketch may convey some idea of its singular character.

The water is intensely cold; yet, in the severest winter it never freezes; trout are never found in it, although they are plentiful enough in the stream that runs out of it—the stream that Sir Richard called the "Styx," which supplies the Tore Waterfall. The peasant, of course, attributes this peculiarity to the influence of his Satanic majesty; but from its position it is never calm, being in a state of agitation on the mildest summer day. As it is chiefly supplied by springs that pass over the surrounding peat-beds, the water is of a very dark colour, and its depth is said to be unfathomable. A footpath marks the way to the summit of the mountain. It is a perfect level of considerable extent, covered with a deep stratum of peat moss; into which the foot sinks some inches, even in the driest weather.

The view from the mountain-top defies any attempt at description; it was the most magnificent sight we had ever witnessed, and one that greatly surpassed even the dream of our imagination. In the far away distance is the broad Atlantic, with the river of Kenmare, the Bay of Bantry, the Bay of Dingle, and the storm-beaten coast of Iveragh; farther off still, in another direction, are the Shannon, Tarbert, and Kilrush. Midway are the mountains, of all forms and altitudes, with their lakes and cataracts, and streams of white foam. At our feet lie the three Killarney lakes, with Glena, and Tore, and even Toomies, looking like protecting walls girdling them round about. The islands in the Upper and Lower Lake have, some of them, dwindled into mere

DEVIL'S PUNCH-BOWL.

---

* Tourists complain terribly of the perpetual annoyance to which they are subject by the boys and girls, who follow them everywhere, and sadly mar the grace and quiet of the scene. Well, it is an annoyance, but not "altogether so," for they are often picturesque, and must be considered as essential parts of the "scenery."

specks, while the larger seem fitted only for the occupation of fairies. The river Flesk winds prettily along the valley; and the Flesk Bridge, with its twenty-one arches, resembles a child's toy. We were peculiarly fortunate as regards the weather. Against the intense cold that prevails at all seasons on the heights we had been duly warned and prepared; and our guide was loaded with matters we might have sadly missed if they had been withheld till our return. We had scarcely reached the top, when the clouds came suddenly round us—around, above, and below; we could not see our companions, although they were but a few yards from us, and the rough play of the wind prevented us from hearing their voices. At length Sir Richard crept to our side, and as if infected by the solemn expression of our countenances, he abstained for a while from breaking the reverie in which we indulged. After a time, however, he murmured some words of alarm lest the clouds should continue, and prevent our seeing the glorious prospect he had promised us. The dark light, for it is scarcely paradoxical to say so, continued about us for many minutes. It was a bright white mist in which we were enveloped; and, as we attempted to peer through it, we could compare it to nothing but lying on the ground and looking upwards when the sky is unbroken by a single cloud. After a time, however, the clouds gradually drifted off; and the whole of the magnificent panorama was displayed beneath us. The effect was highly exciting; the beautiful foreground, the magnificent midway, and the sublime distance, were all taken in by the eye at once. While we gazed, however, the clouds again passed over the landscape, and all was once more a blank; after a few minutes they departed, and gave to full view the whole of the grand and beautiful scene; and in this manner above an hour was occupied, with alternate changes of darkness and light. On our way down the mountain, we deviated from the accustomed track to visit Coom-na-goppol—"the Glen of the Horse;"—so called, according to Mr. Weld, "from the excellence of its pastures;" but, according to Mr. Windele, "from the circumstance of one of these poor animals having been accidentally precipitated over a craig into a dark lough at its base." The glen may be likened to a gigantic pit, surrounded on all sides by perpendicular mountain-rocks, in which the eagle builds its nest without the fear of man. It is inaccessible except from one particular spot, where its superabundant waters have forced a passage into a still lower valley. To reach it from the heights above would be almost impossible. Following the course of the stream we are conducted through rich pasture ground to the borders of a spacious lake—Lough Kittane; in extent it nearly equals Tore Lake, but Nature has left it without adornment—surrounded by rude and barren hills.

Let the Tourist be as stout a mountaineer as ever trod on heather, he will not, after ascending and descending either Carran Tuel or Mangerton, set foot in the valley quite as "fresh" as he was when he commenced his journey. The sauce for Kerry mutton will have been brought down from the mountain; and this day, especially, the Tourist will be little disposed to question the accuracy of the waiter—be he who he may (if our old friend, Jerry Connor, who now holds the chief place at "the Lake," so much the better), who will be sure to announce it as "the *sweetest* mutton in all Ireland." It is, however, so remarkably small, and the appetite will—for once at least—have grown so outrageously large, that the guest will stare as he looks at the dish when dinner is over.

The exertion of the morning will prevent a very strong desire for renewed activity in the evening; yet the remainder of a summer's day must not be lost. Advantage

should therefore be taken of the opportunity to hear an Irish piper play, and to make acquaintance with the Irish bagpipes—so long famous in story and song. The pipes are delicious or abominable—just according to the skill of the hand that rules them: and unhappily at Killarney now there is no one who can do them full justice. Still, as one of the peculiarities of the place, they ought to be seen and heard here.

The bagpipes are said to have been introduced into Ireland from Caledonia; though, if such be the case, a very early period must be assigned for their introduction, as we find them alluded to in the very ancient tale of Deirdre, supposed by the best judges to be an undoubted relic of Pagan times. It had the same use among the ancient Irish armies that it now has among the Highland regiments. But the Irish made, in the course of time, an improvement—by using a bellows to fill the chanter instead of the mouth, and continued making various additions until they produced the comparatively pleasant instrument, the union pipes.

The accompanying figures represent the Irish bagpipes in their primitive and improved form. We have here the earliest pipes, originally the same as the Scotch, as appears from a drawing made in the sixteenth century, and given in Mr. Bunting's work; but now differ in having the mouth-piece supplied by the bellows A, which being blown by the motion of the piper's arm, to which it is fastened, fills the bag B; from whence, by the pressure of the other arm, the wind is conveyed into the chanter c, which is played on with the fingers, much like a common pipe.

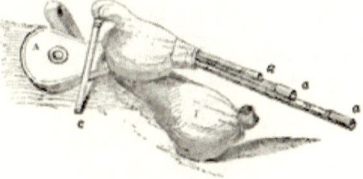

COMMON BAGPIPES.

By means of a tube the wind is conveyed into the drones *a*, *a*, *a*, which, tuned at octaves to each other, produce a kind of cronan, or bass to the chanter. The cut represents the improved or union pipes, the drones of which, tuned at thirds and fifths, by the regulator A, have keys attached to them, which not only produce the most delightful accords, but enable the player to perform parts of tunes, and sometimes whole tunes, without using the chanter at all. Both drones and chanter can be rendered quiescent by means of stops.

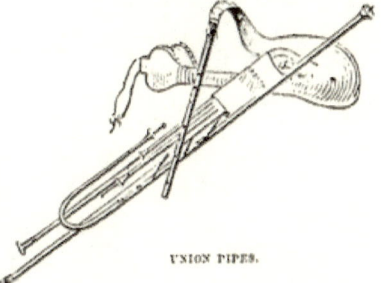

UNION PIPES.

The Pipers were at one period the "great originals" of Ireland. The race is gradually departing, or, at least, "sobering" down into the ranks of ordinary mortals; but there was a time when the piper stood out very prominently upon any canvas that pictured Irish life. Anecdotes of their eccentricities might be recorded that would fill volumes. For many years past their power has been on the wane; temperance committed sad havoc on their prospects; and, at length, the introduction of "Brass Bands" effectually destroyed the small balance that remained to them of hope.

The king of Irish pipers—one who was worthy of his throne, and was the equal of the best of the old race—GANDSEY—is gone: he sleeps calmly in the mid aisle of Mucross, and his spirit, no doubt, roams among the pleasant places he knew and loved so well. He was full of intelligence, point, and native humour; but his humour was never coarse, and he had been so much among the high-born and the high-bred as to have caught much of the manner that proclaims the gentleman.

The Tourist cannot now hear this admirable player and excellent old man, whose mantle has not descended upon any of his successors in the art. A reasonably good substitute, however, may be found in the piper, Daniel O'Leary. You will, perhaps, hear him when you visit beautiful Glena; for he is fond of tuning his pipes among its sweet woods of arbutus, albeit he is "dark." He will convince the most sceptical as to the rare powers of the Irish pipes, when in hands able to sustain their long-established repute.

In no district can acquaintance with Irish native melody be so profitably and pleasantly cultivated as at Killarney. Many will visit the Lakes whose knowledge of the national music of Ireland is limited to "Jullien's quadrilles," and a few melodies married to the immortal verse of Moore; but the wild, unearthly character of some of the finest airs renders them unsuited to English words; and they are even yet in a great degree secreted among the glens and fastnesses of the wildest parts of the country, where those who would fain gather them have never gone. Be it remembered, Irish music was never the offspring of fashion or caprice; it was literally *the voice of the people*. Whether excited by joy, or sorrow, or love, or injustice, their feelings found vent in music: their grief for the dead was relieved by a dirge; they roused their troops by song, and offered their prayers in chorus and chant: their music was poetry, and their poetry music.

THE THIRD DAY'S TOUR.

AGHADOE; GAP OF DUNLOE; BRANDON'S COTTAGE; UPPER LAKE; LONG RANGE; EAGLE'S NEST; WEIR BRIDGE; TORC LAKE; LOWER LAKE; GLENA.

PREMISING that the day must be a fine one, let it be commenced early; for the Tourist who undertakes to follow us will have much to do; so much, indeed, that—if it be all done—no after-evil of ill-weather can greatly diminish his power to become acquainted with the "Lions" of the Lakes; for when he has seen those we have named at the head of this chapter, the rest may be visited easily, inasmuch as they are accessible "between showers." * Let us start at

---

* It is probable that during the drive the Tourist will have an opportunity of visiting one of the rustic schools, which have been for the most part displaced by the National Schools. They are now rare, even in Kerry; they were called "Hedge Schools," because the boys usually studied under a hedge, the cabin of the schoolmaster being generally too close and dark for the purpose. The "Poor Scholars" of Kerry have been long celebrated; they picked up knowledge when and where they could; moving about from one school to another, and gathering English, Latin, and sometimes Greek, as they went, always free of charge.

once, then. We shall first go a mile out of our way to visit Aghadoe; it is not in the direct road to the Gap, but is about two miles from Killarney Town. If not to-day, some time or other Aghadoe should certainly be visited, for the ruins are very interesting as well as venerable. They consist of the remnant of a round tower, the walls of a small cathedral church, and the base of a round castle, called sometimes "the Pulpit" and sometimes "the Bishop's Chair." The church is a low, oblong building, consisting of two distinct chapels of unequal antiquity.* The ornamented

AGHADOE.

doorway, although much injured by time, is still graceful and beautiful. The graveyard is "neat and clean;" formerly it was in a disgraceful state, the relics of mortality being scattered everywhere about it; they are shown in the engraving, but happily they will not now meet the eye of the visitor.

The round castle stands at the hill side, within a square "bawn" or enclosure, fortified by a foss and earthen ramparts. It bears tokens of considerable strength; the walls are seven feet high; the height of the structure is now about thirty feet. It contains a flight of stone steps, formed in the thickness of the wall. The corbels that supported the timber joists, which formed the floor of the first chamber, still remain. It was evidently a small building, used, perhaps, merely as a defensive fortress to the church; its age, probably, is not more remote than the twelfth century.

The round tower, although a very small portion of it remains, cannot fail to be a subject of deep interest to all strangers.† Let the Tourist climb to "the top,"—the task is not a very difficult one, and see what a glorious view he will have of "the Lakes;" a view, by the way, which most visitors prefer to any other within convenient reach.

Descending the hill, we continue the road along the northern borders of the lake until we reach the LAUNE BRIDGE, from which there is a fine view of the rapid

---

* "Aghadoe continues to give title to a bishop. Amongst the Roman Catholics, the diocese is still preserved distinct; but in the Established Church it ranks as a secondary one, attached to the see of Limerick." The remote antiquity of the Abbey is supported by reference to the Annals of Inisfallen, where it is emphatically styled the OLD Abbey, although the Abbey of Inisfallen was founded in the seventh century.

The Ogham stone described by Vallencey, and referred to by Mr. Weld, as "in the north-west corner of the church of Aghadoe," is now in the grounds of Aghadoe House. It was stolen from the churchyard by a Killarney butcher, to make a stone for his "hall door;" and was luckily discovered in time to be rescued, although not before it was broken.

† It stands sixty feet from the N.W. angle of the church, and is called "The Pulpit" by the peasantry. All that now remains of this ancient structure is the basement, reaching from the sill of the door downward. The height is about fifteen feet; it measures in its outer circumference fifty-two feet; the diameter within the walls is six feet ten inches; the wall is four feet six inches thick. The stones are large, regular, and well-dressed. The greater part of the facing stone of the north side has been unfortunately taken away for the erection of tombs in the adjacent burying-ground. Within and without the spoliator has been effectually at work, aided by those worst of pests, the gold-seekers, whose unhallowed dreams are most fatal to our antiquities. This tower must have fallen previously to the last century; but no notice of it in its erect state has survived."—WINDELE.

THE BOOK-CAVE OF DUNLOE. 109

river, on both sides. We drive through a very wild country, hilly and boggy, until we near the entrance to the Gap. A short distance before we reach it, the Tourist will be called upon to visit a singular cave: if he be an antiquary, he should on no account omit to examine it. It may be classed among the more remarkable objects of antiquity in Ireland.

It is situated in a field immediately adjoining the high road; and was discovered in 1838 by some workmen who, in constructing a sunk fence, broke into a subterranean chamber of a circular form, the walls of which were of uncemented stones inclining inwards, with a roof, also, of long transverse stones. In the passage were found several human skulls and bones.*

This Cave of Dunloe must be regarded as an ancient Irish library, lately disinterred and restored to the light. The books are the large impost stones which form the roof. Their angles contain the writing. The discovery opens a new page concerning the hitherto disputed question touching the acquaintance of the ancient Irish with letters. The *Ogham* writing, as it is called, is stated to have been known and practised in Ireland long before the era of Christianity; it is to the Irish antiquary what the *Runes* are in the north, and the *Arrow-headed* or *Wedge* character is in Babylonia and Persepolis. It is more intelligible, however, than the latter, but far less known and elucidated than the former. As we have said, it has been a much disputed question amongst Irish writers; and as, until a late period, it was nowhere found on monuments, there were not wanting persons disposed to treat the claims of its upholders with contempt, and to regard the character as the imposture of idle bards and sennachies. The scale consists of four series of scores, each series embracing five characters, and each letter ranging from one score to five. The position of these groups in reference to a main or medial line, called *Fleasg*, constitutes their power. It has been called the *Craoc* or branch Ogham, because it has been assimilated to a tree; the *fleasg* answering to the trunk or stem, and the scores at either side, or passing through it horizontally, or diagonally, to the branches. On the majority of the monuments on which it has been found, the angle is availed of to form the *fleasg*. On the Callan-stone, and on one other hitherto discovered, the medial line is cut on the centre of the stone.

The scale originally consisted, and indeed properly does so still, of but sixteen letters. This must also be regarded as an additional proof of its high antiquity. Such was the Phœnician, Pelasgic, Etruscan, and Celtiberian number. O'Halloran has given us the Ogham in its original extent.

O'HALLORAN.

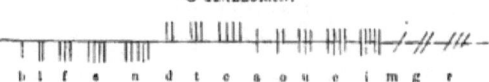

b   l   f   s   n   d   t   c   a   o   u   e   i   m   g   r

---

* The entrance to the field which contains this singular assemblage, is by a gap near a small bridge which crosses the river Loe. To examine it, however, it will be necessary to mount a wall and tread through the wet grass—difficulties which few Tourists will be inclined to surmount, but which are capable of easy removal, and which ought to be removed. A short cut to the gap, however, divides the road where this marvel is to be seen. The field is closed up, "because" Tourists spoilt the bit of land. Mahoney, of Dunloe, is the landlord, and ought to direct his tenant to sacrifice the quarter of an acre. Moreover, anybody would gladly pay sixpence to see the cave.

In subsequent ages it was corrupted or improved by the addition of compounds, diphthongs, and letters of foreign extraction, so that the present scale consists of twenty-five primitive and compound characters.

```
 ┃ ┃ ┃╴ ┃┃┃ ┃┃┃┃   / ┃/ ┃// ┃┃┃┃ ┃┃┃ ┃┃┃ ┃┃┃┃   ×  ○  ⊖   ╪
 b  l  f    s    n h d t   c  æ r m g ng cr    r   æ o u e   ea   oi   ui   ia   æo   p
```

The earliest written piece of Ogham writing, at present known, is in an ancient vellum MS. of the eleventh century, which had been at one time in the hands of Sir James Ware, and is now preserved in the British Museum.

The very entrance to THE GAP is a sudden introduction to its marvels;* the visitor is at once convinced that he is about to visit a scene rarely paralleled for wild grandeur and stern magnificence; the singular character of the deep ravine would seem to confirm the popular tradition that it was produced by a stroke of the sword of one of the giants of old, which divided the mountains, and left them apart for ever. Anywhere, and under any circumstances, this rugged and gloomy pass would be a most striking object; but its interest and importance are, no doubt, considerably enhanced by the position it occupies in the very centre of gentle and delicious beauty. The varied "greenery" of the pleasant glades that skirt the lakes, or line the banks of their tributary rivers, has hardly faded from the eye, before the bleak and barren rocks, of forms as varied and fantastic as they are numerous, are placed before it; and the ear, in lieu of the mingled harmony of dancing leaves, and rippling waters, and song of birds, is compelled to listen only to the brawling and angry stream rushing onwards, wasting its strength in foam, but continually changing its form—here a creeping rivulet—there a broad lake—and there a fierce cataract. Along the banks of the river is a narrow, and, of course, circuitous path. On the right, the Reeks, with their grand-master, Carran Tuel, look down upon the dark glen: while on the left, Toomies and the Purple Mountain rise above it, and with a more gracious countenance; for their sides are not so steep but that the goat finds sure footing and pleasant pasture; and the cow—if it be Kerry born—may also wander and ruminate

---

* As you approach the Gap, you will be arrested by some of the thousand and one women, boys, and girls, who will gather like a rolling snow-ball as you proceed. They will try to tempt you with goat's-milk and "mountain dew;" but some of them will offer you stockings of their own knitting: in all ways they will try to wile the visitor out of halfpence —with a good supply of which he should therefore be provided. A poor blind man will meet you, and solicit something for a tune on his fiddle; and here and there men with small cannon will expect you to exchange a sixpence for a shot; a good bugler is always in the Gap, and will accompany any Tourist through it. Just before you reach the glen you will be asked to visit the cabin of Kate Kearney, who will invite you to drink "goat's-milk and—something warmer," and farther in, just where you leave the carriage and take the ponies, is a slated house, where a man, Tim Connor, has a small public. About the centre of the Gap is a "nate Cabin," at which a poor woman will be found busy netting ladies' collars, or working bed-quilts. Dear lady visitors, see and help her, for God has afflicted her so that she cannot walk, although she can work. This immediate locality is said to be the scene of a remarkable description in Gerald Griffin's novel of "The Collegians."

Something more than a line, however, seems to be demanded by Kate Kearney—a name famous in song. The tourist will pass the dwelling of the grand-daughter of that Kate Kearney, who—we care not to say how many years ago—inspired the muse of Miss Owenson—Sydney, Lady Morgan:—

"Oh! did ye ne'er hear of Kate Kearney?
She lives by the Lake of Killarney."

The grand-daughter—herself the mamma of a fine family, Irish in number and in growth—is not unworthy the high fame of her grand-dame. She is what in Ireland is called a "fine fla-hu-lagh woman,"—meaning that she has "blood and bone," but as for the "beauty"—we shall not be ungallant enough to question her legitimate right. The Tourist will find cakes and goat's-milk at her cottage, which neatness and order might very much improve. The cottage is close to the entrance to the Gap of Dunloe, so that he will be sure to see her; for he may be quite certain that she will be at hand with her—"offerings."

at leisure. The road, or rather bridle track (the pony that treads it must not be a stranger), often passes along the brinks of precipices, and then descends into absolute pits; the roar of the rushing torrent is heard plainly all the while—now and then in the depths below, and now and then as a talkative and warning guide by the side of

IN THE GAP OF DUNLOE.

the wayfarer. The dark stream is the Loe; and in its limited course through the Gap it expands at several points into lakes of various and unequal magnitude, and again contracts itself to gather force for a new rush through the valley. The rocks along the pass are of forms the most grotesque; and each has received some distinguishing name from the peasantry.* The one we have pictured is called "The Turnpike." Soon after passing the Turnpike, the wildest part of the Gap is reached; and not far off, the ear is suddenly arrested by a "concord of sweet sounds" produced by the water gurgling through a subterranean channel, on its way to the "serpent lake"— but it will be easy to discern the winding channel, rendered black by its depth, and marked out by the green water-plants that grow underneath the water beside it. Although the mountains on either side are for the most part bare, they present occasionally patches of cultivation, "few and far between;" but sufficient to show that even in this savage region the hand of industry may be employed with

---

* One of them is christened, from its singular shape, "O'Donoghue's Heart." The guide may perhaps tell you that though everybody knew his heart was a big one, they never thought it was so hard. One of them is the Serpent's Lake; it obtains its name, according to John Spillane, from an obvious cause—a serpentine channel that conveys the river into it, and when under water, the black mark assumes the form of a serpent.

advantage. From some crevices peep out the gay evergreens—high up, and often so far distant that the eye cannot distinguish the arbutus from the prickly furze. Occasionally, too, the deep gloom of the pass is dispelled by the notes of Spillane's bugle—waking the echoes of the mighty hills; and now and then the eagle soars above the valley. Still it would be impossible for the very lightest-hearted to be otherwise than sad while passing through this dark and deep ravine; it oppresses the spirits with exceeding melancholy. Yet it has its own peculiar sources of pleasure.

THE "LOGAN STONE."

When the Pass terminates, and the Tourist is, as will be supposed, wearied in heart and foot, he suddenly comes upon a scene of unrivalled beauty. A turning in the narrow pathway brings him just over the Upper Lake; and high above "the black valley"—the Coom Dhuv. The reader will obtain, from the pencil of Mr. Creswick, a happier notion of the excitement produced by the change, than our language can give him. It was with an uncontrollable burst of enjoyment that we gazed upon the delicious scene. On the side of a lofty hill is the "Logan Stone"—about twenty-four feet in circumference. The peasants call it the "Balance Rock," and it is doubtless a druidical remain of remote antiquity. Moore likens it to the poet's heart which—

"The slightest touch alone sets moving,
But all earth's power could not shake from its base."

From near this stone (to be reached by a by-path, and with some caution in treading over the moss and bog) a most magnificent view is to be obtained of the Upper Lake on the one side, and of the whole of Coom Dhuv on the other. Spillane knows the spot well where the prospect is the grandest and most beautiful; and moreover, he knows the safest path by which it is to be reached: it is a "short cut," that is to say, "the longest way round;" but the detour will be rich in compensation for the labour.

From the black valley are seen the back of the Reeks, and a footpath, very rugged and almost inaccessible, leading to Carran Tuel. A fall from the neighbouring mountains supplies three small lakes, and then runs into the RIVER GARAMEEN, crossed by a foot bridge, and so, running to Brandon's cottage, joins the Upper Lake.

GARAMEEN BRIDGE.

Leaving "the Black Valley," the Tourist passes through "Lord Brandon's demesne;"* and having found his boat waiting in one of the sweet and lonely creeks of which there are here so many, he takes his seat, and prepares for pleasure of a less fatiguing character—the oars rapidly convey him through the Upper Lake.

And now let him look leisurely around him. He is in the midst of mountains—bleak and barren, but mighty in their magnificence.†

> "Abrupt and sheer the mountains sink
> At once upon the level brink,
> And just a trace of silver sand
> Marks where the water meets the land."

Their dark shadows are thrown upon the water, so as to give it a character of gloom, in perfect keeping with the loneliness of the scene. One feels as if the sound of a human voice would disturb its solitude: and wishes the oars that row him over

---

* Lord Brandon, who built a cottage here, and also an imitation of the Round Tower, has long ceased to own any property in the neighbourhood. The place, however, still bears his name.

† "To my mind," says Inglis, "the Upper Lake is the most attractive; the mountains are nearest to it; it has not one tame feature." "Once fairly embarked on its waters," writes Windele, "and looking back, the illusion of its being altogether landlocked, and enclosed without any opening, or mode of egress, seems nearly complete." "On entering the Upper Lake" (we quote from Webb), "attention is at first wholly engaged by the vastness of the mountains, and next by the extreme ruggedness of the scene."

the Lake were muffled. He passes along by the small islands: neither of them tempt him to land, unless it may be Rossburkie, to look for the tree round which the milkmaid tied the spancel.* Here are Arbutus Island, Eagle Island, M'Carthy's Island (covered from base to summit with the arbutus, and singularly graceful in form and character), Duck Island, Stag Island, Ronan's Island, and the Knight of Kerry's Island.† We must refer him to the guide for the origin, real or fanciful, of each name. That called after the heir of the Kerry Geraldines we believe actually belongs to him, although he has no other acre of property in this neighbourhood.

Passing the "big" promontory called "COLEMAN'S EYE,"—and so named after a giant, a saint, or an English gentleman—it is uncertain which—he enters "THE LONG RANGE." But before he arrives there, he will often look back. The mountains, between which lies the "Gap," are directly behind him; to the left are the "tails" of the Purple mountain; to the right is rugged Cromagloun; all about him the mountains rise from the lake, and seem as if they would shut him in for ever. To convey an idea of the rude magnificence of this scene is impossible. Presently its savage grandeur is passed; and we enter the realm of Beauty. The stream carries us rapidly homeward. It is running through the Long Range; and the men have merely to guide the boat.‡

The channel is charming and full of interest; the water is clear and rapid; and on either side it is amply wooded, "patrician trees" happily mingling with "plebeian underwood," through which glimpses of the huge mountains are occasionally caught. Enormous water-lotus, white and yellow, throng both sides of the stream, and giant ferns spring up from every square foot that is not rock-covered, sometimes out of crevices in the rock itself; here and there you may pull a branch that would shelter you from a shower. About midway, in "the Long Range," we reach the far-famed EAGLE'S NEST—the most perfect, glorious, and exciting of all the Killarney echoes. The rock (for in comparison with mountains that look down upon it, it is nothing more although, when at its base, it appears of prodigious height) derives its name from the fact that, for centuries, it was the favoured residence of the royal birds, their eyry being

---

* "She was milking the cows just as the sun was rising. A fine early little girl she was, rowing her boat and her pails with her own hands to the Island, before the dew was off the grass, or the birds awake, and singing—for she had a light heart, singing like a thrush; when all of a sudden, she turned her head, what should she see but a crock of shining gold, under a tree, just at her elbow. Keeping her eyes on it, she walked over, stooped down, and, to make sure that what she saw, poor thing, was not bewitchment, she took up two of the pieces, and dropped them into her bosom; she tried to lift the crock, but it was too heavy for her entirely; so to make sure of the spot she took the spancel off the cow she was milking, and tied it round the tree, then ran off to her boat, determined to bring her friends to help her home with her treasure; the last thing she did when she took up the oars to row to the mainland was to look back at the crock, and there it was—the dethother—smiling and shining in the sunbeams. Well, when she got home she told what she had seen, and one looked at the other, until she gave her mother the two gold pieces; and then father and mother, and brothers and sisters, all crowded into the boat, and maybe they didn't pull hand and fast to reach the Island. 'There's the spancel!' shouted the girl, pointing to the nearest tree; 'there's the spancel!' and sure enough there was a spancel. 'No,' said her brother, 'there's the spancel.' 'Not at all!' exclaimed her mother, 'it's on that tree.' 'I wish,' put in her father, 'that you'd all hold your nonsense, here it is round the rowan-tree.' The poor gold-finder looked bewildered; and well she might, for round every tree in the island a spancel was fastened. Then she asked her mother to show the two gold pieces she had given her, and the poor woman pulled them out, and laid them on the palm of her hand, that they might all see them: but in less than a minute, while their very eyes were on them, they were changed into dry leaves, and whirled off her hand by a light breeze; while from every tree in the Island rose a laugh so merry and so full of fun and mischief, they could hardly help laughing themselves."

† There are about twelve islands in the Upper Lake; some of them, however, are islands only in summer. Ronan's Island is the largest. It was so called, according to Mr. Webb, from an enthusiastic Englishman, who, "liking the situation," made it his home, and lived for some years the life of a recluse here, avoiding all society, and seldom leaving the island, except to shoot or fish, by which he procured his chief sustenance. There are no remains of a house.

‡ Sails are very rarely seen on the Lake. They are at all times dangerous, in consequence of the frequent occurrence of wind and squalls.

secured by nature against all human trespassers.* The rock is of a pyramidal form, exactly 1,103 feet high, thickly clothed with evergreens, but bare towards the summit, where the nest of the bird is pointed out, in a small crevice nearly concealed by stunted

IN THE LONG RANGE.

shrubs. We put into a little creek on the opposite side of the river; but remained in our

---

* The peasants relate several amusing stories of attempts to rob the "Aigle's Nest;" and many feats are detailed of the efforts of daring mountaineers to make property of the royal progeny. The boatmen tell an illustrative anecdote of a "vagabone" sodier, "who says, says he, 'I'll go bail I'll rob it,' says he. 'Maybe you will, and maybe you won't,' says the aigle; and with that she purtinded to fly off wid herself. So the sodger, when he sees that, lets himself down by a long rope he had with him; and, 'I have ye now by your sharp nose, every mother's son of ye,' says he. When all of a sudden out comes the ould aigle, from a thunder cloud, and says very civilly, says she, 'Good morrow, sir,' says she; 'and what brings ye to visit my fine family so airly, before they've had their break'est?' says she. 'Oh, nothing at all,' says the sodger, who ye see was grately frightened; 'only to ax after their health, ma'am,' says he, 'and if e'er a one of em has the tooth-ache, for which I have a specific that I brought wid me in my pocket from furrin parts.' 'Ye brought some blarney in the other pocket then,' says the aigle; 'for don't I know ye came to stale mee childre?'

boat, having been recommended to do so. Our expectations of the coming treat had been highly raised, and we were in breathless anxiety to enjoy it. The bugle-player, Spillane, landed, advanced a few steps, and placed the instrument to his lips: the

THE EAGLE'S NEST.

effect was MAGICAL—that is a poor word to convey an idea. First he played a single note—it was caught up and repeated, loudly, softly—again loudly, again softly, and then as if by a hundred instruments, each a thousand times more musical than that which gave its rivals birth, twirling and twisting around the mountain, running up from its foot to its summit, then rolling above it, and at length dying away in the distance until it was heard as a mere whisper, barely audible, far away. Then Spillane blew a few notes—ti-ra-la-ti-ra-la: a multitude of voices, seemingly from a multitude of hills, at once sent forth a reply, sometimes pausing for a second, as if waiting for some tardy comrade to join in the marvellous chorus, then mingling together in a strain of sublime grandeur, and delicate sweetness, utterly indescribable. Again Spillane sent forth his summons to the mountains, and blew, for perhaps a minute, a variety of sounds; the effect was indeed that of "enchanting ravishment"—giving

"Resounding grace to all Heaven's harmonies."

It is impossible for language to convey even a remote idea of the exceeding delight communicated by this development of a most wonderful property of Nature: sure we are that we shall be guilty of no exaggeration if we say that this single incident, among so many of vast attraction, will be sufficient recompense to the Tourist who may visit these beautiful lakes. When Spillane had exhausted his ability

'Honour bright,' says the sedger, 'do ye think I'd be doing such a mane thing?' 'I'll have it to a neighbour o' mine whether ye did or no,' says the aigle. So wid that, she bawls out at the top of her voice, 'Did he come to rob the aigle's nest?' In coorse the echo made answer, 'To rob the aigle's nest.'—'Hear to that, ye chief!' says the aigle; 'and take that home wid ye,' giving him a stroke wid her bake became the two eyes, and sent him rowling into the lake—and I'll go bail mone of his progenitors ever went to rob an aigle's nest after that day.'

to minister to our enjoyment—and the day was declining before we had expressed ourselves content—preparations were made for firing off the cannon. As soon as they were completed, the match was applied. In an instant every mountain for miles round us seemed instinct with angry life, and replied in voices of thunder to the insignificant and miserable sound that had roused them. The imagination was excited to absolute terror: the gnomes of the mountains were about to issue forth and punish the mortals who had dared to rouse them from their solitude; and it was easy for a moment to fancy every creek and crevice peopled with "airy things." The sound was multiplied a thousandfold, and with infinite variety; at first it was repeated with a terrific growl; then a fearful crash; both were caught up and returned by the surrounding hills, mingling together, now in solemn harmony, now in utter discordance; awhile those that were nearest became silent, awaiting those that were distant—the echoes of echoes; then joining together in one mighty sound, louder and louder; then dropping to a gentle lull, as if the winds only gave them life; then breaking forth again into a combined roar that would seem to have been heard hundreds of miles away.* It is not only by these louder sounds the echoes of the hills are awakened; the clapping of a hand will call them forth; almost a whisper will be repeated—far off—ceasing—resuming—ceasing again. The most eloquent poet of our age has happily expressed the idea we desire to convey:—

> "A solitary wolf-dog, ranging on
> Through the bleak concave, wakes this wondrous chime
> Of airy voices lock'd in unison,—
> Faint—far off—near—deep—solemn and sublime."

Yes, good reader; if you had but this one recompense of your visit to Killarney, it would suffice.

About a mile from the "Eagle's Nest" † is the old WEIR BRIDGE, a bridge of two arches, only one of which affords a passage for boats, and through this the water of the Upper Lake rushes into the other lakes on its way, through the Laune to the sea. The current is exceedingly rapid, and it is usual for Tourists to disembark and walk across the isthmus, meeting the boat on the other side, the passage being considered one of danger to persons who are either easily alarmed or indisposed to take the advice of the boatmen—"Plase to sit quiet." Our helmsman was, however, anxious to try the strength of our nerves, as well as to exhibit one of the Killarney lions in its wrath and power, shaking its mane in angry vigour; he, therefore, gave us no warning

---

* "We gazed at the wood, the rock, and the river, with alternate hope and fear; and we expected with a pleasing impatience some very marvellous events. . . . . . Angels from the sky, or fairies from the mountain, or O'Donoghue from the river, we every moment expected to appear before us."—OCKENDEN (1760). "Our single French horn had the harmony of a full concert, and one discharge of our little piece of cannon was multiplied into a thousand reports; with this addition, that when the sounds seemed faint, and almost expiring, they revived again, and then gradually subsided. It equals the most tremendous thunder."—DERRICK (1760). "Each explosion awakes a succession of echoes resembling peals of thunder, varying in number and intensity according to the state of the atmosphere."—WINDELE. "Our imagination endues the mountains with life, and to their attributes of magnitude, and silence, and solitude, we for a moment add the power of listening and a voice."—INGLIS. "The mountains seem bursting with the crash—now it rolls, peal upon peal, through their craggy hollows, till at length, dying away in the distance, all seems over; hark! it rises again; other mountains mimic the thunder, and now it is lost in a low growl among the distant hills."—CROKER. "It is scarcely in the power of language to convey an idea of the extraordinary effect of the echoes under this cliff, whether they repeat the dulcet notes of music, or the loud discordant report of a cannon. Enchantment here appears to have resumed her reign, and those who listen are lost in amazement and delight."—WELD.

† A good and industrious girl, Debby (Deborah) Connor, will be invariably found located on the small island opposite this rock. She is seen busily at work, and does great good with her "earnings," maintaining her mother and more than one of "her people." She makes neck-chains of plaited horsehair, and half-a-crown will be well laid out at her "establishment"—her lap—by thus procuring a reminder of Killarney, and the most beautiful of all its beautiful scenes.

until we were actually within the fierce current. We shot through it with frightful rapidity; and it seemed that a very small deviation either to the right or the left would have flung us among the breakers, the result of which must inevitably have

OLD WEIR BRIDGE.

been fatal. The men, who had rested on their oars, were watching us with some anxiety, and the moment we were in safety they woke the echoes with a loud shout, and congratulated us on our "bowldness." We can claim but little merit for our heroism; for, in reality, there is no peril in the "voyage:" and we had forgotten the disasters that Mr. Weld records, and to which Derrick made reference half a century before him.

At Dinis Pool the current divides; one branch, to the right, enters TORC LAKE; the other, to the left, runs between Dinis Island and Glena Mountain, and joins the Lower Lake at the BAY OF GLENA.*

---

* In Dinis Pool, at a particular point, the visitor's attention is arrested by the boatmen ceasing to pull, and lying on their oars; and on asking the reason why, their touching answer is, "Sure you would not have us disturb poor Ned MacCarthy's grave!"

"Where weeping birches wildly wave
The boatmen show their brother's grave;
And while they tell the name he bore,
Suspended hangs the lifted oar."—LOVER.

BEAUTIFUL GLENA.   119

Tore Lake should be more visited than it is; the rocks here are the most beautiful anywhere, and are perforated in all possible ways. There is but one island—The Devil's Island. There are otters in the Devil's Island. A cave of some length is called the Whiskey Cellar; and there, at the end, is O'Donoghue's arm-chair; his butler is close by Jacky Boy's Bay. Here also is O'Donoghue's wine-cellar. In fact,

THE DEVIL'S ISLAND.

a row round Tore Lake may be a rare treat for a long summer evening; landing occasionally, to walk among the woods of Mucross, but more especially with a view to examine the singular formations of the limestone rocks. The lake is usually calmer than its sister lakes; the surrounding shores are high, and on one side it is completely overlooked by mountains. Hereabouts, as well as at Glena and in the Long Range, the ferns grow to enormous size, and in profuse luxuriance. There are, indeed, many who will think the Tore Lake more attractive than either the Upper or the Lower.

In 1861 the Queen christened a rock in Tore Lake. It now bears the mark, "Victoria, August 28, 1861." Heartily we hope that Her Majesty will again visit Ireland, and again gladden the hearts of her loyal and loving subjects there.

But we have yet a word to say concerning GLENA. There is, we think, nothing at Killarney, where nature is everywhere charming to absolute fascination, equal to this surpassingly lovely spot—beautiful Glena. The mountain of Glena, clothed to luxuriance with the richest evergreens, looks down upon a little vale endowed with the rarest natural gifts, and which the hand of taste has touched here and there, without impairing its primitive character. Glena, a name that signifies "The glen of good fortune," is the property of Lord Kenmare, whose lady has

THE COTTAGE AT GLENA.

built a cottage-ornée in this delicious valley; it is in happy keeping with the beautiful and graceful scene, and the walks and gardens that surround it are so formed and disposed as in no degree to deduct from its simple beauty. Here, also, a pretty and convenient cottage has been erected for the accommodation of strangers: it is placed in one of the forest glades, close to the shore. Here we rested awhile; enjoyed a plentiful dinner, which Mr. Goodman had prepared for us; and here O'Leary "played the pipes," while Jerry Clifford danced a jig with a pretty colleen. The day was fine, and it was indeed a happy day—a day to remember as long as we live.*

We had with us on that delicious day a pleasant companion and a kind and sympathising friend—who has since left earth. He thoroughly enjoyed the scene, his generous nature entering fully into the spirit of tranquil happiness it inspired. His name is in no way known to fame, and we do not here give it record. But his spirit will accept this loving tribute to his memory, and it will surely be with us when we again visit beautiful Killarney.

* Persons are in charge of Glena, whose business it is to provide accommodation for strangers, which they do in a manner entirely satisfactory. O'Leary, the piper, will play any famous Irish air, and gratify the stranger by that which may, at all events, be a novelty. The chances are that a merry Irish girl—the maid-of-all-work to the visitors—will be there also; and, if so, be sure you can see an Irish jig, for there is little doubt that one of the boatmen will call for "Green grow the rushes, O!" and the effect will be irresistible. A dance is as certain to follow it as a bugle sound when you round the corner at parting from beautiful Glena.

Here, then, let us end our Third Day's Tour. For although, probably, those who must make the most of time may even yet be enabled before nightfall to row round Tore Lake, among the island rocks in Castle Lough Bay, and even to enter and examine, briefly, Inisfallen and Ross—we trust that comparatively few will be compelled to *crush* two days into one, and consequently sacrifice to fatigue the enjoyment that may be derived from both.

Now, then, we are journeying homewards—homewards from Glena, beautiful Glena! Its "Bay" is among the very loveliest things about Killarney.* It is "a

IN GLENA BAY. MRS. HALL'S POINT.

good step" to either of the inns. But stay, the boatmen may not yet "pull out," for Spillane must have a word or two with Glena—his "pet" of all the mountains! Who could weary of such words, so answered? To Spillane, who has awakened them a thousand times, it is still a labour of love; and the boatmen, to whom the aerial voices are familiar as domestic sounds, gladly rest upon their oars to hear them once again!

And now, surely we shall have seen enough of the lakes, and mountains, and rivers, and valleys for to-day, to render repose a luxury. We have intimated our belief that the comparative quiet of the grounds about THE RAILWAY HOTEL will produce that "calming" effect which is true pleasure after excitement; but those who seek amusement when evening has closed in will find it here: some of the

---

* In Glena Bay, a little point of rock juts out; the boatmen and guides "christened" it with the usual "ceremonies," and called it "Mrs. Hall's Point;" it commemorates our latest visit—on the 27th June, 1864, and pleasantly associates our memory with the locality we dearly love.

visitors will perhaps look over the photographs, or "bog oak ornaments," that will be submitted to them in great variety; others will gossip with the guide concerning what they have seen and what they have yet to see; others will arrange plans for to-morrow's excursion; others may arrange a day's fishing on the lake, and compare their choice London flies with the comparatively rude imitations that are far more likely to bring trout to the hook.

But when the day is over, let it not be forgotten that the Islands of the Lower Lake are to be visited; and that a rare treat awaits the Tourist from this fertile source; for the shores as well as the islands are full of interest; and he will "voyage" to the entrance to THE RIVER LAUNE, where scenery will await him of a different order from any he has yet examined.

Good reader, let us hope the day will be "calm and sweet and bright;" for umbrellas are unseemly objects, even in a boat.

THE FOURTH DAY'S TOUR.

THE ISLANDS AND SHORES OF THE LOWER LAKE.

This day we spend among the islands and along the shores of the Lower Lake; taking a row round Tore; awakening the echoes of the old mountain; and, resting the oars off many a well-known spot, holding converse with far-famed "PADDY BLAKE." The labour of to-day will not be severe; the remainder of our tour about Killarney we can make easily, and by "short stages." Indeed, tourists whose time is limited may, when the third day closes in, consider the Lakes to have been visited, and prepare for a journey homewards or elsewhere. But many, we hope, will be less hurried, and will give a whole day to the "Shores and Islands." If at "Cloghreen," or at the "Lake Hotel," the

Tourist should first row among the small island-rocks in CASTLE-LOUGH BAY, the bay in which he will enter the boat, and be consigned to the care of four as civil and obliging "Kerry-boys" as ever told a legend—or believed one. All about him are odd-looking rocks and pretty islets; some so bare that not a blade of grass grows over them; others so thick with foliage, that, literally, you see nothing but a clump of trees rising out of the water, and sometimes little more than the topmost branches of these very trees are visible. There are in this Castle-Lough Bay just "a baker's dozen," and very pretty they look; but there is not one of them that will recompense a landing. At Castle-Lough, however, we must pause a moment. The castle perished in the wars of 1652. So completely was it destroyed, that scarcely one stone was left standing on another. Barely sufficient now remains to point out its locality. It may have been of importance, from its position, but never could have been of any extent. North of Castle-Lough Bay the Flesk runs into the lake, passing by the grounds of Cahirnane. It has voyaged a long way, to help the waters at Killarney.

Those who are located at the Victoria will probably proceed to visit the island by a different course; for the boat-house of the hotel lies about a mile almost due north of the Bay. There is, however, a road from the Victoria through the island. And from the Railway Hotel there is a road that leads direct to the castle, where boats are usually taken by those who are located at that hotel.*

Here, then, at ROSS ISLAND, and immediately under ROSS CASTLE, let us embark at the convenient quay built by Lord Kenmare. Before we look at the old castle, let us walk through the gardens and round the island; but—will the visitor believe us?— he will have paced no less than two miles before he arrives at this garden-gate again.†

Ross is more properly a peninsula than an island, being separated from the main land only by a narrow cut through a morass, which it is more than probable was a work of art, with a view to strengthen the fortifications of the castle. The island, for so it must now be termed, is the largest island of the lake. It contains about eighty plantation acres, richly and luxuriantly cultivated; a portion of it is converted into

---

* Here is a list of all the rocks and islands in the Lower Lake, beginning with the most northerly, Brown or Rabbit Island, and so descending to the most southerly, Sugar Island: the reader will of course ascertain their relative positions by looking at the map.

1. Brown or Rabbit Island.	9. Rough Island.	19. Osprey Rock.
2. Lamb Island.	10. Hen and Chickens.	20. Friar's Island.
3. Heron Island.	11. Pigeon Island.	(All in Castle Lough Bay.)
4. O'Donoghue's Prison.	12. O'Donoghue's Table.	21. Otter Rock.
5. Cherry Island.	13. Cow Island.	22. Darby's Garden.
6. Inisfallen.	14. Elephant Rock.	23. Burnt Island.
7. Mouse Island.	15. Jackdaw Island.	24. Stag Island.
8. Ross Island.	16. Crow Island.	25. Drinking Horse.
(All north of Ross Bay.)	17. Yew Island.	26. The Prince's Island.
	18. Ash Island.	

Another island has been lately added—by name—to the list: it is "The Prince's Island," which we have therefore marked as No. 26. It is nothing but a rock; but serves to commemorate the visit of the Prince of Wales in 1858. It was intended to re-christen the Mouse Island—one of the prettiest of the group—and to bestow upon it that honour; but his Royal Highness protested against depriving it of its time-honoured and very appropriate name; although he expressed himself content that his memory should be associated with the rock, which until then had really no distinguishing mark, although it had been usually called the Gun Rock.

There are about half a dozen others that have names; such as Gunnet Rock, Tom Cole's Rock, Currig-a-hecca Rock, and Alexander Rock. Brickeen Island and Dinis Island stand between Torc Lake and the Lower Lake; they belong properly to neither of the two lakes; but if to either they must be assigned, we should give them to Torc, as being the property of Mr. Herbert.

† It is just under Ross Castle that "Paddy Blake" must be talked to: Paddy Blake, the famous Echo, that, when you ask him, "How d'ye do, Paddy Blake?" makes instant answer, "Pretty well, I thank ye." At certain times it is the clearest of all the lake echoes.

a graceful and carefully kept flower-garden, where seats are placed so as to command the more striking and picturesque views; and in every part, Nature has been so judiciously trained and guided, that the whole scene is one of surpassing beauty.

ROSS CASTLE.

The castle is a fine ruin; much less injured by time than the majority of its co-mates in Kerry county. It is a tall, square, embattled building, based upon a limestone rock, sustained at the land side by a plain massive buttress; from the north-east and north-west angles project two machicolated defences. It contains a spiral staircase of cut stone. It was erected by one of the earlier chieftains of the Donoghues.* It forms a conspicuous feature in the landscape from every part of the Lower Lake. During the war, the outbuildings were fitted up as a barrack.† The castle is famous in Irish history as being the last in Munster to hold out against the Parliamentary army. In 1652, Ludlow, the successor of Ireton, assisted by Sir Hardress Waller, laid siege to it. It was defended by Lord Muskerry with a sufficiency of troops, and an ample supply of provisions; yet the castle, so well prepared for defence, surrendered upon articles, without striking a vigorous blow. The circumstance is attributable to the terror that seized upon the garrison when they beheld war-ships floating on the lake, in fulfilment of an ancient prophecy, which foretold that the castle could be taken only when an event occurred almost as improbable as that " Birnam Wood" should

---

* Of course the several legends connected with the name of the O'Donoghue have their source in this, his castle of Ross. The peasantry will point out the window from which he leaped into the lake when he exchanged his sovereignty on earth for that of the waters under it. He was endowed, they say, with the gift of transforming himself into any shape, and his wife requested him to exhibit some of his transformations before her. He warned her that if he did so, and she displayed any symptoms of fear, they would be separated for ever. She still persisted, in the spirit of female curiosity, and in perfect confidence that she could look on unmoved. On his assuming, however, some very terrible shape, she shrieked with terror. He immediately sprang from the window into the lake below, and remains there an enchanted spirit; his enchantment to continue until, by his brief annual ride, his silver shoes are worn out by the attrition of the surface of the water. Of the race of the O'Donoghues, " the Annals of Inisfallen" have furnished various particulars, which give a pretty clear insight into the character of gone-by times, when "might made right," and illustrate the utter insecurity of life and property, that kept the "petty kings" always armed lest the stronger should come and strip them. From the year 1024 to 1200, of the " Kings of Locha Lein," nineteen out of twenty were "slain," some in open fight, some by treachery, and some having been previously driven out of their territories. The last item in the dismal account stands thus :—" Jeoffery O'Donoghue, and Saova, daughter of Donchad Childreach O'Brien, his wife, as also his brother and his three sons, burned in his house at the garden of the Greenfort, by Finech M'Donnell God, being betrayed by his own huntsman." Among the "fierce leaders of battles," nevertheless, there were a few distinguished as " gentle at arms," and some who " never forsook the mass." This list, however, which gives so dark a picture of the age, refers to the O'Donoghue of the Glens, and not to the ancestors of the spirit chieftain. Yet the milder branch has altogether withered and vanished; while of the "turbulent," "the ruthless," the " proud and stern in battle," the representative still exists.

† While a barrack Colonel Hall was quartered there with the staff of his regiment; and in one of the rooms a son was born to him in 1798.

come "to Dunsinane." Although it is very unlikely that Ludlow had heard of this tradition, or would have heeded it if he had, it is certain that, having considered it wisest to attack the castle by water, he had constructed boats for the purpose; "and," as he says, "when we had received our boats, each of which was capable of containing one hundred and twenty men, I ordered one of them to be rowed about, in order to find out the most convenient place for landing upon the enemy, which they perceiving, thought fit, by a timely submission, to prevent the danger that threatened them." General Ludlow does not explain how the boats were conveyed into the lakes; and so great must have been the difficulty of transporting them from any distant part, covered as this district of Ireland then was with bog and forests, that the boat has been generally considered to have been nothing more than a raft. An accident enabled us to remove all doubts on the subject.

In the wall of the ancient church of St. Multose, at Kinsale, we discovered an old tomb, partly concealed by rubbish; and learned that this division of the structure had, until very lately, been blocked up by heaps of stone and mortar. The inscription on a wooden panel, almost rotted away, and fixed immediately over the grave, was in Latin. The word "Kerria" excited our curiosity; and, on clearing the stone, we were amply rewarded for our labour.*

As we have observed, from all parts of the lake, and from every one of the adjacent mountains, the Castle of Ross is a most interesting and attractive point in the scenery, and it amply repays the honour it receives by enabling the visitor to obtain, from the summit of its tower, a commanding view of every important object by which it is surrounded. An hour passed in walking round the island will be an hour pleasantly and profitably spent; and curiosity may be gratified by inspecting the surface of the famous copper mine, the débris of which is scattered in profusion upon the western shore; among them are several huge portions of a steam-engine—the first, we believe, ever introduced into Ireland. When opened by Colonel Hall in 1804, he obtained unequivocal proof that they had been worked previously; but at a period very remote, and when mining, as an art, was utterly unknown.†

---

* The following is a translation of the epitaph:—
 "Here with his father, lies Thomas, by surname Chudleigh,
 For the kings of the English both built ships.
 The father's skill was uncommon: alas! alas! *his* life was short,
 He caused a ship to sail on the land;
 That the ship did sail on the land Kerry well knows,
 The tower of Ross taken with difficulty proves.
 Proceed, Muse, I implore; study to sing the *praises* of the *son*.
 He was very ingenious, skilled in the same art.
 He built a ship for the King to which Kinsale gives a name
 He built, but to another great praise was given;
 He built this, I say, reader, though another bore away the honours.
 Thus, for another, not for itself, the vine affords sweet grapes;
 Thus, for another, not for himself, the horse bears heavy burdens;
 Thus, for another, not for himself, the dog courses over the plains;
 Thus, for another, not for herself, the ship herself sails the seas."

The descendants of the ship-builder are still living, and the name of the ship of war, "the Kinsale," appears in the old Navy Lists.

† THE MINES. It will be impossible to visit Killarney without hearing perpetually of the Mines. The history of Ross Mine is thus given in "Croker's Researches in the South of Ireland:"—"About the year 1804, Colonel Hall, an English officer, who had been some time quartered at Killarney (with a regiment he had raised in his own county of DEVON), conceiving a favourable opinion of Ross Mine, induced one or two gentlemen in the vicinity to join him in re-opening it. Having succeeded in clearing out the water and rubbish, the little company were encouraged by the fluttering appearances to proceed to work it; which they did on rather an extensive scale, notwithstanding the unfavourable circumstances of

During our recent visit we found that the island had undergone great improvements. Portions allotted to most delicious flowers are succeeded by lawns and shrubberies, prairie and wood, the noble ruin of the O'Donoghue giving an air of magnificence

ROSS CASTLE.

to the whole; so that it seems like some fairy enchantment—the island in itself containing a sufficiency of beauty, without looking to the lake or mountains beyond. What visions, too, of old, old times, crowd the memory, when pennon and banner floated on the breeze—when the glen chief received homage and tribute within those walls upon which the green ivy clusters—when abbot and knight passed through the portal, and the mountains echoed the war-pipe or the shout of joyous revellers!

A visit to Ross Island naturally suggests a consideration of the LEGENDS OF THE O'DONOGHUE—the most fertile topic of interest connected with the Lakes. We shall therefore delay the reader while we relate some of the most striking.

Wander where you will in this delicious neighbourhood, either up the mountain,

its situation, nearly close to the lake, the ground not rising much above, and dipping towards it at an angle about thirty degrees from the horizon; so that in a short time the workmen had excavated completely under the lake, with every fear of its waters breaking in on them. The richness and abundance of the ore was, however, a sufficient inducement to counteract this danger and inconvenience, as, during the four years that Ross Mine was worked, nearly £80,000 worth of copper was disposed of at Swansea, some cargoes producing £90 per ton. But this very richness was the ultimate cause of its destruction, as several small veins of pure oxide of copper split off from the main lode, and ran towards the surface. The ore of these veins was much more valuable than the other, consequently the miners (who were paid by quality as well as quantity) pursued the smaller veins so near the surface, that the water broke through into the mine in such an overwhelming degree, that an engine of thirty horse power could make no sensible impression on the inundation; and thus a forcible stop was put to all further proceedings."

The late Col. Hall (the father of the author of this work) discovered and opened no fewer than thirteen mines in the south of Ireland. Some of these he worked for a considerable period; and, although his efforts were in the end unsuccessful, he set an example of enterprise and activity, and supplied evidence of the vast mineral wealth of the country which entitle us to claim for him some tribute of public gratitude, and justify us in classing him among the benefactors of Ireland. He was amongst the earliest of those who laboured to turn to account its great natural resources—to encourage men of larger means—men who will probably reap the rich harvest for which it was his destiny only to prepare the ground, and to direct public attention to a source of profit for the undertakers, and of employment for the people. Like many others who have pointed out the way to fortune, it was his fate to behold the achievement of his hopes only from a very remote distance; but he enjoyed the enviable knowledge that his labour had not been in vain; that he had been the means of spending some hundreds of thousands of pounds in the country; of giving advantageous employment to masses of the people in various districts, and of showing how others might certainly do that which he, as certainly, failed of doing.

along the valleys, upon the water, or in any one of the islands, you are sure to find some object connected with the legend; every rock of unusual form is forced into an illustration of the story; the guides and boatmen will point out to the Tourist O'Donoghue's horse, O'Donoghue's prison, his stable, his library, his pigeon-house, his table, his cellar, his honeycombs, his pulpit, and his broom.

Although its variations are numerous, the original story may be told in a few words. In ages long past, O'Donoghue of Ross was lord of the lake, its islands, and the land that surrounded it. His sway was just and generous, and his reign propitious; he was the sworn foe of the oppressor; he was brave, hospitable, and

THE SPIRIT OF O'DONOGHUE.

wise. Annually, since his death, or rather disappearance, he is said to revisit the pleasant places among which he lived—

" So sweet is still the breath
Of the fields and the flowers in our youth we wander'd o'er."

Every morning he may be seen gliding over the lake mounted on a white steed, richly caparisoned, preceded and followed by youths and maidens, who strew spring flowers in his way; while sounds of unearthly sweetness glide along the waters, and become thunder as they make their way up the surrounding hills. Although he appears in state only on May morning—

" For when the last April sun grows dim
The Naiads prepare his steed for him,
Who dwells, bright Lake, in thee,"—

he is seen on various other occasions: and lucky is the child of earth by whom the immortal spirit is encountered; for be he peer or peasant, good fortune is sure to wait upon him—and therefore many are they who peer with longing eyes along the lake, at sunrise or in twilight, to catch a glimpse of the chieftain, and listen with eager ears for the music that heralds his approach.

We have said that many living witnesses are ready to testify to the appearance of the O'Donoghue, either riding upon the lake, walking on the shore, or playing "hurly" upon the surface of the waters; and we have conversed with so many of them, of credit and repute, that we can have no hesitation in believing them to have actually beheld that which they affirm they *have* "seen with their two eyes." The circumstance, however, is now easily accounted for; although, a few years ago, it was impossible to consider it otherwise than supernatural. The legend, told in so

O'DONOGHUE'S HORSE.

many ways, is a fertile source of amusement to visitors. As we have said, every rock of the Lower Lake is associated with it: the most remarkable of these rocks is "O'Donoghue's Horse," of which the accompanying print will convey an accurate idea; although from some points of view it bears a much closer resemblance to the form of the animal whose name it bears. We were the more desirous of preserving a copy of this natural wonder; for, its base being nearly undermined by the continual action of the water, it is not likely it can long remain on the comparatively slender props that now sustain it. In a few years the "horse" may be an inmate of the chieftain's stable under the waves; but he will cease to be an object of interest and attraction to dwellers upon earth.* The guides and boatmen have all, of course, "had a sight" of the chieftain, and will tell the Tourist amusing stories—but those they have only heard—of their ancestors, who not only saw, but conversed with him, and shared his hospitality in his palace below the waves.

Our guide directed our attention to a scene of surpassing beauty, and exclaimed,

---

* The horse has vanished since this was written; no doubt there is a "legend" to account for his disappearance; but in sober truth it must be said that the frost of a severe winter undermined his constitution, and he sank (to be again with O'Donoghue) into the Lake. We have thought it right, however, to preserve the only portrait that exists of this time-honoured steed.

"That's the place, and a beautiful place it is—a place that any country may be proud of. I've seen people that would float beneath the shadow of those mountain woods for a whole summer day, and then return again in the twilight, and wait to see the moon rise, and then stay out until she had nearly finished her rounds in the heavens. I don't like it, I don't at all alike it; the lakes are mighty lonely, and even along the shores you seldom hear the song of a bird, or any *living* noise except the belling of the deer. It's a lonesome place without the company of one's own kind—though I'm not saying that's the *best* one might have in it—still, it's mighty lonesome in itself."

"There's a spot somewhere about this mountain of Glena, is there not, called 'The Lady's Leap?'"

"There is; and some say it is that point, and others say it is this one, just above us, pushing out there through the trees."

"Do you know the legend?"

"Oh, that's no laigend at all," said one of the boatmen; "but as thrue as that the heavens are above us. Everybody knows that the lady who made the leap was never afterwards seen upon earth, any way."

The legend we gathered from the various versions of our guide and boatmen is this:—Long, long ago it was, that a beautiful young lady lived out yonder, in an old ancient castle, which, like many a fine place that was among the hills, and in the glens of Ireland, isn't there now. She was more lovely to look upon than all the other fair daughters of Kerry—bright as a sunbeam, gentle as a dove, light-footed as a white roe; her hair was darker than midnight, and her young heart spotless as snow when falling; her voice was so full of music that the bards used to listen, and echo it upon their harps, then throw them aside in despair, and call them tuneless; the poor blessed her as she passed them, for she came of a generous race, and added fresh glory to their names; and the rich honoured her, though she did not honour *them* because of their riches. She was the only child of her father; and when he said, "Oh, my daughter, wilt thou not choose for thyself from amongst the princes of Erin one to be a protector and friend to thee, and a father to my people when I am gone?" she turned the light of her bright blue eyes away from her father's face, and wept. It seemed as if, with the power of making all hearts love her, she thought not of love towards man, but closed her heart against all earthly affection. Upon this, the holy people, priests and nuns, said, "The fair maiden will be one of us,—she has no love for the vanities of the world." But the more experienced among them answered, "Not so: behold the fashioning of her robes, their varied colours; and see the blue of her mantle, the curious embroidery, and needle-work, and the jewels that glitter on her brow and in her hair: those who think of cloisters do not delight in gauds." There was only one among her maidens—Una, of the raven locks—that kept silence, and opened not her lips; the others called their mistress a second Bridget, and chattered of how they would not use their lovers so—if they had them; but Una, her chosen follower, her humble friend, made no comment; thinking, doubtless, like all of quiet tongue, so much the more. Now every one knew that wherever her lady went, Una followed; and the two maidens would wander days and nights together along the borders of the lakes. Sometimes Una would carry her lady's harp; and when the fishermen heard their voices in conversation or music, they would row far from them, respecting them too much to disturb their retirement. Sometimes the lady would sit in her boat, which was lined with purest gold, and Una would row her

along the silvery lines traced by the moonbeams on the waters; and the lady would play and sing in that lonely way, until the first rays of morning warned her that the night was past. The month of April drew near its end, and when the last day came, the lady said to her attendant, "Una, sleep on to-night, for I mean to work a spell, and discover if it can be given to mortal to converse with him who dwells beneath the glorious waters of the beautiful lake." And Una was sore afraid, and trembled; yet she laid down and tried to sleep. But she could not sleep, for she wondered why she should be told to do so; and she followed her mistress secretly and in silence. When Una arrived at the margin of the lake, she concealed herself behind an arbutus; but the lady stood beneath the cliff, and Una could see only the star that glittered on the top of her silver wand as she moved it to and fro.

Una was not long there before she heard a noise as of foaming waters; and then it came nearer and nearer, until she beheld the form of a knight on horseback, his white plumes waving above his helmet, which seemed one huge diamond, his armour laced together with all manner of coloured jewels. The horse was half hidden by the foam of the wave; but Una said it seemed as if the knight bestrode a rainbow. The softest, sweetest music that ever was heard accompanied him to the shore; and when he sprang upon the bank where her lady stood, every tree on Glena bowed down its branches to do homage to their native prince. Una was not so overcome with the sight but that she heard the knight praise her lady's beauty, and promise that if she would be faithful to him, and him alone, for seven years, meeting him on that spot every May morning until the seventh morning, that on the seventh he would bear her away to his lake-guarded palace, and make her his bride. This she promised to do; and sorry was Una to hear her, for she thought within herself how sad it would be for the country to lose so fair a blossom, the poor so good a friend, and her aged father so dutiful a daughter.

For six May mornings, following each other with their flowers, and wreaths of hawthorn, and tender lambs, and singing-birds, and maids as innocent as the one and as blithe as the other—for six May mornings, before the lark sung its carol, or the thrush left its young to seek for food, did the lady meet her royal lover in the same place. The seventh morning was at hand. She changed not, she thought of no other. Her heart was with the Water-king: and every other suitor was dismissed, to her father's grief and the disappointment of her people.

Una counted the days of April with sorrow; mingling her tears with its showers, and watching her beloved lady with more than usual anxiety. "Surely," she thought, "she will never have the heart to leave her old grey-headed father;" and she thought this the more when she saw how her lady's eyes filled with tears when the good old man kissed and blessed her—alas! for the last time. This night, also, she permitted Una to receive her saffron robe and jewelled coronet, and, then taking her hand, she told her she had been a faithful servant, and, she knew, had kept her secret; and Una fell at her feet and embraced them, and lifted up her voice and wept bitterly; and she felt her lady tremble, and hot, large tears fall upon her brow; but she said, "Una, I am pledged to my love to be his bride, and I go to keep my word—do thou be a child, unto his death, to my father, and divide my jewels and garments amongst the poor. I shall take nothing with me save this white robe—my bridal robe—and this wreath upon my head:" and the wreath was made of the white water-lilies—their cups more pure than silver, and their threads more bright than gold. This wreath she placed upon her brow with her own hands, and then walked out into the balmy air, while the stars were alive in the sky, and the wood-pigeons dreaming over their nests. Una followed at a distance, and saw that the Lake-king was waiting for his bride. For a moment her lady stood upon the bank, and waved her arms towards the home of her youth; then paused, and turned towards her lover, whose noble steed stood as firmly on the liquid waters as if his silver shoes had pressed the earth—the white plumes of his helmet waved and danced in the morning air—he stood in his stirrups to receive her, and the same moment the sweetest music floated all around. The lady sprang from earth for ever; and away—away—away, swifter and brighter than a thousand sunbeams—the Prince and his beautiful Bride flashed across the lake!

"And spirits, from all the lake's deep bowers,
Glide o'er the blue wave, scattering flowers."

We have not done with the O'Donoghue legends; and whether the reader weary of them or not, we must give two or three more.

"And did you never hear of O'Donoghue's pigs? Sure, the pigs he had war wonderful—so fat and large and handsome, broad-backed and deep-chested—more like cows—the wonder of the whole country they were. Well, he was a little a' one side for want of money; and he said to his wife, 'My darlin,' he says,—for he was very fond of her, always,—'My darlin,' he says, 'the times are bad enough, and there's so much talk about the pigs that I'll sell 'em.' 'Sell 'em!' she says, looking all ways at him—for she knew her own now—' is it sell them?' 'Whisht!' he says, 'and don't be talking of what you don't understand; keep to your little parlour, my dear, and leave O'Donoghue to manage his pigs!' Well, whatever she answered, she said half to herself; and by that token it wasn't, maybe, agreeble—for when a woman doesn't care to spake out, there is something she wants to keep in, you may be certain sure of,—and O'Donoghue put a frown upon himself that would terrify the lake into a storm at any hour of the day or night; and so she made a curtshey to him by way of obadience, and left him to himself. Well, he thought to himself, while he was taking a turn in his library (you may see it in the lake now), that, as he only wanted the money for present use, he might as well sell the pigs; and so off he druv them to market the next morning. Ye think it quare he'd drive the pigs? Bedad! and so it was; but he had a rason for it—*they wouldn't be druv by any one else.* So presently a travelling pig-merchant came up to them, as well as he could through the fair—for the crowd round the pigs went beyant all, to see O'Donoghue on his white horse standing at the tail of a hundred o' pigs. Well, he offered for the pigs; and O'Donoghue, when he buttoned up the money, says, 'My good man,' he says, 'if yer discontinted wid yer bargain, jist let me know, and I'll give ye yer money back again.' But the vagabone thought how soft O'Donoghue must be, for he knew he got the pigs for half their value. And one went home, and the other went home; but the home of O'Donoghue and the home of the pig-driver did not lie the same road. Well, the man drove off his pigs; and they most broke the heart in him and his men, from the unasy way they wandered—here and there, up and down, in and out. Still, when he thought of the fine bacon they'd make, he went on, never heeding the trouble. After two days' weary journey he came to a river ford; and if ever there had been a bridge there, it was broke down, and the river was foaming and dancing over and around the rocks, cutting and slashing like fun, and glittering like diamonds. Well, the very minute the pigs saw the wathur, they dashed into it; and sure enough as they did, every pig became a rush——"

"A what?"

"A green growing rush, rooted under the wathur—quite natural-like, waving, with its little tuft of brown bud at the top.—There war his beautiful pigs—his broad bacon turned into green rushes! First of all, he set up an ullagawn that would shake the Rocks; and then he turned back fairly and softly towards Killarney to get his money back from the O'Donoghue. When he reached the castle, he knocked at the hall door wid the Dane's hammer that hung there; and out comes the lady. 'And what do ye want, my good man?' she says; so he explained to her. 'Then,' she says, 'you must go up to the Prince's bedside and shake him up,' she says, 'for he is asleep; and if you find that won't do, pull him by the foot.' He did as she bid him; but sorra a wake he'd wake. So lifting up the golden quilt that covered the bed, he pulled his foot; and if he did, as sure as Glena is darkening the wathur, foot, ankle, leg, and thigh came away in his hand. Oh! how he blessed O'Donoghue and his pigs—*the wrong way*—as he stood holding the limb, and the Prince sleeping as sweet and as quiet as if the May breezes were playing round his head. So he tucks the leg under the tail of his coat: and though he was trembling from head to foot, he walks past the lady as *bowld as a ram*, and says, 'Thank yer honor,—I've finished my business.' He flew off like the wind, and the leg slipped from under his arm; and as sure as it did, it took to running before him! Whichever way he ran, it was before him. More than once he raised his hand to make the blessed sign, *but he had no power*. And sure his condition was not bettered when looking back, he saw O'Donoghue hot foot after him. 'Stop,' he cries, 'ye beggarly pig-driver. What ails ye, that ye can't stop when a gentleman tells ye? Give me my leg, he says; and I think it a very unmannerly thing of ye, and a proof of yer ill-breeding, to come to a gentleman's house, and to stale the leg off his body without his lave, and he asleep. Give me my beautiful leg,' says he, coming up to him. 'Plaze yer honorable honor's glory for ever!' says the fellow, stopping. 'Sure, it run away, sir—it's on before, sir.' 'Where?' thundered out the Prince; and every echo from the Eagle's Nest to the Gap of Dunloe shouted 'Where?' 'There,' answered the nagur. 'Oh! oh!'—and the O'Donoghue laughed—the leg was in its own place. 'And there,' said the Prince, throwing a purse towards him. 'My pigs are at home, and there's yer money. I only wanted my turn out of the Saxon's goold.'"

We have yet another legend :—

"It was sleeping he was, the poor innocent boy with not enough brains in his head to make it ache—an innocent chap intirely—sleeping sometimes—and sometimes watching the cows' tails to see if rain was coming, and sometimes counting the stars, or hallooing to the echoes, the only company he had, the craythur, on the mountain. Well, he was sleeping; and all of a sudden some one shuck him by the showlder.

"'Wake up, Jerry!' says a fine dark gentleman in black, 'Wake up, Jerry, and take this letter for me to the Emperor of Proosha.'

"'De Emperor of Proosha, is it!' says Jerry, rubbing his eyes—'Oh! by dis and by dat, I don't know where to find him.'

"'Get up, you fool,' said the dark gentleman, 'get up,' and he shook his head, with a three-cocked hat upon it, at the poor boy—'here's my horse standing ready, and he'll take you to him at once.'

"'I'll go wid all de pleasure in de world,' replied Jerry—'if yer honour'll just tell me who'll be mindin' de cows till I come back.'

"'I'll mind them,' says the dark gentleman.

"'Oh! yer honour's glory, I'd be sorry to thruble de likes of yer honour.'

"'If you don't be off to Dublin this minute,' says the dark gentleman, 'and give this letter to the Emperor of Proosha, who you'll meet wid the King of Roosha, and the Prence of France, all walking arm in arm into the Parliament house in College Green; if you don't fly this minute, and give it to the Emperor of Proosha—the shortest of the three he'll be, with sandy whiskers, and a stoop in his neck; for his crown'—goes on the dark gentleman, with a bit of a wink—'his crown is like many another crown in the world, more than he can convaynently carry; give him the letter, and don't wait for an answer, and if you don't do it, I'll—!' and as he shook his fist in the poor boy's face, every single mountain, even the three reeks that form the crest of the Macgillicuddy, trembled like young rushes. 'It's done, yer honour!' shouted Jerry, brave as a lion and bould as a ram, springing on the horse's back as a kid springs to its mother's side, and off went the horse, making the mountains his stepping-stones, until he stopt in College Green, and then turning his head like a Christian to Jerry, he says, 'Get down, you fool, and don't be keeping me waiting, for the smoke of the city makes me sneeze.' So poor Jerry got down, and sees the King of Roosha, and the Emperor of Proosha, and the Prence of France, all walking into the Parliament house, and he up at once to the Emperor of Proosha, and making a bow, gave him the letter, and then mounted his horse that was trying to keep in the sneeze, and away they went, till he came to where he had left the dark gentleman, who was no other than O'Donoghue himself—and, 'Ye'r a nate boy,' says the chief to him, 'mighty nate, and if you want to see raal sport, come down to-morrow morning to Castle Lough, and make this sign over yer eyes, and its there you'll see fun—only, if you dare to open yer lips it will be the worse for you.'

"So Jerry thought he'd take one day's divarshun out of himself; and sure enough he was earlier than the sunbeam at Castle Lough—and doing as he was bid—and there he saw the Emperor of Proosha, and his hurlers—and the Prence of France, and his hurlers—and the King of Roosha, and his hurlers, all walking on the lake, and trying their bits of hurleys; and of a sudden up rose O'Donoghue and his boys, with black oak hurleys, and every man of them had a white silk shirt tied about his middle with green, and the pipers playing O'Donoghue's whistle as grand as Gandsey; and wasn't Jerry, by the same token, as proud as a red deer that he belonged to the kingdom of Kerry. Well, it was O'Donoghue against Roosha, and Proosha, and France —and one Kerry boy to three furriners—but Kerry had the best of the day, until— but Jerry—for he was but soft, you understand—Jerry never could tell *what* turned the luck, but it *was* turned—and whir-r—the Irish were bet—just for a while—and the poor boy clapping his hands in a fair agony, he shouted out, 'Oh, O'Donoghue, are ye going to live and stand *that?*' And as he spoke something *rowled* in the heavens above his head, and he was *struck* down between the two eyes; and when he did rise up, he rose up a blind boy upon his own mountain, and remained blind to the day of his death. Some said he was struck by lightning; but, considering everything, it was more natural to suppose he was struck by O'Donoghue for not minding what he told him."

And another legend still:—

Killarney is no more exempt than other parts of Ireland from "*hard men*,"—sub-letters of the soil, who extort to the uttermost farthing. One of these had been "very hard intirely" upon a widow—a lone woman—who had been industrious but unfortunate. He had come to her "little place," and told her that unless her rent was paid the next morning, he would distrain forthwith—there should be no more delay. The widow knew that, as the man had no pity, her time was come. She sat for a few minutes, watching the turf ashes smoulder upon the hearth, wondering if they would go out or continue burning until after twelve—and then, throwing the hood of her cloak over her face, she thought she would just walk down to the quay of Ross Island, and "see if the air would raise her heart." She came to the quay, and sat down, praying (if it was God's will) that He would take her out of her trouble —that she might be as calm as the lake; and she prayed also for patience, and when she arose, she felt stronger both in body and mind than she had been for many a long day. She turned her steps homeward, but, just as she raised her eyes, "she was struck," by seeing a tall fine-looking gentleman before her. She curtsied, and was passing on, when he bid her good evening, very kindly, and asked her what she was doing there by herself so late, just as the moon was rising; so she told him how her little place was to be taken from her in the morning, and how she had come out just to breathe the fresh air, and be alone with God and her own heart for a while, and was going home to sleep, maybe for the last time, under her own roof. The gentleman watched every word she said, and asked her how much she owed; and she told him, and it was both a long *gale* and a heavy rent. So he made no more words, but pulling out a purse that looked both long and heavy, "Take these," he says, "and go home, and pay your rent before a witness, and take a receipt." Well, they were gold pieces she held in her hand, and while she was down on her knees blessing him he was gone. So she went home, and calling on a neighbour, they both went to the hard man's door. "It's no use," he says—and he smoking his pipe like a gentle-man *forenint* his tumbler of punch—"it's no use, ma'am, coming to me;—the money —or the road." "Here's the money, sir," she says, "if you'll be pleased to give me the receipt." Well, to see the look he gave at her, and then at the money—and then at her again—and how he tested the gold, and was mean enough to ask her how she got it—for the rich of his kind are mighty fond of thinking the poor are thieves— but she scorned to give him any satisfaction beyond the money;—her neighbour saw her pay it, and she took her receipt, and the hard man locked up the rent in his strong box: but the next morning—never was there anything higher than the "ullagawn" he raised—for in place of the ten gold pieces the widow gave him, what had he in the strong box but ten "arrabutus leaves!"—and then all the town knew it was O'Donoghue himself that righted the poor widow, and punished the hard man."

Our readers may believe as much or as little as they please of these stories of actual interviews between children of earth and the spirit of the disembodied prince: but that he has been seen, accompanied by "troops of friends," there can be no rational doubt. Among other witnesses to the fact, we summoned one who was very unlikely to be influenced by pre-established superstition—an Englishman, a Protestant, and moreover, a soldier of the 30th regiment, of the name of Thomas Reynolds. We sent for him to our hotel, and found him a plain-spoken native of Devonshire; a sturdy ploughman, who had won the first prize at a ploughing-match. The man had evidently no imagination, and was as little likely to invent a fiction, or to give it currency, as any one we have ever seen. His story was this:—He was ploughing at Inisfallen with another man, an Irishman; they were engaged in ploughing up the ancient churchyard of the island—a labour which Reynolds disliked, and to which his comrade strongly objected, but Lord Kenmare's steward insisted on its being done. The morning following the day on which they commenced their work, they were mooring the boat in which they had proceeded to the island, when they saw a procession of about two hundred persons pass from the old churchyard, and walk slowly and solemnly over the lake to the mainland. Reynolds was himself terribly alarmed, but his companion fainted in the boat. This circumstance occurred at daybreak, when it was almost twilight. He affirmed that he saw, repeatedly afterwards, smaller groups of figures; but no crowd so numerous. In answer to our questions, he expressed his perfect readiness to depose to the facts on oath; and asserted that he would declare it if he were on his death-bed. The people, he added, were astonished to find him—an Englishman and a Protestant—confirming their story. The man had certainly no object in coining a deceit; we have not heard of his ever having previously told it to any stranger: it was mere accident that made us acquainted with it, and he was evidently indisposed to satisfy the inquiries of the curious.

Before the science of the optics was well understood, these very curious and very interesting appearances were supposed to be the result of supernatural agency. We now know that all such phenomena are the effects of natural causes, and can even be reproduced artificially. They are caused by refraction or reflection of the rays of light, and sometimes by both combined, and differ from "the airy child of vapour and the sun" (rainbow) only in being more rare; because they require more unusual atmospheric changes, and uncommon localities, of hill and plain, land and water, to produce them.*

Of the islands, next in importance is INISFALLEN—sweet Inisfallen! It receives from all Tourists the distinction of being the most beautiful, as it is certainly the most interesting, of the lake islands. Its peculiar beauty is derived from the alternating hill and dale within its small circle; the elegance of its miniature creeks and harbours;

---

* This tradition, therefore, is founded upon natural causes, and the spectre of O'Donoghue is a real vision. Many such illusions are on record. The mirage of the sands of the East exhibits distorted images of real objects, so as to deceive all travellers. M. Monge, who accompanied the French army in Egypt, and Dr. Clarke, witnessed and have described those phenomena—lakes, trees, and houses in the midst of a naked desert; and so great was the optical deception, that they would not believe it such till they passed through the lovely spots, and found nothing but a few miserable Arab huts and stunted shrubs in a waste of arid land. Similar appearances are recorded by Scoresby and others as occurring in the Arctic seas: one of the ships seemed, as by enchantment, floating in the air; which Scoresby afterwards discovered to have been the reflection of his father's vessel which accompanied him in the atmosphere, though the real ship was at a distance far beyond that at which objects could be seen by direct vision.; From a similar cause arise the " Fata Morgana," in the Straits of Messina, described by Swinburne, and others. Beautiful landscapes, with men and cattle in motion, appear on the surface of the seas. It was found to be reflections of objects on the distant opposite coast of Reggio. In certain states of the atmosphere, these spectra are lost as it were on the surface of the sea, and every sheet of water as it passes becomes a distinct mirror reflecting them. But perhaps the most striking of these appearances is the celebrated "Spectre of the Hartz Mountains," which kept the district in terror and alarm from time immemorial, till M. Hause, the French chemist, discovered the cause. He went for the express purpose of witnessing the phenomena; and for thirty mornings climbed the Brocken Mountain, without being gratified. At length, early one morning, he observed on the opposite side of the hill the gigantic figure of a man turned towards him. The distinctness of the form left no doubt of the reality of the figure; while he contemplated the monster with wonder and awe, a sudden gust of wind nearly blew off his hat, and when he put up his hand to hold it on, he observed the giant do the same. He now found that it was nothing more than a dilated image of himself reflected on the surface of an opposite cloud atmosphere. No doubt the legend of O'Donoghue took its rise from some similar optical deception. It is said to be seen at the same hour of the morning, and at the same time of the year, as that of the Brocken Spectre. Some horseman riding along the opposite shore of the lake is reflected by the atmospheric mirror, and seems to continue his course along the surface of the water. Upon this principle it is easy to account for the appearances which from time to time terrify the peasantry—and the scene witnessed by Reynolds is to be thus explained.

and the extraordinary size as well as luxuriance of its evergreens; and it far surpasses in interest any one of its graceful neighbours, inasmuch as here, twelve centuries ago, was founded an abbey, of which the ruins still exist, from which afterwards issued "the Annals of Inisfallen"—among the earliest and the most authentic of the ancient Irish histories.* On approaching it we seem to be drawing near a thick forest: for the foliage is remarkably close, and extends literally into the water, many of the finest trees having their roots under the lake. On landing, however, we find that the lofty elm and magnificent ash, mingled with hollies of gigantic growth, and other evergreens (excepting only the arbutus, of which the island does not contain a single specimen) of prodigious height and girth, only encircle a greensward, of so pure and delicious a colour as to demand for Inisfallen, beyond every other part of Ireland, the character of being pre-eminently "the Emerald Isle." Vistas have been skilfully formed through the trees, presenting on one side a view of the huge mountains, and on the other of the wooded shores of Ross. Of the abbey a few broken walls alone remain; it is said to have been built in the seventh century by Saint Finian Lobhar (the Leper), the descendant of one of the most renowned of the Munster kings; and it was subsequently appropriated to the use of the regular canons of St. Augustin.

In truth, this little island is very beautiful, resting as it does with so much ease and grace upon the surface of the lake; indented with the most fairy-like bays; elevated into rocky, though not rude magnificence at one side, while the opposite shore shelves to the water's edge, and runs out into shallows. It is a miniature of a beautiful country—lawns, and dells, and thickets, and vistas, with the most lovely views of the lake and the mainland, that assume new aspects from every point of view. There are, of course, legends in abundance, connected with this island; one of them concerns the "bed of honour," an indented ledge in the rocky part of the island, overshadowed by a venerable yew-tree. The legend bears much the same moral as the "Rich and Rare" song of him whose poetry is the warmest language of Ireland. The daughter of one of the chiefs in the neighbourhood of the lakes was wooed by two youths, both of renown and noble name: but the one the maiden loved was not her father's choice; and, fearing she would be forced to a marriage in opposition to her affections, she flew with her lover to the island of Inisfallen; dreading either from its being of easy access from the shore, or from superstitious feelings which would prevent their liking the proximity of the abbey, with its stores of graves and legends of supernatural appearances, for a resting-place, they wandered to the opposite side. The lover pulled a quantity of long grass and moss, and made his lady a couch

---

* The original work, written, and for several centuries preserved, in the abbey of Inisfallen, is now in the Bodleian Library. It is on parchment in medium quarto, and contains fifty-seven leaves. The earlier portion consists of extracts from the Old Testament, and a history of the ancient world down to the arrival of St. Patrick in Ireland in 432. From this period it treats exclusively of the affairs of Ireland—terminating with A.D. 1319. It appears to have been the production of two monks; one of whom carried it to the year 1216, and the other continued it to the year 1320. There are several copies of it extant; one of which was in the collection of his Grace the Duke of Buckingham, at Stowe; part of this was translated and printed in 1825, by Dr. O'Conor. The facts are narrated in the smallest compass, and present a dry, but sad "succession of crimes, wars, and rebellions." Sir James Ware selected and published several passages, to which he refers as authorities, a single quotation may satisfy the curiosity of our readers—"Anno 1120; this abbey of Inisfallen being ever esteemed a paradise and a secure sanctuary, the treasure and the most valuable effects of the whole country were deposited in the hands of the clergy, notwithstanding which, we find the abbey was plundered in this year by Maoldiun, son of Daniel O'Donoghue. Many of the clergy were slain, and even in their cemetery, by the Mac Carthys. But God soon punished this act of impiety and sacrilege by bringing many of its authors to an untimely end."

T

upon the ledge, whereon she slept, while he watched lest they should be followed by her father and his rival. The sun had hardly risen when the breeze brought the sound of the war-pipe to the lover's ears—the gathering cry of the hostile clan; and presently boats were seen visiting and searching the various islands; the war pennon floated, and the music came towards Inisfallen. First of all the angry father set foot on the holy isle, then the rejected lover, and a troop of retainers: all, as huntsmen, seek the hare, fifties to one. The fugitives were soon discovered. "You will not take her now?" said to his rival the youth who had kept watch in Inisfallen. "Surely you will not take her now?" "I know," was the reply, "that holy priest has not blessed you, nor united you; but such is my faith in her virtue and your honour, that if twelve months instead of twelve hours had passed, I would take her as trustingly as if she had never left her mother's side."

The lady, however, was for once constant, and was united to the object of her love; and the ledge of the rock has retained its name until the present time.

Our guide, "Sir Richard"—we cannot write of Inisfallen without recalling to memory the Prince of Guides—conducted us up and down the tiny hillocks, and through the miniature vales, of this delicious isle, and listened with evident pride and pleasure to our expressions of exceeding delight. And then he and the elder Spillane took advantage of our disposition "to sit awhile and rest," for the day was very fair, and the sun was sinking "with a pure light and a mellow," to enlighten, and interest, and amuse us, by relating some of the legends of the Lakes. Although we have no design to detain our readers for so long a period as these capital raconteurs kept us, under the shadow of the venerable tree, we design to incur the hazard of wearying them by compressing some of their tales.

They told us—How St. Patrick never came into Kerry; but only looked into it, holding his hands out to it, and saying, "I bless all beyond the Reeks."——How Fin Mac Cool kept his tubs of goold in the lake under Mucross, and set his dog Bran to watch them; this was ages ago, long before the Flood. An Englishman—a grate diver intirely—came over to try wouldn't he get the goold; and when he went down, the dog woke from his slumbers and seized him; and I'll go bail he never tried th' experiment agin.——How, when O'Donoghue leaped out of the windy of Ross Castle, his enchanted books flew after him—and there they are—O'Donoghue's library, to be seen this day; only turned into stone, and like the Killarney guidebooks—rather heavy.——How, right under the Crebough there was a huge carbuncle, that, of a dark night, lit up the rocks under the lake and showed the palaces and towers of the ould ancient city that the waters covered.——How Darby got his "garden"—a group of barren rocks in the Lower Lake. He asked ould Lord Kinmare to let him cut wattles out o' the trees of Inisfallen. "I will," says my lord, "as many as ye plase between an hour before and an hour after midnight." So Darby took him at his word, and went to work. But no sooner did he touch the bark of one of the blessed trees, than he was whisked away in a whirlwind, and flung with a skinful of broken bones upon the bit of bare rock that we call Darby's Garden to this day.——How a holy hermit fell into sin, and did a hard penance for seven long years, just where the trees under Mucross dip into the water. He walked straight into the lake, and stuck his holly-stick into the gravel at the bottom, and made a vow never to leave the spot until the kippen threw out branches and leaves. And for seven years he stood there, without sleep or food; till at last the stick blossomed, and in one night became a grate tree, and then the holy hermit knew he was pardoned; and 'twas he that did the wonderful cures from that day out, till all the country was running after the "Hermit of the holly-tree."——How the first O'Donoghue was a tall slip of a boy; and he was sitting in his ould nurse's cottage, when she set up a screech that the O'Sullivans were staling the cattle. So up he gets, pulls an ould sword out of the thatch, and kills every mother's son of the thieving blaguards. When the fight was over, up comes his gilly, and "Didn't we do that nately?" says he; and "Were you helping me?" says O'Donoghue. "I was," says the gilly. So with that, O'Donoghue goes out and sticks one of the dead men agin the wall, with his eyes staring open, and his spear in his fist; and he calls to the gilly, "Kill me that big fellow," says he; and the gilly was frightened, and tried to skulk off. "I knew ye were a coward," says O'Donoghue; and hauged him on the next tree.——How the Englishman inquired of a Kerry peasant, by what means Ireland happened to have so many mountains—to which the Kerry boy made answer thus, "Ye see, Ireland being the finest and the best country in the world, in coorse was the last country that Nature made; and when Ireland was finished, Nature had a dale o' stuff to spare; so she left it there—and that makes the mountains."——How the giant Eel, that lives in a goulden palace in Lough Kittane, walked one midsummer night into the Lower Lake, kicking up a bobbery in the halls of the O'Donoghue; for which impidence the Eel is chained for ten thousand years to the rock we call O'Donoghue's Prison; and many's the man that's heard its moans, and seen the water rise and fall above it, as it twirled and twisted, trying to squeeze itself out of its handcuffs.——How Fin Mac Cool fought at Ventry Harbour, the battle that continued without interruption three hundred and sixty-six days. And Dulav Dura, the champion of the Monarch of the world, slain six hundred of Fin's best troops in six days, all in single combat; so Fin successively killed Fion M'Cuskeen Lounibunig, Finaughlaugh Trackluskeen, and the champion Dulav Dura; and fought so long and so lustily that his limbs would have fallen asunder if they hadn't been kept together by his armour; till, in the end, Fin totally destroyed his enemies, and took possession of the field with trumpets sounding, drums beating, and colours flying, having been fighting for it one whole year and a day.——How Macgillicuddy of the Reeks was a boy or gilly to the Mac Carthy Mor; and he went into Connaught to seek his fortune; and he fell in love with a young lady, and she with him; and he boasted to her father that he had more ricks than the father's land could grow hay enough to cover with haybands; so the father sent a messenger into Kerry to know the truth of his riches, and whether the young stranger had the grate fortune he spoke about. And, to be sure, the daughter gave the messenger a hint; so he thraveiled to Kerry, and saw young Macgillicuddy's father ating his dinner on his knees, with heaps of rats all about the cabin he lived in; so he goes back and tells the fair maid's father, that the Macgillicuddy had more live cattle about him than he could count, and was ating off a table he wouldn't part with for half Connaught. So, in coorse, the boy got the girl.——How Ossian used to see white horses riding through his fields. "So," says he, "by Jakers, the next time they come I'll mount one of 'em," says he. And he did. And they took him to the Thierna na oge—that's the land of eternal youth; and a mighty pleasant place he found it, wid beautiful ladies, fresh and fair as a May morning. Only after a while, "I'll go home," says he, "just to ax how my friends are." "Och, they're dead!" says the king; "dead these fifteen hundred years," says he. "Pooh!" says Ossian; "sure I haven't been here more than a year?" "Well, go and see," says the king; "mount one o' my white horses; but mind, if ye get off his back, ye'll be ould, shrivelled, and withered," says he, "and not the fine bould gorsoon ye are now." So Ossian went; and he wondered greatly to see such a many ould castles in ruins—for ye see, yer honours, 'twas after Cromwell went through the country like a blast; bad luck to his seed, breed, and generation; Amin! Well, Ossian meets an ould clargy, going home to holy Aghadoe, and he trying to lift a sack o' corn on his back; and "help," says he, "for the sake o' the Virgin." "Faiks, I will, honest man," says Ossian; "for the sake of virgin or married woman, or widdy," says he; for ye see Ossian was a hathen, and didn't know what the holy father meant by "the Virgin." So he leaped off his horse, and in a moment he was an ould, shrivelled, withered man, oulder looking a dale than the priest he was going to help wid the sack o' corn. So the blessed monk of Aghadoe knew that the spell of the enchantment was broke; and he convarted Ossian—made a Christian of him on the spot: and by the same token, it was to a dale finer and better country than the Thierna na oge, that Ossian was carried that same night.—— How the blessed Abbot of Inisfallen walked for two hundred years about the little island that wasn't a mile round. And the way of it was this:—He was praying one morning early, before the sun was up; and he heard a little bird singing so sweetly out of a holly-tree, that he rose from his knees and followed it, listening to the music it was making; and the little bird flew from bush to bush, singing all the while, and the holy father following, for so sweet and happy was the song of the little bird, that he thought he could listen to it for ever; so where it flew he went; and when it changed its place, he was again after it, the little bird singing all the while, and the holy father listening with his ears and his heart. At length the abbot thought it was nearing vesper time; and he blessed the little bird and left it. When he stepped back to his convent, what should he see and hear but strange faces and strange voices; the tongue of the Sassenach in lieu of the wholesome Irish. And the monks asked him what right had he to wear the habit of the holy Augustines? And so he told them his name, that he was their abbot, and that he had been since day-break following the music of the little bird that was singing sweetly among the branches of the holly-tree. And they made answer, that two hundred years ago the holy abbot had left the convent, and was never heard of afterwards—and that now the heretic and the stranger was ould Ireland's king. So the holy father said, "Give me absolution, some of ye, for my time is come;" and they gave him absolution: and just as the breath was laving him, they heard at the lattice window the sweetest song that ever bird sung; and they looked out and saw it, with the sun shining on its wings that were as white as snow; and while they were watching it, there came another bird; and they sung together for a while out of the holly-tree, and then both flew up into the sky; and they turned to the holy father—and he was dead.

But we have surely stayed too long at Inisfallen—"fair Inisfallen!"—we must away among the other islands. There are few, however, and none of them remarkable. Here is O'Donoghue's Prison, a rock covered with a thick layer of peat, and containing only a single stunted tree; here, on the other hand, is Lamb Island, a mass of underwood and finely-grown forest trees. Here is the tiny morsel of evergreen called Mouse Island; the chances are that we shall see a craven cormorant issue from its half a yard of sedge.* Passing Brown or Rabbit Island—so called from the myriads of coneys that formerly peopled it, and were all drowned in a single night by a sudden flood—and leaving the river Laune a mile or so to the right, we cross the lake to visit O'Sullivan's Waterfall. Many prefer it to that of Old Tore; it has a more solitary character; has been evidently left more completely to self-government: there is, in short, more of nature about it. Rowing southward, we pass Stag Island, then Burnt Island, and pause a minute or two to look at "Darby's Garden"—a low ledge of rocks, out of which grow a few meagre arbutus-trees. Here we are again right under Glena Mountain, floating through Glena Bay, looking once more at Glena Cottage, and listening yet again to the echoes of Glena—beautiful Glena!

We have a choice of water-paths into the Lake—one straight before us, under Brickeen Bridge, the other round by Dinis Island, passing again through the narrow channel, which extorted a compliment from the great Magician of the North. Let us enter Tore by one way, and pass out of it by the other.

And now for a rich treat—a delicious termination to a day of luxury—A Row ROUND TORE LAKE. We have already made some reference to this great pleasure; but probably the Tourist will have postponed it until visiting the Islands. Some time or other it must be enjoyed, and this day cannot be closed better. Luckily it is evening. Bright and glorious as the Lakes look in sunshine, there is something sweetly soothing in a row upon their waters just as the twilight is deepening into night. Fortunately, we asked Spillane if Tore had any echoes. "Of course," he said, "it had; but so few, comparatively speaking, went round Tore Lake, that its echoes were not so celebrated as they deserved to be."

The evening was clear and grey; and our boatmen, Myles Mac Sweeny and the elder Hurley—just the boatmen fitted for the scene—knowing when to keep silence, and most anxious to arouse and display all the Lions of the Lakes for the Tourist's enjoyment.

Respectfully Spillane saluted Tore Mountain, as we entered his domain, with one of his native airs. There was neither ripple on the lake, nor breeze from the mountain—all was hushed: there was a pause—lowly and faithfully were the notes echoed: another pause—more faintly it sounded in the distance: another pause—the echo this time was imperfect in the semitones; but faint though the next repetition was, it seemed correct.

And now we are fairly in the lake—shut in by those "eternal hills;" our oars skim the water, so that we go very gently along—softly, and then pause, our boatmen resting on their oars, while Spillane again summons the "air-maidens," by the magic sound of the "Meeting of the Waters." At the end of each bar he pauses, and then it is repeated—again—and again the answer comes in the luscious voice of "Sweet echo—sweetest nymph!" The Tore Waterfall appeared but as a silver ripple, straying down the mountain. We thought of the delicious view we had enjoyed

---

* Cormorants were formerly great pests of the Lakes; but Mr. Herbert has taken care to thin their ranks by ordering his gamekeepers to shoot them wherever seen. They used to destroy enormous quantities of fish. Their successors are "*the cross-fishers;*" i.e. unfair anglers, who do incalculable mischief to the fishery. This atrocious mode of poaching is thus practised:—Two boats go out, each with a line, rod, and reel; their lines are joined and depending upon them are a score, sometimes threescore, of flies. A vast number of fish are thus hooked; and several are landed, although a large proportion of them escape, in consequence of the inutility of skill to "play" them. It is a butchering libel on the art; and an angler who practises it ought to be expelled the "gentle craft."

from the top of that same Fall, and how the lake looked from the summit of mighty Mangerton, the water over which we were then floating seeming as if it would all hold in the palm of a giant's hand! The Tore cottage was seen to great advantage, its smooth lawns undulating, and then extending to the lake, the smoke curling up the mountain, imparting a *silent life* to the landscape, while suddenly the dinner-bell rang forth its cheerful summons, and then the boatmen plied their oars bravely, for we were anxious to view the caves on the opposite side.

These caves are exceedingly picturesque, the summit frequently so slightly covered with clay, that you wonder how the trembling London-pride can find sustenance. Having been introduced, of course, to "Jackey Buee,"—Yellow Jackey, a "manly-looking rock"—we proceeded slowly round the lake, examining first one cave and then another, until, when we came again beneath the mountain, our boatmen paused:—"Now, Mr. Spillane!" said Myles, "now's a fine time for the laugh—O'Donoghue's laugh." There was an instant hush, while Spillane rose, and, placing his bugle to his lips, blew strongly a succession of discords—an imitation of what might be called "Satanic laughter." Crash, crash it went, and roused the angry echoes, which repeatedly, now loudly, now faintly, then in the distance—far, far off—the phantom-like sounds. Certainly, it was most unearthly music—ringing sharply, and then deeply—as if the echoes, retired to their slumbers, were enraged at a rude waking; and their voices gave existence to a succession of bitter curses.

Out again we issue, right across the lake, on our homeward voyage. Once more we pass by Inisfallen; once again we listen to Spillane, as he plays, while we repeat the words,

"Isle of beauty, fare thee well!"

But although our row round the lake was after sunset, it does not follow that others will postpone it to an hour so late. Those who are voyaging earlier may row by Inisfallen, and enter the river Laune—the river where the naiads meet the mermaidens of Old Ocean; for it connects Killarney with the broad Atlantic.

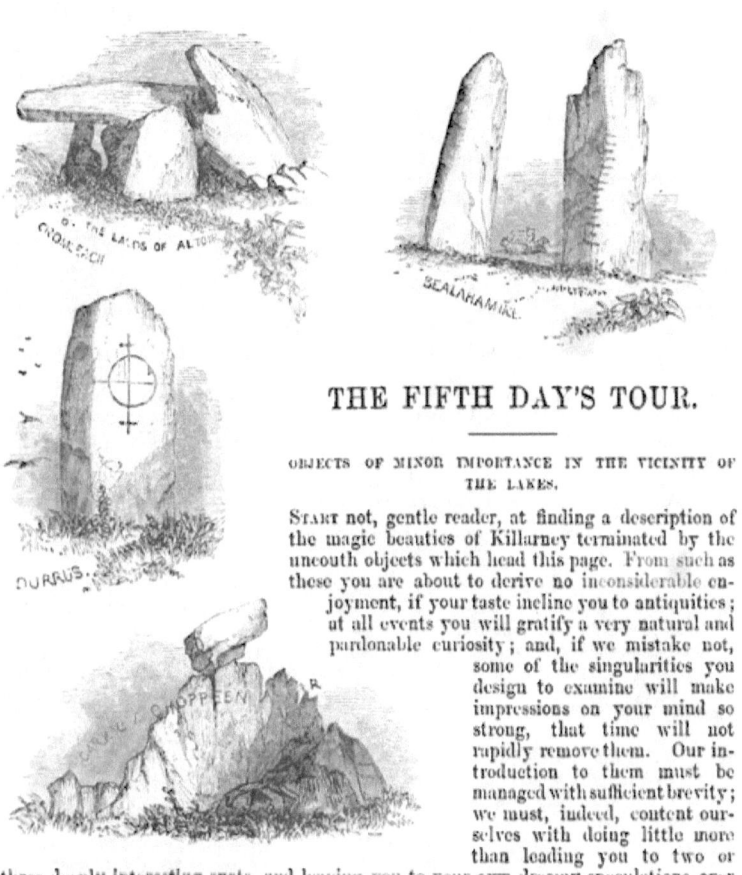

THE FIFTH DAY'S TOUR.

OBJECTS OF MINOR IMPORTANCE IN THE VICINITY OF THE LAKES.

START not, gentle reader, at finding a description of the magic beauties of Killarney terminated by the uncouth objects which head this page. From such as these you are about to derive no inconsiderable enjoyment, if your taste incline you to antiquities; at all events you will gratify a very natural and pardonable curiosity; and, if we mistake not, some of the singularities you design to examine will make impressions on your mind so strong, that time will not rapidly remove them. Our introduction to them must be managed with sufficient brevity; we must, indeed, content ourselves with doing little more than leading you to two or three deeply interesting spots, and leaving you to your own dreamy speculations over themes and heroes of many centuries ago. The value of Killarney to the Tourist is unquestionably augmented by the fact that the

"Work of Druid hands of old"

may be inspected in the midst of so many natural beauties.

About two miles from Killarney, and a quarter of a mile perhaps from the main road, is the singular Cuiart or circle of Loisavigeen. It is situated in the centre of a field, near the summit of a hill, and consists of "seven low upright dallans, or pillar-stones, each between three and four feet in height, and forming a small court, the diameter of which is fourteen feet; that of the outer earthen circle is thirty-four feet." (We adopt the measurement of Mr. Windele.) About sixty feet south of the entrenchment stand two other dallans, the tallest of which is eleven feet high. They stand nearly east and west, and are distant from each other seven feet. Circularity in their stone monuments was a favourite form with the pagan Irish. It is observed not only in their temples, such as these circles and fire-towers, but even in their dwellings, their Cahirs, forts, &c.

The hill overlooks the Glen of Ahahunning. It is a pretty glen. Through the soft grass and moss appear numberless grey stones, which the people say were used in fairy warfare. It is planted with trees, which thicken into a wood if you follow the winding of the river to any distance. At one side the banks slope to the water, on the other they are abrupt and broken into ravines. A pretty gentle little girl guided us to both the hill and the glen, and to the tree that has a melancholy notoriety amongst the peasantry, from the fact of a young and beautiful woman having hung herself from its branches—a rare occurrence in Ireland. "You see, ma'am," said the girl, "that it happened, when the wood was first planted, that one of the Mac Sweeneys deluded a poor young girl from some part of Munster into this glen, promising to make her his wife, which he could not do, for a reason that he had a wife of his own. When she found how it was, her heart was crushed altogther; and stealing out into the glen, she cut those words, as you will see, upon the stone:—

'Mac Sweeney took me from my place;
May he, like me, meet sure disgrace.'

And then she hung herself out of the bough of the tree—the largest tree in the wood it was then: and now you see—for there it is—it is the smallest; it never grew a stroke since—a stunted, ugly tree."

No wonder the tree should have a legend attached to it, for it is very singular. Every branch, no matter how small, has a crooked bend; and certainly, at its foot lies a stone, on which a little trouble will clearly trace the couplet our little guide repeated to us. There is nothing traditionary in that.

The Tourist is on his way to Glenflesk; and let him visit it. Its beauty will amply repay the trouble, to say nothing of the interest attached to "Labig-Owen" —the Bed of Owen—a huge crevice in Phil-a-dhaoun, the Demon's Cliff. It is a "good step" from the road, up a very steep hill, or rather a succession of rocks— some pointed, others flat and smooth; here and there the foot sinks into patches of bog, and the hands grasp for help the feathery birch-boughs or gigantic heather. The way to the "Labig," the "easy way," as it was called, is greatly intersected by roots of trees, crossing and recrossing the various passes, some overgrown with moss; while from every crevice spring up the broad green leaves and thin transparent stems and blossoms of the London-pride. When near the summit the visitor will look down upon the valley, which from this point of view is of exceeding beauty; the straggling course of the tremulous river is masked, and its murmurs supply appropriate music; while the opposite sides of the mountain show their bared and craggy sides, in contrast to the rich but wild luxuriance of the foliage at our feet. At length, by climbing, scrambling, and crawling, the foot of the Outlaw's Rock is reached. A ladder having been previously obtained at one of the surrounding cottages, the "bed" is entered. It is a flat space of about twelve feet square in the side of the hill; a crevice is pointed out as the sleeping-place, and a jutting rock as the table of the outlaw. A safer asylum can scarcely be imagined; it is completely screened by naturally planted trees, some of which are very aged; completely inaccessible on three sides; and on the fourth the entrance might be defended by one man against a hundred. Here several outlaws have taken shelter; the last was a commonplace murderer, about fifty years ago: to an earlier seeker of its protection, however, an interesting story is attached.

Owen, the real hero of the Phil-a-dhaoun, was of the noble race of the Mac Carthys, and, as in duty bound, an ally of the O'Donoghues of the Glens. He was a rover of the most daring character, a man of great personal strength and beauty, bold and brave, possessing the qualities which even now exercise an almost unbounded influence over the Irish peasant. It is said that one of his followers was so devoted to him, that he left kith and kin to companion his wanderings; and when trouble (*i.e.* justice) was in pursuit of the mountaineer, and he found it necessary to retreat like the fox to his lair, or the eagle to his eyry, when he made Phil-a-dhaoun his resting-place, and slept upon the heather-covered rock, his friend would sit at the entrance to the cave and watch his slumbers. With the assistance of this untiring comrade he kept possession of the heights, the peasantry supplying him with food, placing goat'-milk, oaten cakes, and whisky in the crevices of the rocks, or beneath the thick moss. Thus he subsisted for a long time; but although a price was set upon his head, he became weary of restraint, and also thought that by retiring into the wilder and deeper glens of Iveleary he might withdraw suspicion from his favourite Phil-a-dhaoun. His follower resolved to maintain his post, so as to divert attention, and enable Owen to make good his retreat to the house of one Reardon, in the glens of Iveleary, who, while professing the greatest devotion to the outlaw, cherished a bitter hatred towards him. The determined bravery and great personal strength of Owen Mac Carthy prevented the false coward from resorting to open violence; but he resolved to ensnare what he dared not combat: he placed the bed of the gigantic glensman over a trap-door, and when he slept secure in the hospitality of an Irish roof, Reardon and his accomplices lowered the bed, murdered their guest, and cut off his head. The disgrace of this cold-blooded and treacherous action clings to them still, for the Reardons of that district are still called *Reardane na ceau*, meaning "Reardon of the head." Owen's faithful follower, who had remained at the *Labig*, when he heard of the murder flung himself off the ledge in a fit of despair, and was found dead among the rocks in the glen.

The Tourist should return from Glenflesk by the old road, which, leaving to the right the ancient Castle of Killaha, runs for some distance by the side of, or at least not far from, Lough Kittane. It is a barren lake on the eastern side of Mangerton, or rather at the base of Crochan Mountain, and is supplied by the streams which run from both; its own waters are poured into the Flesk by the river Finou. The pedestrian may examine many magnificent objects among the neighbouring glens. We refer to it chiefly to indicate the locality of a wonderful cave, or rather series of caves, of which we may claim the merit of discovery. Raths abound in the neighbourhood of Killarney ; and our curiosity was naturally excited to ascertain if any one of them contained excavations—which it is said are the common characteristics of all.*

It was rumoured that an ancient house of the O'Donoghues, in this vicinity, was abandoned soon after it was built, as "unlucky," in consequence of the builder's erecting it "convenient to a Rath." This was a clue: we followed it up, and, under the guardianship of "Sir Richard," proceeded to make our inquiries. The result was the proceeding about half a mile from this ruined house, with half a score of candles, and a couple of stout fellows with spades. We found the Rath easily—a green mound on the summit of a small hill, perfectly circular, the circle formed by a hedge of mould ; of the artificial character of which there could be no doubt. We saw what we supposed to be the entrance to the chambers underneath ; it was nearly in the middle of the enclosure, and open as they all are—to the east. With some difficulty we persuaded our workmen to aid us in the task of clearing away the stones that had been flung into this opening. After a couple of hours' hard labour, we had the satisfaction to find the passage clear, and wide enough to admit the body of a man.† As the service was one of some little danger, we drew lots with Sir Richard who should adventure first. The task fell to him. Lighting each a couple of candles, and bearing each a small stick, we entered as nearly together as we could. Having descended about ten yards—a gradual slope—there was a sort of landing, upon which we took rest: the passage was so narrow that we could not sit upright.

The descent was resumed. Presently some loosened stones fell, and informed us that beneath us there was water: about twelve yards lower, and to this water we came. The stick assured us that its depth was not dangerous ; and so, into the cave we went—the first of human beings, most probably, who had entered it for two thousand years. The cave was a perfect circle, about sixty feet in diameter, and in height not above five feet; we could not stand upright: the water was about two feet deep, so that, unfortunately, it was impossible for us to ascertain if any object of interest was to be found on the floor, for the water became mudded very rapidly.‡ Probably some remains of bones might have been discovered ; for the best authorities seem to consider these excavations sepulchral. Peering about us, we perceived a hole that looked like a fox-hole. It was, however, barely big enough for us to crawl through ; and we entered another cave, smaller, but similar in form and character. Another such passage led us into another such cave. We could find only these three,

---

* There is no object which the peasantry regard with so much superstitious dread as the Rath, from the belief that it is the especial property of the fairies. It is difficult to find a labourer who can be tempted by any reward to put his spade into one of them. They have consequently remained undisturbed for ages; and often a large space is therefore suffered to continue an unprofitable waste in the centre of a fertile meadow. Stories in abundance are told of punishments that have followed attempts to open or level these Raths, and of scenes and objects witnessed by persons who have unconsciously slept beside them, or passed them at night. They are always circular. They are vulgarly attributed to "the Danes." That they are structures of very remote antiquity is apparent from the circumstances of their being found in places where the Danes never settled; as also from the cromlechs and stone circles sometimes found on their summits, plainly identifying them with the age of heathenism.

† One of the men caught a very severe cold, in consequence of his visit below; and of course his illness was attributed to the effects of the curse upon all who put a spade in a Rath.—It is the invariable custom to fill up all such openings: first, because it is considered unlucky to the land to leave them open : and next, because occasionally they break the legs of cattle, whose feet stumble in them.

‡ The weather had been exceedingly wet for some days before our visit ; water had therefore made its way into the cave ; but that in dry seasons there was no water there, we had conclusive proof. On examining closely, we found the sides of the cave scraped in a singular manner, the marks being evidently fresh ; a little reflection convinced us that this arose from the rabbits, who had made their way in, and had been searching about to find a way out.

but have no doubt that others exist; indeed, we felt quite certain that another hole in the Rath, much about the size and character of the one we opened, would lead to precisely the same results—the discovery of a line of subterranean chambers; and we have little doubt that they go all round the hill. An old man pointed our attention to a spot somewhat distant, both from the entrance we explored, and that to which we now call attention, which he said he recollected to be named "the chimney," and which assuredly was an opening into a room under ground. The chambers we explored appeared to have been merely scooped out, and in a very rough manner; there was no evidence of the exercise of skill, except that the corners of two of the rooms were formed by a wall of uncemented stones, each about 14 inches by 7, and evidently selected with some care. These had been laid one above another from the floor to, we imagine, within two feet of the roof; they of course passed considerably higher than the rooms, which, as we have observed, were only five feet high.

A question will naturally occur—what was the motive for forming this singular, and apparently useless, excavation? if constructed for human habitation, it would be difficult to devise one more unnaturally uncomfortable. In fact, no one who examines this series of chambers will for a moment entertain the idea that they were formed for human beings to live in. To determine their uses—whether for concealment, for religious rites, or for sepulchral purposes—must rest with others. This cave, so near a neighbourhood where many persons will have leisure to gratify curiosity, may be considered as an acquisition of some value to the locality.

We have still another Druidic remain to introduce to the reader. Those who walk in Lord Kenmare's beautiful demesne should on no account omit to visit the famous "CLOUGH-NA-CUDDY," the stone of Cuddy. It is surrounded by trees, chiefly hawthorn, of immense age and growth, and planted in a circle. From time immemorial this stone has been considered holy by the peasantry. It is visited continually by the ailing—the blind particularly, who wash their eyes with the water contained in two holes here indicated.

When the Tourist has examined CLOUGH-NA-CUDDY, the circle of Loisavigeen, the Logan Stone in the Gap, the Ogham Library, and our cave, he will have, perhaps, a clearer notion of the works of the Druids than he can have within an equally limited space elsewhere.

CLOUGH-NA-CUDDY.

Another of the beautiful drives about Killarney is the drive to Lord Kenmare's Deer Park. The road to the right leads to a very extensive view, but that to the left conducts to a delicious little glen, through which the coquettish Deenagh meanders—dimpling, and brawling, and eddying.

Let no one leave Killarney without rowing a mile or two down the Laune, and visiting DUNLOE CASTLE by water;—as we did, in the "gloaming" of a summer evening, when the lake was calm—the grey fly floating on its surface, and the salmon and trout springing from the waters. As you turn into the Laune, the current flows so silently that you wonder how it is you rush past the ferry, and then float on through a wilderness of water-beauty. The river widens at each side into little bays, over-arched by trees of the most luxuriant growth, and foliage of every tint; then turns, so that you get another view of the mountains of the Gap to the left; while on the right all is of the most soft and sylvan beauty; then "the bittern sounds his drum,"

"Booming from the sedgy shallow;"

or a heron flaps past; or the grey hawk screams from the mountains; and the small shriek of the plover is answered by the plunge which the wild duck or the coot makes into the water—disturbed from the rushes by the stroke of our oar, fall it ever so lightly; or perchance an eagle comes soaring from the cliffs, where his eyry has been time out of mind, not deigning to notice the world beneath; the small trout spring on both sides, so that the river is dimpled all over; every bush and brake is full of existence:—you hear the low of the mountain cattle, and the bleat of the wild goat; and you see the thin wreath of cottage smoke toiling through the atmosphere; and then there are fresh bays, and creeks, and huge trees lying almost across the stream; and a troop of ponies shake their ragged manes at you, and then neigh and gallop into the thicket; and the clouds that float above you, and above the glorious Reeks, are "fresh from the pavilion of the setting sun,"—some pale as the leaves of mountain-roses, or tinged with a faint primrose, or so filmy, and white, and tender, that you see the blue sky beyond them, and a star or two glancing therein; and then—but here stands the castle on its bold promontory above the river—a firm, fearless looking keep, approached by a steep hill-road, recalling one of the Rhine towers.

When we re-entered our boat, the mists were rolling up; the mountains, and the water, and atmosphere, appeared of the same tone of colour—almost of the same quality. Occasionally a distant bugle would tell the return of some party who had been rowing on the lake. As we passed the ferry, we could hear the chorus of a song, while the figures of the singers were dim and "phantasmagoriac." On the flat beyond, lights sparkled through the windows of the picturesque residence on "Mahony's Point;" and so dim and indistinct had all things become before we reached the landing Pier, that the glancing lights in our hotel seemed dancing in mid-air.

There must be limits to every human work; and in book-making they are specially prescribed. Our space is exhausted before the subject.* Yet we cannot conclude our

---

* Among the inducements to visit the Lakes, there is one we cannot omit to notice. For a description of it we must draw upon a friend, as we were not ourselves fortunate enough to witness it: we allude to one of Killarney's far-famed stag-hunts. Our visits to the Lakes were paid during months when the young fawns were about, and when a "stag hunt" was impossible without doing much mischief. It is not generally known that the mountains abound with red deer. Tore alone contains many, and in the summer evenings they may be heard belling on all sides of its lake. The hounds are now kept by Mr. Herbert;—a famous pack, well suited to the wildness of these glens. The place of meeting on this occasion was Derricunnihy, the beautiful cascade on the Upper Lake. The morning was fine, and we procured one of the many fine boats which are to be hired at Killarney. They were all in requisition: nothing could surpass the beauty of the scene as we threaded along the various windings between the Upper and Lower Lakes; boats, lustily manned, filled with ladies, whose gay attire and cheerful faces caused even the mountains to sing with pleasure,—for a merry laugh from each boat as it passed the far-famed Eagle's Nest was returned tenfold by its echoes, which kept up a constant reply to the view-halloo of the boatmen, the bugle of the helmsman, and the fainter cadence of the female voice. At length we reached the Upper Lake, and were surprised at the number, beauty, and appointments of the various boats;—Lord Headley's with his crew, Mr. O'Connell's, O'Sullivan's, &c., &c., the flags bearing their respective mottoes, all eagerly awaiting the moment of action. At length Mr. Herbert arrived in a splendid cutter, manned by some old college friends, himself pulling stroke—his blue banner bearing the title of his bark, the "Colleen Dhas" (the beautiful maid). The hounds were now laid on, and soon made the echoes ring with their music. We pulled along shore parallel with their cry; at length we turned into a bay at the bottom of the lake, and then lay-to by the advice of our boatmen. We had scarcely reached the spot when the helmsman raised his hand in silence, and pointed towards the glens; we saw a majestic stag bounding towards us. Within a few yards of our boat he dashed into the lake, and was quickly followed by the hounds, tracking him with fatal accuracy. They soon reached the opposite shore, and climbed the mountain side; at length the bugle sounded, and a hundred voices proclaimed that the monarch of Tore had fallen. The novelty of the scene, the excitement of the peasantry, the beauty of the rowing—all contributed to render interesting this novel pastime.

introduction to "the Lakes" without giving some account of that which every Tourist is pretty nearly certain to encounter—A WET DAY.

We shall picture one—or rather two—and require no aid from fancy.

Pour—pour—pour—a thorough day of Killarney rain—pour—pour—pour—unceasingly. The noble trees of Mucross absolutely bend beneath the weight of waters. The cock who crowed so proudly yesterday, and carried his tail as if it were a banner, has just tottered past, his crested neck stooped, and his long feathers trailing in the mud;—the hens have disappeared altogether. The pigs!—no one ever did see a pig at liberty about Cloghreen; compulsory stay-at-homes! We are at the hotel—"The Herbert Arms"—and there, in our pleasant chamber, this is written. There is a pony waiting to carry some one up to Mangerton—his ears laid back, and the water flowing down his sides. Three of the glen girls, with their goats'-milk and potteen, have stood for at least two hours under what, in ordinary weather, would be called "the shelter of the trees,"—but now the trees look as if they themselves wanted shelter. And so the glen girls—with their yellow streaming hair—and piggins, and bottles, and cracked tea-cups—have disappeared. Dill, poor little fuzzy-faced dog, has crept into the parlour, wet and shivering—and is now looking up at the fire, composed of logs of holly and huge lumps of turf—in a *distrait* sort of way—not grinning, as usual, the nearest approach to a human laugh we ever saw on a dog's face. The men who passed and repassed yesterday, carrying hampers of turf slung across their shoulders—what has become of them? certainly they did not hurry at their occupation, but took it easy—"very asy;" lounging along in a somnambulist sort of style, indicative of a strong desire for repose. A few of the village children have passed to the pretty school; and they have either galloped through the rain like young rough-shod colts, or gone in detachments—threes and fours—sheltered beneath their mother's cloak—a moving tent of grey or blue cloth. Everything appears shivering and nerveless—Nature's energies seem washed away—the calf that was "mooing" all yesterday to its mother has not the spirit now to move its tasselled tail, or raise its ears, or ask for a drop of milk. The gentle patient "fishing gentleman," whom three years ago we left in a boat on Tore Lake, and discovered on the very same spot this summer—he whose name is never mentioned without a blessing—has come forth—looked up—shook his head twice at the clouds—then disappeared altogether, to tie flies—or perhaps count, as we have been doing, the number of rain-drops hanging from the window-frame—and wondering which will fall first. A little shock-headed girl, whose wild eyes glitter from out her hair, her cloak hanging in what artists call *wet drapery* around her, has just brought in news that the bridge is under water.—"The Flesk Bridge!" we repeat in astonishment. "No, de road ladin' from Klarney town to de bridge." "And how did you come?" "Trough de water." The little girl's arrival is an event; for we seem shut in from every external thing this morning, save the sound of the pouring rain: even the arbutus girls, Killarney "accompaniments," have not made their appearance. If we open a book we cannot read, for we are watching to see if there is any chance of the clouds breaking; we look out of the window, grumbling, and discontented, instead of being thankful that we are not undergoing quarantine in the dirty beggar-crowded town of Killarney, instead of at the pretty hotel at Cloghreen—or, as it was once called, Droumirourk—at the foot of broad-backed Mangerton, almost within sound of the thunder of Tore Waterfall, and opposite the bowers and groves of Mucross. How different is the soft splashy sound of the bare-footed peasants, who, at long intervals, slop past the windows, to the sharp clinking pattens of English dwellers in country villages! We have heard no baying from the deep-mouthed hounds this morning, though usually they make the village ring with it—especially if either Spillane or Gandsey sounds a bugle. If the rain ceases even for a minute, thrush and blackbird burst into a loud song of joy—and Jerry Connor, most attentive of waiters, watchful of the weather, pops in to tell us, "that though it's a terrible rain intirely for the time of year—glory be to God!—yet the glass is rising, or—going to rise." Then our landlord comes in with the information, that never was anything so magnificent as the boiling flood at the Old Weir Bridge caused by last night's storm; and that we really must drive to Dinis Island, and see it—no matter "the pour;" we might come to Killarney a hundred times—and never see the Old Weir in such real glory; the foresters have been in the woods since daybreak, tearing away the branch-wracks of the hurricane; and the torrent wreaths itself into foam—curling above the arches. Our landlord says it is worth enduring a week's confinement from rain and storm to see the Lakes fuller than they have been for twenty years; to see the Old Weir foaming and shaking—and to see Tore Waterfall dashing down his eighty-foot torrent—with as much zeal and energy as if he "was got up" to please the Queen! It is therefore decided that though the rain pours as violently as ever; that though Jerry—always ready to hope in the very teeth of despair—can only say he thinks "the glass has a *mind* to rise;" still we are to drive to Dinis Island in a covered car—and there get out and look at the Old Weir in his "flurry." At what hour are we to set out? Our guide, good Sir Richard, said at twelve; but then comes the question, by which of the TWO CLOCKS are our movements to be decided? Our landlord shook his head and smiled—he, or some one else, had regulated the clocks yesterday; and yet—the clocks would not keep together!

Clocks have been remarkable for having a will and a way of their own since their invention: one would almost fancy it impossible for so much obstinacy to be enclosed in such proper, discreet-looking mahogany cases. But these *two clocks* appear to us to be more opposed to each other's opinions than any clocks we ever met before. When first we came, if the hall clock struck three, the clock on the landing would remain most obstinately silent for about three quarters of an hour, when it would, in a loud and decided tone of voice, proclaim the hour to be two; in another quarter the hall commander would maintain the justness of his own opinion by striking four, which statement the landing clock would reply to some time after by saying it was three; the housemaids seemed to think the landing clock was the most correct, because "it was the ouldest." The waiter, Jerry, put faith in neither, but, treating both with disrespect, always appealed to his "own repater," which he said kept good Cork time. We thought the cook must have had an oracle of her own, for she certainly did not keep time either with the hall or the landing. The three-quarters opposition had ceased during the last two days: but the two clocks had gone off on another tack; the hall clock would begin gravely and soberly to tell forth the hour, and, supposing it was five, when it struck as far as three, whir! bang! the landing clock would begin—strike, strike, strike, as fast as possible, until it got on to the insane number of thirteen or fifteen, when, as if out of breath from the exertion, it would make a sudden pause, and then mutter one or two click clicks, as much as to say, "I talked him down." We asked the housemaid what she had to say to her favourite after that; and she replied, that "the hands were right enough, but that it had grown weak inside from hard work." The clocks were evidently of opposite parties, so opposed to each other that they would not work together: whatever one proclaimed right, the other protested to be wrong. The one in the hall had four anchors at the four corners of its fair clean face, emblematic, doubtless, of its maker's hope that it would keep good time. There are castles and a ship at the top—Black Rock Castle, perhaps; the maker's name, "James Byrom, Cork," a right good name. Now for the one, the opposition clock, that will not hear what his neighbour has to say, but *will* talk him down; while the other, just as violently, continues on his own course. The landing clock is simply ornamented with a bunch of roses, "James Byrom, Cork!" both by the same maker, both made in the same town, both probably by the same hands, both perhaps out of the very same tree!—yet—no harmony between them; rather than go together they will both go wrong: if the clockmaker set them alike, and we think they are proceeding harmoniously together, some shake, or "filthy pebble in the wheel of justice," is sure to set them at loggerheads again: if they jog on in clicking amity for half an hour, be sure they differ upon some mite, some flaw, some thread of time, in which neither is right; and so away they go, in error both, and, what is worse, setting the whole house by the ears, because of their trumpery party differences, which, like those of the Big-endians and Little-endians of Gulliver, lead to nothing and end in nothing.

But it is a thing of moment to be ready in time for our car—inculcating a lesson of punctuality in others by being punctual ourselves. So we agree to "never mind" the clocks, but attend to Jerry's watch, which is "always with Cork;" and the driver, Jerry Sullivan, being as quick and anxious to gratify us as the waiter, Jerry Connor, we migrated from the dwelling-house to the covered car. It is a sort of miniature waggon; and though the wind still blows, and the rain still pours, we heed neither, but drive through the Mucross gate. Certainly the Kerry people are the civilest and gentlest in all Ireland—ever ready and good-natured. It pours incessantly; yet the driver, Jerry, heedless of the rain, only hopes we shall get a view of something, for we deserve it. The beautiful cows are grouped under the trees that so often afford them shelter—but now each leaf is a water-spout. We can only distinguish the outline of the Abbey—pour—pour—the lake has overflowed all its banks, and we splash through the water where the road is generally high and dry. Suddenly, as we arrive at Brickeen Bridge, the rain ceases, and while we get out of the car the sun bursts forth through the gorged clouds; the face of nature has a damp, drowned aspect, yet words convey no idea of the effect of the sudden sunshine on the landscape; the view, both to the right and left, created, as it were, in a moment by the sudden burst of light, is magical; the clouds roll up the mountains—woods, hills, valleys, rocks, cascades, are all illuminated: but, in less time than we have taken to write this line, the sun is again enclosed by a wall of black clouds; the vapours pour down the mountains, and we are thankful, as we ought to be, for the shelter of the "covered car." We dash through the drive that girdles the beautiful demesne; up hill and down dale; Jerry pausing every now and then, and exclaiming, "Oh! den, but it is a pity! dere is a beautiful view, just dere!—Well, praise to de Almighty, but it is a wonderful day of rain, and no end to it." We get out at Dinis Island, and walk through the pouring shower to the best point for seeing the Old Weir. Ay! that is indeed worth seeing—it is almost impossible to believe we have ever glided under that arch, as if floating on air; the mountain streams are rushing down on every side; they have roused the lake; torrent meets torrent in fierce encounter; they lash each other, and foam and raise their crested heads, until the Old Weir bridge seems to sink into the raging flood. It is really very glorious—"well worth the trouble?"— yes, certainly—*very* well worth seeing, although it be of all others the thing in nature most distasteful—a beauty in a passion!

Again the rain has ceased—paused suddenly. According to Jerry, "de day has taken up for good;" and, after a little more driving, we arrive at the gate that admits to the path leading to the Tore Waterfall. We climb the ascent, slippery though it is; and certainly the waterfall is magnificent—roaring in its pride of power as it dashes on—one mass of crystal foam over the ledge; we never saw it in such perfection. The surrounding woods are so dark and heavy from recent rain that the foaming torrent looks doubly bright; in general, there is a yellow tone of colour, as if some clayey matter was mingled with the water; but here every drop is clear —pure—transparent—pellucid. From the height where we stand to the lowest fall it is one mass of sparkling crystal: the sunbeams fall occasionally upon the haze that floats like a halo above the falls, imparting the hues of earth's brightest gems to the trembling dews—violet and amber—a hundred tints of light and glory.

As we entered our hotel the clocks were at loud variance; the hall clock deliberately beating three, while that on the landing rattled on—ding—ding—ding—until it paused, from fatigue it is supposed, at twelve.

"The clocks are gone to folly," said Jerry; "but it is well to have a repater in the house that keeps Cork time."

Courteous reader! Has our wet day wearied you? Not, perhaps, if you have been actually shut up, because the pour, pour, has kept you a prisoner; and, if you have had no rain, you have been better occupied than in testing the truth of this picture. We shall try your patience, however; for having described a wet day at Cloghreen, we must, in common fairness, describe one at the Victoria!

We had attended service in the pretty church of Aghadoe. After service we had a delightful drive through the Headley Woods, catching occasional glimpses of the lakes and the surrounding scenery; the coney and the hare crossing the road and bounding up the tangled banks every moment. We hastened through the drives; for the mountains were backed by a deep lurid light, and huge drops of rain splashed amid the trees—mountain mutterings told of the coming storm. We had hardly reached the shelter of our hotel when the thunder began in right down earnest; and glorious it was—commencing behind the Reeks, rushing through the Gap of Dunloe —then, bursting forth anew above the Toomies, and shaking the echoes of Glena, pealing hoarsely through the glens and fastnesses of Mangerton—broad hoary Mangerton!—while the lightning played like a diadem around the beautiful brow of Tore. We sat at the open window of the Victoria, which commanded a panoramic view of the mountains we have named—Inisfallen sleeping in the dark waters of the lake beneath. Every other sound was hushed—even the rail ceased its croaking;—all was silent, save the eagle, whose broken wing secured its liberty in the grounds of the hotel; and as it sat upon the garden-seat, its head outstretched to the mountains, to which it could never soar, it answered each fresh peal of thunder with a scream, bending as if to listen for the echoes, which, rolling amid the mountains, now loudly, now indistinctly, were indeed most glorious! Sometimes the thunder crashed as if one fierce cloud encountered another—and then the royal bird clapped his wing, as if in triumph. We would have given much to have seen him soaring away through the storm—one of the grandest, the boatmen said, they had witnessed for many years.

And now that we have advised the reader how even out of a wet day at Killarney he may obtain some enjoyment, let us bid the pleasant subject farewell; in so far as the Lakes are concerned, that is to say—for we have yet to take the Tourist round the wild sea coast.

The Tourist who follows in our track will not require to be told that we have rendered very insufficient justice to the exceeding beauty of the Killarney Lakes; or that we have passed over some objects of great interest and value, from which he will not fail to derive amusement, instruction, and enjoyment. It is indeed difficult, if it be not actually impossible, to convey a notion of the numerous and wonderful attractions of these Lakes. The pen of the writer and the pencil of the artist will equally fail to picture them, for they are undergoing perpetual changes that cannot be described; and it will not be easy to recognise at noon, or at evening, the scenes that may have been closely examined, and even copied, in the morning; so infinitely varied are the effects produced by the peculiar fluctuations of light and shade that occur over the whole district—the islands, the shores, the water, and the mountains.

Yet, we trust, our main purpose has been worked out;—to supply an agreeable and useful Companion to those who visit the district, and to increase the number of Tourists thither, by exhibiting the almost inexhaustible fund of enjoyment supplied by the "Killarney Lakes."

x

THE TOUR ROUND THE COAST
FROM KILLARNEY.

OUR duty is by no means done, although we have left "the Lakes." We shall ask the reader to accompany us to the wild sea-coast of the south-west, and the Tourist to follow us into a district where the graceful beauties of Killarney may be contrasted with the wild grandeur of scenery certainly unsurpassed in Ireland. That district is now visited by a large number of those who visit Killarney; and one of the special objects of our latest tour was to describe the routes to it, with the facilities for travelling and accommodation; and at the same time, to picture its peculiarities, as well as our limited space and opportunities permit us to do.

In this book we have already described the road between Killarney and Kenmare; that which, passing through Cloghreen, by the Tore Waterfall, close to Derricunnihy, up the hill, to the "Constabulary Barrack," and by the side of Lough Luis-na-earagh, conducts to a wild and barren district, along a good and level road, to the town of Kenmare, distant twenty miles from "the Lakes." * It is from this town we shall begin our tour; although, as we shall explain, the sea-coast may be reached by other routes.

There are, perhaps, few towns in Ireland which possess so many capabilities as KENMARE: the Bay is among the largest, safest, and best; there is a good quay; the river is crossed by a pretty suspension bridge—numerous streams run into it; its situation, as regards England, is convenient; the sea, and rivers, and lakes are stored with fish; it is on the high road from two populous and much frequented districts. In fact, Nature has abundantly enriched Kenmare with all that can furnish wealth and increase prosperity. Yet it has no trade, nor the semblance of any; neither does there seem to be a prospect of turning its vast natural advantages to account, either by fisheries, mines, or manufactures. Yet there is ample evidence of

---

* We adopt the following description of a new road from Kenmare to Killarney, which we regret to say we neglected to visit. "There is also scenery of great beauty to the west of the Lakes of Killarney, at present very little known, partly from want of roads, and partly from want of hotel accommodation. A new road has just been opened by Mr. George Preston White, through his estate, of about two miles in length, near the upper lake, which now enables tourists to drive all round the lakes, which they could not do formerly, and which was a great disadvantage. This new route opens up scenery of the most charming character; the new drive round the lakes is about thirty miles in length, and there is certainly not in the Queen's dominions a more charming tour than this route unfolds. The tourist had better first proceed through the Gap of Dunloe, rather than return that way, because the view which bursts upon the sight on reaching the summit of the Gap, would not have the same effect by reversing the route. It possesses the advantage also of presenting another view of the lakes near Luiscacnagh Lough, which comes suddenly into view, and which does not present the same advantage in coming in the opposite direction. For these and other reasons, therefore, the tourist is recommended first to drive or ride through the Gap of Dunloe, when on reaching the summit of the Gap, that glorious view unexpectedly and suddenly bursts upon the spectator. Here the upper lake is, as it were, mapped out at your feet, displaying its beautifully irregular outline with its wooded islands, whilst on the left, in solemn grandeur, lies the Purple Valley, the most decided approach to the sublime of anything at Killarney." It is intended to build an hotel on this estate; it will add materially to the accommodation and enjoyment of tourists.

unexplored mineral wealth; the productive mines of Berehaven are not far off; and from its lakes into the sea there is wasted water-power sufficient to turn every spindle in Manchester.

Our business, however, is to guide the Tourist on a pleasure excursion, and not to tell him how and where to mourn over the sins against Nature, which those commit who, possessing power to "do good and to distribute," forget that "to whom much is given from him much will be required."

While resting at the comfortable "country" inn at Kenmare, the Tourist (especially if he be an angler) should give a day to the southern side of the bay, visiting the lovely lakes of Clonee, that of Glenmore, the harbour of Killmichaeloge, and the adjacent mountains, from the summit of which we look upon the Bay of Bantry; that beautiful bay is seen on the one side, while the almost as beautiful Bay of Kenmare is in full view on the other. We cannot find space to describe minutely this charming route; but we must say to the Tourist a word or two of entreaty that he will visit the Lakes of Clonee: they are distant but seven miles from Kenmare, and the road to them has many attractions—the mountains to the left, the bay to the right, midway in which is Dinish Island with its ruined church. A rugged hill by-road leads along a wild valley to these lovely lakes. Lower and upper Clonee and Lough Inchiquin are united by small but rapid rivers: they contain islands gracefully wooded. Huge mountains look down upon them; and at the extremity is a rich tract of alluvial soil, on which there is a farmhouse, inhabited by a "strong" farmer, who is ever willing to assist the angler—to lend his boats, to lend his flies, to lend (in the Irish way) his bacon, his potatoes, and his whisky. From all we could learn there is no "water" in Kerry more full of fish—the salmon in their season, the white trout generally, and the brown trout always. The place is little known, and seldom trodden. Fair fishing is free, or at least only taxed by the duty of a message to the agent of the Marquis of Lansdowne, to whom the property belongs. But if the angler threw his fly all day without "a rise," his day will not have been ill-spent if he look about him. From all the hill-sides pour contributory streams:—

" And rushing from their native hills,
The voices of a thousand rills
Come shouting down the mountain sides!"

Tourist or angler, let him ascend the mountain that bounds Lough Inchiquin: visiting on his way the dark and gloomy lake of Napeasta, surrounded by rocky, barren, and precipitous steeps, and completely hemmed in, except at the small opening by which its waters find a passage to the lower lakes. Having climbed this mountain—what a prospect! The view obtained from the summit is indeed sublime; it is scarcely possible to conceive aught grander than the expanse of ocean, lake, and mountain. In the immediate foreground is Kenmare Bay: then appear the Macgillicuddy's Reeks, with the fantastic peaks of Carran Tuel; a little to the right is the Gap of Dunloe, its mountain barriers seeming like huge perpendicular walls; in fact, from this point of view, you look right through "the Gap." To the west are Ballinskellig Bay, the Skellig Rocks, and Valencia Island; and more to the north the magnificent Bay of Dingle, with its great mountain barriers; to the south is Bantry Bay, with Glengariff —the whole district being covered with innumerable mountain lakes. But the leading feature of the scene is the broad ocean, which presents itself, broken by great projecting headlands from this point of view. The journey of a day, made on this, the southern side of Kenmare Harbour, might in truth supply materials for a full volume; but we must hasten back to Kenmare, for it is by the northern road the Tourist will usually travel unless he cross the bay—boats being obtainable at Colleras, Ardgroom, or Ballycrovane—charming bays in miniature, that afford shelter from all winds; they will convey across to Sneem Harbour, where there is a convenient country inn, and where the inn-keeper has a horse and car "ready," or a boat if the Tourist desire to make excursions seaward ; or to visit the opposite, from this, side of the Bay.* But it may be, and is, a question whether on the northern side we may not visit or examine scenery as wonderful and beautiful as that we have described.†

By this—the northern—road the Tourist is on his way round the coast. A mile or two out of Kenmare are the ancient ruins of Dunkerron Castle, once the hospitable seat of the O'Sullivan Mor ; and Cappanacuss, another shattered castle, of the same family. The mind will, however, soon seek and find relief, gazing on the chimney tops of Dromore Castle—the seat of "the Mahoneys"—a family long renowned, and still famous, for hospitality. A mere glance at the stately residence will suffice to convey assurance that the lord is a resident, improving not only his land but his tenantry, rendering the one productive and the other prosperous ; yet losing none of the ancient repute which describes the gate as ever open to the stranger, and the sympathy ever ready for all. Farther on, the river Blackwater flows into the bay. The river rushes through a deep ravine, the steep sides of which are thickly wooded. Its source is a small dark lake—LOUGH BRIN—among the Dunkerron mountains ; and near its mouth it is crossed by a bridge of two lofty arches, passing over a chasm of great depth. This is *the* river which the angler in the south knows and loves best. There is usually here a certainty of sport, although its length is but four miles from its source to its mouth. A very neat and comfortable inn is established here, and

BLACKWATER BRIDGE.

---

* We may here take advantage of an opportunity to state that all along this coast, and, indeed, along the whole coast of Ireland, will be found, at certain intervals, the stations of the coast-guard ; they are usually occupied by three or four of the men—invariably steady, well-conducted, and obliging, and always ready to advise and assist the Tourist. These men are seamen of the navy ; generally one of them is married, and the wife superintends the domestic arrangement of the "settlement." The officer in command is, of course, somewhere in the district, and, it is needless to say, will be ever at hand to assist the traveller in case of any difficulty. It may be worth a note to add that, in this force, the country has eight thousand "able seamen"—trained and disciplined, hardy, healthy, and in the prime of life—available at a day's notice, in the event of their services being required to man a fleet.

† In a nook which leads to Lough Glenmore and overlooks the charming harbour of Killmicheolge, resided in 1860, and probably does so still, in a small and very poor hostelrie, which he keeps, the lineal representative of the Mac Sweenys—once lords of the whole of the district on which the tourist looks from either of the adjacent hills. The family were dispossessed of their estates so far back as the reign of Elizabeth, when they became, by right of conquest, the property of the ancestors of the Marquis of Lansdowne, to whom the Mac Sweenys then and thereafter became tenants. The history of their eventual transfer from the tenant to the landlord is just the "old story"—want of forethought and prudence, and a reckless disregard of "to-morrow." The chief of a principal branch of the O'Sullivans, another princely family of the district, now "fallen from their high estate," resides in the immediate neighbourhood, and occupies a position no higher than that of a snug farmer. There is, surely, here matter for history that might surpass romance.

perhaps no locality combines so many attractions: the angler is not only free to fish, but the liberal owner of the water will rejoice to learn his success.* The village of SNEEM is soon reached, and then West Cove; the road is but a continuation of delicious scenery—mountain, river, lake and ocean. If the pleasure of the Tourist tends that way, he should diverge a mile or two from the road to visit the singular ruin of STAIG FORT; a circular building, of massive stones, without mortar, although so closely knit that it is scarcely possible to remove one of them. Antiquaries have no data as regards this remarkable ruin: but it is unquestionably among the most ancient remains of the country, and was no doubt constructed as a place of shelter during wars between chiefs who have long been dust.

From West Cove, the Tourist will proceed to DERRYNANE, *en route* to WATERVILLE, where he will rest awhile, for here there are two "hotels"—one of them fitted up entirely for his special accommodation. But Derrynane cannot be dismissed in a paragraph; it has, and will long have, a place in history. It was here "the Liberator" or "the Agitator"—call him which you will—had his only real home; here, where the waves of the Atlantic gave him health and strength, "the great advocate of Ireland" threw off the shackles of politics and party, and became the hospitable host, at whose board every comer, hostile or friendly, was a welcome guest. The Tourist, no matter what may be his creed, religious or political, who walks the paths of this demesne, listens to the wild rush of ocean against huge cliffs, visits the small ruin on a small island close by, or stands in the little bay, where the waters seem hushed as if listening to the fierce clamour of the waves outside—cannot do this without homage to the memory of one of the most remarkable men of any age or country. A shame it will be to Ireland if this "bit of land" be suffered to pass away from his descendants. The family reside at Derrynane; and there will be no difficulty, we believe, in the way of any stranger visiting the place.

The road that passes above the dell in which lies Derrynane House, is now one of the best roads in Ireland; but the Tourist will see "the old road," and wonder how it was ever possible for horse or carriage to ascend or descend the hills and the valleys over which it passes: yet, until within a few years of his death, O'Connell had no other way to his home by the ocean among the mountains.

To enjoy a full view of the all-glorious scene that now presents itself, the visitor need not leave the car—he is high enough above it; to mount one of the adjacent hills is needless: he looks out upon the ocean—the broad Atlantic; that distant island is "Scariff:" that nearer to him is "Dinish:" nearer still are "Melaun" and "Headed" islands: immediately below is the Abbey Island, no doubt a dependency on the great abbey of Ballinskellig; the remains of a ruined chapel are still there, and still it is a place of pilgrimage, the interest of which has been augmented a thousand-fold. There are a score of islets thereabouts—all of which have names, and they shelter one of the prettiest harbours that can be found on any coast; it is ever tranquil, no matter how fiercely winds and waves may rage without. We look down on the whole of this magnificent scene; the huge cliffs that enclose the small haven and the islands that protect it, the bold headlands, the venerable ruin, the clump of trees that hide the house, the grand sweep of rugged heath, and rock, and bog that lie between us

---

* Among the other attractions of the Blackwater, it may be mentioned that there is a regatta here every year, and that yachtmen find "good anchorage" from Blackwater to Kenmare.

and the sea; there will be no hesitation in pronouncing this scene as among the most magnificently beautiful to be found in any country of the world.

We must hurry on; a few miles and we arrive at WATERVILLE, distant ten miles from West Cove, West Cove being distant from Kenmare thirty miles. A good day's work has been done, therefore, and the Tourist will look for rest.

The proprietor of large estates in this district has built a neat and sufficiently large house beside Lough Currane for the express accommodation of Tourists; it was a wise thought. It is about a mile distant from a poor village. In this village there is an inn of the old class, where those will go who consider active zeal and ready service as "sets-off" against modern improvements. The stately hotel is "The Hartopp Arms;" the comfortable inn is "The Butler's Arms;" the traveller will take his choice. Here he is within reach of many of the principal coast and inland views

THE HOUSE IN WHICH O'CONNELL WAS BORN.

of Kerry; the former we have in part described, and the remainder are before us. Lough Currane has been long famous for its attractions to the angler; in the season—indeed, in all seasons—the lake is full of trout, but the salmon is the temptation here. As usual, there are in attendance men who have boats and furnish flies.*

---

* To those who have experience in the art, it is hardly necessary to say that to take a book of flies to any of these lakes is idle; they are at once put aside as useless; but the angler will do well to be provided with feathers and the "materials" of various sorts. He will be always sure to find in the neighbourhood—wherever he may happen to be—some fisherman who will be his guide, and tie for him the flies fittest for the water over which they are to be thrown.

Lough Currane is a charming spot, only partially wooded, but containing several pretty islands, on one of which is a group of interesting ruins—that of an ancient chapel being still used as a burial-place. It is one of a chain of lakes; those among the surrounding hills being, we understand, still more beautiful and more productive of sport. If the Tourist look across the bay, he will see the ruins of Ballinskellig Abbey; it is but six miles distant, and will amply repay a visit.

We continue our route, and at the end of a few miles come in sight of Cahirciveen: this is *the* town of the district, commanding the whole trade of the country within a circuit of nearly forty miles, north, south, and east; while to the west is THE ISLAND OF VALENCIA. Yet Cahirciveen is little better than it was thirty years ago—a dull town, that conveys no idea of either activity or prosperity, although its advantages are large and many. It has one object that may interest the Tourist. A mile or so distant is a ruined house, overgrown with ivy, pleasantly situate in a wooded dell beside a river. It is the birthplace of Daniel O'Connell; and the remains of the room in which he was born are still shown to the curious or patriotic visitor.*

Before we reach Cahirciveen, proceeding from Waterville, we turn off to the Ferry—less than a quarter of a mile in length—by which we cross to reach the renowned island of Valencia. Valencia is the property of Fitzgerald, the Knight of Kerry. He is an excellent, considerate, and enterprising landlord; and if there be, here and there, in his "dominions" evidence of misery, or, at all events, of indifference to decency and comfort, the evil arises from circumstances he can, as yet, neither change nor control. The Knight resides at Glanleam, a charming wooded demesne at the north-east shore of the island, and finds ample occupation in striving to make contented, happy, and comparatively prosperous, the isolated, simple, and interesting people, numbering about two thousand, whom Providence has placed under his rule. It is not too much to say that the heroic qualities of this branch of the Geraldines have remained with their descendants.†

The island is six and three quarter miles in length by two and a half miles in breadth. It has been long famous for Kerry cows—a very beautiful little animal, when of the pure kind, which gives an abundance of rich milk. The Knight has been very studious to preserve here the true breed, that has much deteriorated in nearly all other parts of the county. One of the neatest and best inns of the south of Ireland is at Knightstown, which adjoins the Ferry, and which, indeed, is the only collection of houses on the island. It is not our business to do more than allude to the controversy that has long been carried on as to whether Valencia ought or ought not to be the great "Packet Station" of the two hemispheres; but if it do not belong to us to report concerning the depth of water, the haven in which the navies of both

---

* The house is a picturesque ruin, richly clad in luxurious ivy; it must have been a good house in its prime, and the neighbouring scenery was no doubt attractive; for there is much foliage about it, and it is adjacent to a river. Although restoration is out of the question, it would be well if some steps were taken to preserve the remains, and to keep them with some degree of neatness and order.

† The Tourist in this neighbourhood, especially if he has any knowledge of Ireland in old times, will expect a passing tribute of respect to the memory of the late Knight of Kerry, the father of the gentleman to whom the honours of the race have descended. His lot was cast in an age less favourable than the present; he was a pioneer as regards very many of the recent improvements introduced not only into his county, but into his country. He had large influence which he exercised for the good of both; no man was more respected, and few men have been more beloved, than the Right Hon. Maurice Fitzgerald. He largely shared in all the wiser counsels of later times by which Ireland has been served and its welfare promoted; and his name should be recorded with honour and gratitude by all who have the interests of Ireland at heart—more especially when associated with a district for which he laboured, as a resident, generous, high-minded, and hospitable gentleman, for upwards of half a century.

nations may ride in safety, sheltered from all variations of the four winds, we may, at all events, speak of the picturesque beauty of this fine harbour. Mountain cliffs so completely environ it as to make it resemble a huge lake: yet it is separated but a few yards from the Atlantic ; and the ship will have scarcely weighed anchor before she is in the open sea—exchanging smooth water for the rough billows while the helmsman might count a dozen.* From the Knight's garden-seat there is a glorious view. The "light" is just under him, standing at the end of a line of sea-rocks. Huge cliffs,

VALENCIA.

full of singular caves, are seen on the promontory opposite: far out at sea are those remarkable islands, the Skelligs; and, turning in another direction, are the islands— the Blasquets—among which Mount Brandon seems to rear its lofty crest, although in reality on the mainland some thirty miles distant. Looking to the right—still seated in this lovely little garden, with its trim walks under trees among rocks— are seen the summits of the Reeks, old Carran Tuel rising above them all. It is indeed a charming spot we are picturing—where the Tourist who loves nature may have rare delight.

The slate quarries have long been famous: they are now worked by the Valencia Slate Slab Company, of which Mr. J. G. Magnus is the managing director. They

* The railway at Killarney, by being extended forty miles, would convey passengers from London to the Island in eighteen hours. The island is the nearest point in Europe to the American continent.

are, consequently, now in good hands; the name of that gentleman gives sufficient guarantee that they are all worked to the best advantage. These quarries are chiefly renowned for the very large dimensions of the slabs; which are, consequently, of great value in the important works of Mr. Magnus and others. The blocks are sawn and shaped as well as raised in the island; and we understand the demand far exceeds the supply.

In the island, also, is the "Terminus" of the cable of the Atlantic Telegraph Company. It was worked for a short time in 1858, messages having been conveyed from Valencia to Newfoundland. In October of that year, however, the "wire" broke; but there can be no doubt that ere long a complete restoration will be effected, and we shall know what takes place in America an hour after incidents have occurred; Valencia recovering the proud position it for a time occupied.

But the visit to Valencia must not be too short to forbid a visit to the "westermost" part of the island—Bray Head. The Tourist will pass on his way two of those singular grave-yards peculiar to the south-west; and of which we understand there are in Valencia no fewer than *four*—conclusive proofs that the island must have been thickly populated in remote ages. They are grave-yards devoted exclusively to infants, such as had not undergone the rite of baptism; the graves being formed of stones, with stones at the head and foot, with a single larger slab as the covering; they have continued to this day to keep the forms they received many centuries ago. They lie as close as they can be, and many hundreds may be counted in either of the enclosures—the walls around which can be distinctly traced. In the centre of one of these grave-yards is an Ogham stone, while a hill immediately adjacent contains a cromleach.

The "walker" to Bray Head—although it is distant a few miles from Knight's-town—will receive ample recompense; there is a good car-road nearly all the way. What a glorious view is obtained from the summit! standing beside an old, but not an ancient, watch-tower, you gaze in all directions on objects singular, striking, or sublime. Far out in ocean, are the famous sea-rocks, the Skelligs. They rank among the most remarkable curiosities of the Atlantic.

They were formerly celebrated as the resort of pilgrims; and many a weary penance has been performed upon their naked and inhospitable crags. The great Skellig consists of two peaks, which rise from the ocean so perpendicularly as closely to approximate to the shape of a sugar-loaf: the larger aising in thirty-four fathoms of the ocean to 710 feet above its level; the occasional projections being clothed with grass of "a delicious verdure and remarkable sweetness." The island is, at all times, nearly covered with sea-fowl; a circumstance for which Dr. Keating, the fanciful "historian" of Ireland, thus accounts:—"There is an attractive virtue in the soil, which draws down all the birds that attempt to fly over it, and obliges them to light upon the rock;" a notion of which the poet Moore has availed himself:—

> "Islets so freshly fair
> That never hath bird come nigh them,
> But, from his course through air,
> Hath been won downward by them."

The peasantry have numerous tales to tell in connection with these singular rocks; and a whimsical tradition exists, that every madman, if left to his own guidance, would make his way towards them. They have, however, of late years, lost much of their "sacred" character, and are now-a-days visited by very few penitents.*

We have detained the Tourist at Valencia somewhat long; but he will not complain if our notes induce him to visit the island, to seek and obtain rest in its pleasant inn, to examine its sources of natural wealth, to enjoy its magnificent views of sea and shore, islands and mountains, its relics of remote ages, its fine and very beautiful harbour, its many objects of interest in natural history, and its sure promise of prosperous commerce and in-flowing wealth hereafter.

The Tourist on regaining the mainland will drive into Cahirciveen, about two miles from the Ferry: here he will take either the public or a private car, to drive either to Tralee or to Killarney.

We shall endeavour briefly to conduct him to both.

We are now leading the Tourist from Cahirciveen to Killarney, a distance of forty miles by the coach road. We are travelling by the public car, which runs daily from the one town to the other. It may be well to add, however, that private cars may be obtained at Cahirciveen as well as at Killarney, but it is a common and a wise custom for those who make this tour, and are not pressed for time, to hire the carriage at the hotel in Killarney, and continue with it "all the way round." It is absolutely marvellous what labour these mountain-bred horses can get through, "thinking nothing" of thirty miles a day, for days together, or even fifty miles in a single day; the machines they draw are light, and the driver will always walk up the hills.

For a long way, indeed about half the distance, the road runs above the beautiful Bay of Dingle; often along the very brink of giant precipices, always in sight of the grand harbour, the wild coast opposite, and the mountains, that sometimes seem so near as to throw their shadows over the sea.

From an ascent, as we leave the town, we look back on the small island in Valencia Harbour; it contains one of those singular stone cells, similar to those that are found on the great Skellig, and which are attributed to recluses of the sixth century, with an ancient stone tomb or chapel close by; while on the north-east side of the harbour stands the ruined Castle of Ballycarberry; there is here one of those singular forts, that, like Staig Fort, has no history, and concerning which even tradition is silent. It is this harbour—that of Valencia—which connects Cahirciveen with the sea, and supplies it with natural advantages of which, unhappily, there have been few to avail themselves. We pursue our route, still by Dingle Bay, until we reach Castlemaine Harbour, which is, in reality, but a continuation of that of Dingle, stretching inland. We gaze over a pretty creek, Rossbegh, where, on the main road, there is a good hotel; for this is the bathing-place of the district, with its many neat and pretty lodges for the accommodation of visitors. As we pass along we obtain a charming view of a calm and pleasant nook that, nestling among high hills, draws in the milder sea-breezes, and gives them out in health.

This is the resting-place of those who fish in Lough Carha—a charming lake which we leave to the right in travelling to Killarney. It is environed by hills, some

---

* Dr. Smith gives a striking account of the perils through which the penitents passed. To the top of the Great Skellig there is but one path, and that so difficult that few people are hardy enough to attempt it. Upon the flat part of the island are several cells, said to have been chapels—for "here stood anciently an abbey of canons regular of St. Austin." "They are built in the ancient Roman manner, of stone curiously closed and jointed, without either mortar or cement, and are impervious to the air and wind, having circular stone arches at the top."

of them wooded, with islands also; and, although small, it presents to the eye scenery only less beautiful than that of the Lakes he is approaching. The traveller obtains a fine view of it as he journeys along. The vicinity of Lough Carha has long been a terra incognita; partly owing to the fact that its beauties were unknown to, and consequently undescribed by, Tourists—having been penetrated only by the sportsman, for whom it had, and has, temptations irresistible; and partly in consequence of the bad roads that led to it, and the ill accommodation provided for strangers when there. These obstructions to its fame are now in a great degree removed.

The lake may be reached also by a new road from Killarney, branching off from the former about ten miles from Killarney, and leading through a ravine in the Reeks called Glouncetane, by the very beautiful lake of Coos, and through the valley of Glencar to the upper end of the lake. This road well deserves to be explored, as there are few parts of Ireland which exceed the valley of Glencar in wild and solitary beauty. The lake of Carha, taking its origin in this valley, runs into Castlemaine Bay, by the Carba river, about five miles in length, celebrated for its winter salmon-fishing. The length of the lake is about seven miles, and its breadth varies from two to four. It is divided into upper and lower. The lower, which is widest and least picturesque, is, however, a very fine sheet of water, and contains many objects of interest. From this point is obtained one of the best views of the Reeks.

After journeying about five miles, all the way with Castlemaine Harbour in sight, the Tourist arrives at KILLORGLIN—a market town of no great importance, but exhibiting signs of great misery intermixed with prosperous commerce. Here will commence the journey of those who are proceeding to Tralee or Dingle; and here another public car conveys passengers into the district further to the west. Hence into Killarney there is a good road, which, skirting the river Laune, and passing underneath the Reeks, leaves to the right the pathway to Curran Tuel, and the entrance to the Gap of Dunloe, and conducts into the town of Killarney.*

We lead the Tourist, therefore, back to Killorglin, distant ten miles from Killarney, and conduct him to the several points of interest between this town and the Shannon. We can, however, do little more than indicate this route—our space is already exhausted—and we must pass somewhat rapidly over the remainder of our Tour. It is, indeed, utterly impossible to do it anything like justice; for all we have said of the wild grandeur of the coast between Kenmare and Valencia will apply, with equal force, to that promontory which, stretching between Dingle Bay and Tralee Bay, but running far out into the Atlantic, contains Ventry Bay, Smerwick Harbour, Brandon Bay, and a number of lesser harbours, each of them beautiful: while the sea, rocks, cliffs, and islands along the coast are but poorly pictured by the term "sublime."

He will first pass through the small towns of Miltown and Castlemaine; Castlemaine derives its name from a small river—the Maine—which runs through the town, in which formerly stood a strong fortress demolished by "Cromwell."

Shortly after passing this, the character of the scenery begins to change. The road lies along the edge of the haven, which is bounded by a low, flat shore for some miles; the distant mountains still forming the most attractive feature in the landscape. The mouth of the Laune can be distinguished, where the waters of Killarney Lakes

---

* It is clear that although we have described the route from Kenmare, our description may guide the Tourist who takes it from Killarney. It may be well also to remind the Tourist that there is a railway from Killarney to Tralee.

join the sea. After passing a sandy promontory, which runs out into Dingle Bay, and shuts in the shallower estuary, Castlemaine Harbour, the coast becomes bold and rocky. The road continues along the shore of Dingle Bay, and commands a most magnificent view. Immediately underneath lie the waters of the bay, rolling in, uninterrupted, from the Atlantic, and discharging themselves in long breakers, even on a calm day, over the rocks. In the distance, the view is bounded by the

IN DINGLE BAY.

strikingly picturesque outline of the Iveragh mountains, forming the high grounds of the promontory at the other side of the bay; at the extremity of which can be discerned the island of Valencia. On the other side of the road rises the ridge of the Brandon and Slieve-mish Mountains, which, if it were not in the neighbourhood of Killarney, would be considered very fine mountain scenery.

DINGLE is a town of little larger size than Killarney. It is the most western town in Europe; and its full name—Dingle-i-Couch—is an Irish proverb, expressive of a very out-of-the-way place. There are two moderately good hotels. The visitor will find things here somewhat old-fashioned—as suits the locality.

Let the Tourist rest at Dingle, and prepare for a short journey of singular interest and beauty. We will suppose him to have arrived in the evening. Let him, then, on the following morning, take the road by Ventry to Sybil-head. Ventry is the centre of the earliest attempt at Protestantising in the west of Ireland, and one of the places at which it is said to have been successful. The two adjoining parishes of Ventry and Dunquin now contain several congregations attending Protestant worship, for whom new churches have been built. Whatever the opinion of the traveller may be of the spiritual results of unquestionably zealous and well-meant exertions in this way, there can be but one as to their temporal consequences. The houses about Ventry are generally neat, clean, and whitewashed; the smoke has chimneys to get out through, and the light has windows to get in at; and one at least of John Wesley's doctrines, that cleanliness is akin to godliness, seems to have taken hold of the inmates. The people appear to be more industrious, and therefore more comfortable. The heart-burnings, contentions, and violence which arose at the commencement of the "new reformation" in this district, have now ceased; the numbers of Protestant proselytes are said not to be increasing as they did at first; but, happily, the professors of the rival religions live at peace beside each other.

Passing Ventry, and stopping, if you choose, to look at the ruins of a small castle which shared in the general blowing up of Irish fortresses after 1641, you pursue your road to the northward, by Sugar-loaf Mountains, to Sybil-head. Ascending the slope of the promontory, you expect, when you reach the summit, to descend to the sea, which is shut out from your view until you reach the very top: but you suddenly find that one half of the hill has been cut completely away by the ocean, and the instant you reach the summit you see below you the waves of the Atlantic rolling at the foot of a perpendicular cliff of the most stupendous and awful grandeur. Looking down from this point, you see on your right a romantic bay—Smerwick Harbour—and a portion of the coast, formed by successive hills cut in two by the sea, in the same manner as Sybil-head itself. They are called "the Sisters;" and when first they attract the eye they have the appearance of a row of sugar-loafs behind each other. On the left of the promontory, stretching out into the Atlantic, are the Blasket Islands. If the day be windy, you will see eagles soaring about the cliffs; but if it be calm, you must look for them perched on some of the pinnacles of the rocks rising from the sea below, where you will be sure to discover at least one. There the monarch of the air will sit for hours in solitude, moving nothing but his head, apparently contemplating the sublime scene that surrounds him, and listening to the giant waves that lash their ceaseless spray on the rocks far below his feet, rendering his resting-place unapproachable by any other of God's creatures. In contrast to him, at the inland side of the hill, you will be frequently passed by the familiar chough, with his glossy black body and scarlet legs, shining in the sun. Far out in the ocean, with the aid of a glass, you will discern ships on their way to or from the ports of America. How peacefully and securely these distant specks seem to traverse that trackless waste, whose unknown terrors so long limited the knowledge and enterprise of civilised man! You stand on the promontory which for ages was deemed the extreme west of the world! The most westerly part of it is, however, not Sybil-head, but on the promontory of Dunquin, a little to the south of it, and is called "Tig vourneen Geeran," or "Mary Geeran's house."

On the north-west side of Smerwick Harbour, nearer Drumlin-head, are the remains of a Spanish fortification, called "Fort-del-Or." At the southern side of Cape Sybil, at the head of a small creek, are the remains of another castle, called Sybilla's or Ferriter's Castle.

If the visitor should have time to visit the Eagle Mountain and Blasket Islands, on Dunquin Promontory, he will be rewarded by seeing some very magnificent coast and rock scenery, and meeting on the islands a singular primitive race of people; but this will occupy more time than most tourists have to spare. An additional historic interest is given to these islands from the circumstance that a portion of the Spanish Armada was wrecked among them, including an admiral's ship—" *Our Lady of the Rosary.*" Among those who perished was a Spanish Prince—the Prince of Asculi—whose burial-place is still shown, near the ruined church at Dunquin.

Another of the "lions" of Dingle is Mount Brandon. It lies to the north, between St. Brandon's Bay and Smerwick Harbour. An energetic Tourist may compass visiting this the same day as Sybil-head; but it will be a very hard day's work.

Leaving Dingle by the road over Connor Hill, the traveller proceeds to Tralee.

The way lies through scenery quite as beautiful as, though altogether different from, any which the Tourist passed on the road we suppose him to have travelled from Killarney to Dingle. As he ascends the mountain over Dingle, he still sees below

FERRITER'S CASTLE.

him the town and harbour, with the bay stretching out beyond, until he reaches the summit level of the road, when it begins to descend along the top of a precipice, winding under and above cliffs of much grandeur. The view then completely changes: at the opposite side of the valley beneath, it is partly bounded by another mountain, and partly expands into a magnificent prospect of the shores of St. Brandon's Bay.

There is a well-appointed public car, which runs every morning from Dingle to Tralee, and travels by this very beautiful road.

A glance at the map will show that the Tourist in visiting this fine promontory has diverged much from the road to Tralee; which is not more than ten miles from Killorglin, and twenty miles from Killarney.

TRALEE is the assize town of the county. It sends a member to parliament; its present representative being "The O'Donoghue." It contains nearly 10,000 inhabitants. The new Roman Catholic cathedral of this town is a remarkably beautiful structure, the interior being decorated in much better taste than usual. The remains of several ruins are in the vicinity of Tralee: among others, that of an abbey, in which for several centuries the Desmonds were buried, the first occupants of its tombs being Thomas Fitzgerald, surnamed "the Great," and his son Maurice, who were both slain at Callan, in a fight with the Mac Carthy Mor. The most interesting monastic remains in Kerry are, however, those of the abbey of Ardfert—about six miles north-west of Tralee. Ardfert is a bishop's see, held *in commendam* with the bishopric of Limerick. The ruins of the cathedral are still in good preservation, and bear marks of high antiquity. In the western front are four round arches, and in the eastern front three elegant narrow-pointed windows. On the right of the altar are some niches with Saxon mouldings. A round tower, 120 feet high, and built chiefly of a dark marble, which formerly stood near the west front, suddenly fell down in 1771.

Between Tralee and Tarbert, a distance of nearly thirty miles, the road is inland, yet at no time far from the sea. There are many places of historic note which the

Tourist will pass on his way: the principal being Listowel. It is a poor town, with, of course, the ruins of a castle. In the year 1600 this castle, which held out for

ARDFERT ABBEY.

Lord Kerry against the Lord President, was besieged by Sir Charles Wilmot. Listowel is watered by the Feal, a river which the Irish poet has immortalised in one of the sweetest of his songs; founded on a tradition, that the young heir of the princely Desmonds, having been benighted while hunting, took shelter in the house of one of his dependants, named Mac Cormac, with whose fair daughter he became suddenly enamoured. "He married her; and by this inferior alliance alienated his followers, whose brutal pride regarded this indulgence of his love as an unpardonable degradation of his family."

A few miles "out of the road" are the far-famed caves of Ballybunian. They are not often visited; yet may be classed among the most remarkable of the natural wonders of Ireland. The only county historian alludes to them very briefly:—"The whole shore here hath a variety of romantic caves and caverns, formed by the dashing of the waves; in some places are high open arches, and in others impending rocks, ready to tumble down upon the first storm." A small volume descriptive of them was published in 1834, by Francis Ainsworth, Esq., to whom we must refer the reader. They are distinguished by names, each name bearing reference to some particular circumstance; as, "the Hunter's Path," from a tradition that a rider once rode his horse over it; "Smugglers' Bay," for centuries famous as a shelter for "free traders;" the "Seal Cave," &c. &c.

From Listowel to Tarbert, the distance is twelve miles and a half: there is a good hotel at Tarbert, and here the Tourist is on the mighty Shannon—the largest and broadest of island rivers.

The mouth of the Shannon is grand almost beyond conception. Its inhabitants point to a part of the river, within the headlands, over which the tides rush with extraordinary rapidity and violence. They say it is the site of a lost city, long buried beneath the waves; and that its towers, and spires, and turrets, acting as breakers against the tide-water, occasion the roughness of this part of the estuary. The whole city becomes visible every seventh year, and has been often seen by the fishermen sailing over it; but the sight bodes ill-luck.

Nearly opposite Kilrush is the far-famed island of Scattery, memorable in ecclesiastical history, and celebrated as the residence of that ungallant and un-Irish saint —St. Senanus—who having

> "sworn his sainted sod
> Should ne'er by woman's feet be trod,"

refused even to associate with him in his solitude a "sister saint—St. Cannera—whom an angel had conducted to the island for the express purpose of introducing to him." But, if we are to credit the poet,

> "Legends hint that had the maid
> Till morning's light delay'd,
> And given the saint one rosy smile,
> She ne'er had left his lonely isle."

The coast from Kilrush—on the mainland opposite the island—a pretty and fashionable bathing-place, round to Kilkee, which faces the Atlantic, may vie for sublime grandeur with that of any part of the kingdom. The two towns are distant about eight miles by land; but, to reach the one from the other by sea, a voyage of little short of forty miles would be necessary, for the long and narrow promontory—the barony of Moyarta—stretches out between them, and forms the northern boundary of the mouth of the Shannon.

But the Tourist, who begins to consider his journey as finished, will, instead of making this visit to the north side of the Shannon, make his way from Tarbert to Foynes, with its charming and most convenient harbour; from Foynes by railway to Limerick—through Asheaton, Rathkeale, Adare, and Patrick's Well: thence from Limerick to the Junction, through a rich district; and from Limerick to Waterford, to Cork, or to Dublin.

CONCLUDING REMARKS.

WE have thus conducted the reader through the all-beautiful district that environs Killarney, described the several routes that lead to it, and the various and varied incidents that will add attraction to the journey.

Those who voyage and travel to the Lakes, and who are not "hurried," will have seen much of Ireland and of Irish character on their way. We again express our conviction that they will return to their homes in happier and more prosperous England, with a higher estimation of, and a kindlier feeling towards, the country and its people: nevertheless, they will be often startled, saddened, and pained by the knowledge how much must yet be done for both, to enable both to take the position that God and Nature intended them to occupy—and which, of a surety, they will occupy at no very distant period.

The purpose of these remarks is to strengthen, and not to discourage, hope and faith in the future of Ireland. That may be best done by describing the *past* and contrasting it with the *present*: a task of which those only are capable who knew the country under far more dismal and disheartening prospects than it now presents.

We believe we cannot better close this book than by some reference to the unequivocal evidence of improvement our own experience enables us to supply: following up the observations we made at the outset, concerning the ease, comfort, rapidity, and certainty with which THE VOYAGE across is now made, as compared with its serious evils when it was uncertain, dangerous, and often of so long a duration, that weeks were sometimes spent between Port and Port.

The existing generation can have but a very limited idea of the changes for the better that have taken place in Ireland during the last forty—twenty—even ten—years. Those who are old may make comparisons of Ireland as it was and Ireland as it is, and rejoice at the result. Who of them will fail to recall the beggars that used to beset him on every highway—in every street. Standing at any hotel door, entering or withdrawing from any shop, a terrible crowd was that through which he had to make his way. Noisy beggars of both sexes, and of all ages—exposing frightful sores and parading miserable diseases—barred the passage; giving wit, indeed, for money, but paining the very soul by wretchedness it was impossible to relieve, and from the sight of which there was no escape. But what else could be? The poor had no other resource; they must beg or starve; it was their only means of life; and, ever and always, in Ireland, charity is a fountain never dry. The Legislature had given no thought to the multitude who were aged, maimed, or afflicted with diseases that prevented work. There was no Poor Law in Ireland until the year 1838. While, in England, the poor had food and clothes and shelter, as natural rights, the Irish had none. Now, there are in every district "poor-houses," where every man, woman, and child, unable to labour, is provided with a home and its accompaniments—where industry is taught as a virtue, and cleanliness inculcated as a luxury. The beggars —at all events the more appalling classes of them—are found nowhere throughout the country.

The Tourist who is not young, and can remember *old* Ireland, may picture the Irish dwellings as they were: so deplorably wretched that an English farmer would have rejected the best of them as habitations for cattle; the mud floor, seldom dry; the dilapidated thatch, rarely impervious to rain; the broken window, "stopped up" to keep out wind and air; the ever-occurring dunghill before the door; the familiar friend the pig, "who paid the rent,"—these were but the lesser evils of the cabin of one room, in which often a dozen, sometimes twenty, fellow-beings lived. They are departing fast: lime is now used profusely; the pig is rarely the inmate of "the parlour;" the dunghill is generally behind the house, and not before the door; the cabins of the Irish peasant are gradually approximating to the English cottage. They are, indeed, still miserable enough; and to the inveteracy of habit may be traced much of the degradation to which those who inhabit them are subjected. "Our nature is subdued to what it works in;" but those who can compare them with the "cabins" of thirty years ago, will see a great change for the better, both in the exterior and interior of an Irish peasant's "castle."

In old times—nay, not very old—there was meaning in the sarcasm of the traveller, that "he never knew what the English beggars did with their cast-off clothes until he visited Ireland;" and in the story of the Irishman who thought himself "in luck" when he exchanged dresses with a scarecrow in an English field. Rags are now exceptional cases; generally the peasant is decently, and often comfortably, clad. At least, there is a material diminution of those external signs of penury and suffering that not long ago offended the eye and pained the heart of the Tourist in that country.

No doubt, to English eyes, there is yet much that requires "change;" comparisons between the outer aspect of England and Ireland will be discouraging, and perhaps humiliating. The yellow "bouchlawn" is still the pest of the fields; and an English farmer may even yet complain, as an English grazier did, of the country being "brutally used;" but all the means and appliances for making land productive are the introductions of recent periods—the spade, the hoe, and the flail did the work of the agriculturist thirty years ago. It is but just and reasonable, we repeat, to compare the Ireland of to-day with the Ireland of forty, twenty, even ten, years ago; to arrive at right conclusions concerning that country, there must be some knowledge of it in the past. We who have been acquainted with Ireland, by occasional and sometimes prolonged visits, since the year 1820, can see and appreciate the great improvements that are, in so many ways, perceptible there. It demands no great stretch of memory to carry us back to a time when, politically and socially, the Irish were treated as a "conquered" people; forty years ago there was not a Roman Catholic member of any Corporate body in Ireland; a Roman Catholic could not be a "Scholar" in Trinity College, a Judge, or a Queen's Counsel—or, in short, be found anywhere on the road to preferment: no Roman Catholic could be a Member of Parliament—none a Lord of the Treasury—none a Governor of a Colony. There are now five Irishmen on the *English* Bench, and one of them is a Roman Catholic; and of the twelve Irish Judges, eight are Roman Catholics. The Englishman and Protestant enjoys no privilege, no advantage, from which the Legislature debars the Irishman and Roman Catholic. Forty years ago, it was forbidden, under penalties, to ring a bell in any Roman Catholic "Chapel" to call the people to prayer. "Middlemen" farmed more than half the lands of Ireland: devouring locusts they were; generally a low class, insensible to any touch of humanity—greedy, remorseless—grinding the poor, and amassing wealth out of misery. The middleman is now hardly known in Ireland: that curse has been removed. The spirit of the age—so resolute in advancing and extending freedom and equal rights—has marvellously changed for the better the character of Irish land-lords. For one bad landlord now, there were ten thirty years ago. Hard and inconsiderate task-masters are still plenty enough; but public opinion would consign to instant ignominy such merciless exterminators as "flourished" when the fathers of the present generation took land. The eternal truth that "property has its duties as well as its rights" is now universally admitted, and very generally forms the basis of new engagements. Thirty years ago, wages for labour were seldom beyond fivepence a day; the peasant never eat meat, and rarely bread; he raised his potatoes and *lived* —that was all. The Police were mockeries, notoriously inefficient—made up, chiefly, of rogues and spies; it is now, perhaps, the best force in the world, not only for the detection of crime, but for its prevention. As one of them expressed himself to us, they "take off the match before the shell explodes." For discipline, order, activity, and integrity they are unsurpassed. Thirty years ago, drunkenness was a distinction, and not, as it is now, a shame—to the higher, as well as to the lower classes, it was anything but dishonour; in truth, he was "an Irishman all in his glory" who was unable to walk home from a feast. Faction fights disgraced every *fête* day. Hedge-schools were the only seminaries of education. There are now schools in every part of the Island, supported, as they ought to be, by annual national grants. In a word—forty, thirty, nay twenty, years ago, Ireland was indeed a *wretched* country—made wretched, and kept so, from a cruel and foolish policy that has long been bearing its natural fruit.*

But to say that England *continues* to act unjustly towards Ireland *now*, is to say that which is false and wicked. There is in England, generally, nay, universally, an earnest and sincere desire to do *Justice to Ireland;* and although evil tongues in Ireland may rail at England in 1865 more foully than they did—or dared to do—in 1820, they fail to excite the hatred they design,—simply because there is no grievance to redress,—certainly none for which the British Government and people are unwilling to supply a remedy.

* If hatred of the English was strong forty years ago, it was in a measure natural and justifiable; there was "cause shown." When an Irishman was pictured, represented on the stage, or displayed in works of fiction, it was always as a person unfitted to be either intimate or friend; as one in whom the vices of social life greatly overbalanced the virtues; while those who sought service, and consulted advertisements in a newspaper, found, in nine cases out of ten, that "no Irish need apply." These, and other evils of the kind, were but the lesser evidences of a systematic study to keep the Irish away from respect and advancement—forty years ago.

Twenty years ago, travelling in Ireland had many drawbacks; now there are admirably managed railways through all the principal districts. Twenty years ago, the "hotels" were very badly conducted; now in all leading cities they vie with those of England; while in minor towns they are clean, comfortable, and in many ways excellent.

We trust, therefore, the Tourist in Ireland—when he sees, as he undoubtedly will see, much that must lower his spirits and postpone his hopes—will bear in mind that not many years ago the state of that country was infinitely worse than it is now.

We might go to much greater length into statements of the benefits conferred upon Ireland by time and enlightened policy, and especially by the *will* of the English people; but our leading, if not our sole, object at this moment is to remove an impression which still, to some extent, prevails, that there will be any annoyances in Ireland—such as can lessen the enjoyments of travellers.

To the "safety" of travelling in Ireland, we have borne the testimony of our own experience; it is sustained by that of every writer who has communicated with the public concerning that country and its people. We trust we shall not weary the reader if we for a moment recur to this topic.

The stranger in Ireland is sure of a cordial reception; whatever domestic "squabbles" there may be, they never affect him. Journey where he will, he may calculate on a welcome. There is no country in the world where the traveller is so safe from annoyance; we repeat, to that fact every tourist who has written earnestly deposes; there is no exception to the rule.

We have travelled much in every part of Ireland, visited every one of its thirty-two counties, having posted, indeed—usually on the common jaunting car—more than six thousand miles in the course of our various tours, by night as well as day, along its by-paths as well as its highways, over mountains and through miles of bog, in very lonely places, sometimes the guest of the humblest cotter. We never met the slightest interruption or insult, and never lost the value of a shilling, during any one of our journeys. To state this may be needless; but we write for readers who may have drawn back from contemplated visits when they hear of "agrarian disturbances," and of "agitators" who strive—in vain—to excite hatred of "the Saxon" in the people. The tourist may be sure that he is safer in the wilds of Connemara, or in the *terra incognita* of Donegal, than he would be journeying from Hyde Park Corner to Richmond.

We tender on behalf of the Irish "people," earnestly and strongly, our testimony —to their enduring fortitude, their self-sacrificing generosity, their indomitable energy, their keen sensibilities, their honesty unyielding under any pressure of actual want; and we believe the "raw materials" of the country are even less fruitful of recompense than the minds and hearts of the Irish people—needing only proper management and wise direction to be made of prodigiously productive value.

We repeat—our hope is to make the English better acquainted with the Irish where they are best seen—at home: knowing well that every visitor, be his visit brief or prolonged, will return from it with a better appreciation of, and a kindlier feeling towards, the country and its people; that, in a word, for every new visitor Ireland will obtain a new FRIEND.

Nothing can be so valuable to England, and nothing so beneficial to Ireland, as *frequent intercourse* between the two countries,—so essentially and so emphatically ONE!

It is, therefore, a duty, as assuredly it may be a pleasure, to visit that country, and it will be a shame to those who prefer a search on the Continent for enjoyment they may obtain with infinitely greater certainty so near at hand, while advancing the great cause of "Union," between the two countries. The old prejudices that kept the people of England and Ireland too long apart have, in a great measure, vanished; *frequent intercourse* will entirely remove them, and the benefits to be thence derived are incalculable. Huge steamboats, so large as materially to diminish all dread of sea-sickness, convey the voyager from Holyhead to Kingstown in less than four hours; London being thus brought within little more than ten hours' reach of Dublin; while "Excursion Tickets" render the "trip" easy to persons of even restricted means, and the railroad authorities, from the highest to the lowest, consider it a primary part of their duty to minister to the wants and wishes of tourists; the ticket being, indeed, a letter of recommendation.

We are in no degree exaggerating inducements to visit Ireland. We might quote opinions nearly as strong as our own, advanced by a score of English writers, who would be accepted as "authorities" on the subject. We quote but one of them—a passage from the *Times*, printed during the past year :—

"There is nothing in these isles more beautiful and picturesque than the South and West of Ireland. They who know the fairest portions of Europe still find in Ireland that which they have seen nowhere else, and which has charms all its own. . . . . The whole coast, west and south, indeed all around the island, has beauties that many a travelled Englishman has not the least conception of. The time will come when the annual stream of tourists will lead the way, and when wealthy Englishmen, one after another, in rapid succession, will seize the fairest spots, and fix here their summer quarters. . . . . If a tourist should visit the spots we have indicated, he would return with the conviction, that beautiful as continental scenery may be, there are points in Ireland which may stand competition with the show districts of any other country."

We by no means desire it to be understood that Ireland has reason to be entirely satisfied. There is much yet to be done for Ireland by England, not alone on the ground of policy, but as just compensation for centuries of misrule. When Ireland was oppressed, goaded, and socially enthralled, disaffection was natural and inevitable; but of late years the system of government has been altogether changed; perhaps, too much so rather than too little; prejudices on both sides have materially diminished, and Ireland has been gradually becoming more and more "part and parcel" of England—it will eventually be as much so as Wales and Scotland, as much so as Devon and York. The next generation, possibly the young of the present generation, will marvel at the miserable wisdom that sought to make the interests of the one distinct from those of the other; when the latest relic that keeps up the delusion of "separate kingdoms" will be a portion of history gone by, and the Viceroy of Ireland will be as obsolete as the Lord of the Marches in Wales, and the King's Lieutenant in Scotland, and when Her Gracious Majesty the Queen, or some member of her illustrious and beloved family, will have a residence in Ireland as well as in Scotland.

We are not beholding a vision nor indulging a wild fancy, if we see in the prospect —not very distant—advantages to which those obtained from time and enlightened policy are but mere fragments of justice: bigotry loosing its hold—the undue or baneful influence of one mind over another mind ceasing—habits of thrift and forethought becoming constitutional—industry receiving its full recompense—cultivation passing over the bogs and up the mountains—the law recognised as a guardian and a protector—the rights and duties of property fully understood and acknowledged —the rich trusting the poor, and the poor confiding in the rich—absenteeism no longer a weighty evil; in a word, CAPITAL circulating freely and securely; so as to render the vast natural resources of Ireland available to the commercial, the agricultural and the manufacturing interests of the ONE United Kingdom of England, Ireland, Scotland and Wales.

We cannot better close these remarks than by quoting some words addressed to us long ago by Maria Edgeworth, and which we address to all Tourists in Ireland, and all who are interested in the progress, and welfare, of that country—"HAPPINESS IN IRELAND IS ALWAYS CHEAP:" it is so easy to give and to receive it!

www.ingramcontent.com/pod-product-compliance
Lightning Source LLC
Chambersburg PA
CBHW021727220426
43662CB00008B/733